YOUNG AL CAPONE

Also by William Balsamo:

Under the Clock: The Inside Story of the Mafia's First 100 Years
(with George Carpozi Jr.)

YOUNG AL CAPONE

THE UNTOLD STORY OF SCARFACE
IN NEW YORK, 1899–1925

William Balsamo and
John Balsamo

SKYHORSE PUBLISHING

Skyhorse Publishing books may be purchased in bulk at special discounts for sales promotion, corporate gifts, fund-raising, or educational purposes. Special editions can also be created to specifications. For details, contact the Special Sales Department, Skyhorse Publishing, 307 West 36th Street, 11th Floor, New York, NY 10018 or info@skyhorsepublishing.com.

Skyhorse˚ and Skyhorse Publishing˚ are registered trademarks of Skyhorse Publishing, Inc.˚, a Delaware corporation.

Visit our website at www.skyhorsepublishing.com.

10 9 8 7 6 5 4 3 2 1

Paperback ISBN: 978-1-62087-109-6

Library of Congress Cataloging-in-Publication Data
Balsamo, William.
Young Al Capone : the untold story of Scarface in New York, 1899-1925 /
William Balsamo and John Balsamo.
p. cm.
Includes index.
ISBN 978-1-61608-085-3 (hardcover : alk. paper)
1. Capone, Al, 1899-1947. 2. Criminals--New York (State)--New York. 3.
Criminals--Illinois--Chicago. 4. Gangsters--New York (State)--New York. 5.
Gangsters--Illinois--Chicago. I. Balsamo, John. II. Title.
HV6248.C17 B35 2010
364.1092--dc22
[B]
2010034682

Printed in the United States of America

This book is dedicated in memory of our beloved mother, Helen Balsamo-Martinez (1915–1994) and John's wife, Johanna (1938–2006).

"I'm a spook, born of a million minds."

—Al Capone, commenting on his tax trouble

Contents

CONTENTS

Authors' Note

MANY YEARS AGO, we began to realize that all of the books written about Al Capone (we think we have most of them in our possession) offer only cursory descriptions of the most exciting period in the life of the man known as "Scarface." It is no wonder that the subject's early days have been shrouded in mystery. Even the most exhaustive research would fail to bring never-before-published material to light for one important reason: None of the previous biographers had the opportunity to live with and to work with people (on the Brooklyn waterfront) and elsewhere who actually knew Alphonse Capone. We can reliably state that no one else can match the years of research we incurred in chronicling young Capone's remarkable existence unless they wish to hold their interviews at so many gravesides.

Collecting personal data and piecing together *Young Al Capone* has been more than a hobby for us. It's been a family tradition, with relatives and friends sometimes supplying leads. Most of them turned out to be dead ends. Others, such as the interviews with Frank Galluccio, the man who put the knife (and caused the scars) to Capone's face and lived to tell about it, were truly startling and the sessions with Frankie Yale's henchman, Gido Bianco, painted intimate and revealing insights into Capone's early days, when young Al learned all there was to know about strong-arming, thievery, and extortion in Brooklyn, on the banks of the Gowanus Canal. Mr. Bianco was a fantastic source of information pertaining to Capone's younger years. Having known Alphonse since childhood, Bianco's powerful accounts provided the impetus for us to invest countless hours toward composing this book, which is a result of numerous personal interviews, tape recordings, newspaper articles dug out from the public libraries, and facts compiled through court records and other official documents.

We also claim a distinct advantage over other Capone historians, as we are related by blood to Batista Balsamo (1868–1940), generally regarded as the first godfather of Brooklyn, New York, where Capone's roots lay. A search of our family tree has verified that our great-uncle, Batista was a descendent of the infamous Giuseppe Balsamo, a.k.a. Count Allessandro Di Cagliostro (1743–1795), an alchemist and noted mystic who was prosecuted in the affair of the diamond necklace that involved Marie Antoinette and Prince Louis de Rohan.

Perhaps Di Cagliostro's shady résumé also included an association with the Sicilian Mafia in the mid-1700s, because we subsequently learned that the mention of our great-uncle's name to selected mob associates opened doors, as well as mouths, for us in our attempts to ferret out details from those who knew Alphonse Capone or who had dealings with him.

The dialogue in this book is written with the hopeful intention of providing a plausible discourse to the events as defined by the historical record. When a character's jargon seems atypical, bear in mind that Al Capone was bilingual, as were many of his contemporaries. They often communicated in Italian, though sometimes in English with Brooklyn slang thrown in the mix. When Capone's cousin Sylvester Agoglia thinks something is "unpretentious," that doesn't imply that he utilized words of more than three syllables in his speech. Most of these criminals were grade-school dropouts. However, neither Agoglia or any other unsavory thug in this book should be limited in their expression of thought, for although they were uneducated, many of them were dangerously clever.

Introduction

"SCARFACE" AL CAPONE was a phenomenon who first saw light of day less than one year before the dawn of the twentieth century, January 17, 1899. He was baptized Alphonsus Capone in St. Michael the Archangel Church, in NYC's borough of churches, Brooklyn. For most of his life he was called Alphonse, Big Al, or sometimes Big Fellow, by those who knew him or had occasion to address him other than by Mr. Capone. The nickname "Scarface" was used only behind his back, when he was out of earshot.

As a small child, Capone was brought to live in a cold-water apartment in a dwelling constructed some fifty years prior to his family moving in. The Navy Yard district where it was located was a thriving blue-collar community comprised mostly of hard-working citizens. But it had its share of wise guys, too. Capone came on the scene when industrious immigrants were not finding "gold in the streets" as some were led to believe, but who chased their dreams of a better life in America through back-breaking labor. A few corrupt individuals found the lure of easy money generated by the public's incessant demand for sinful pleasures too compelling to ignore, and Capone, in time, would fall in with them. It was as if fate had ordained Capone's rise to both physical and criminal maturity to coincide with the Prohibition Act of 1919.

Opportunity knocked at the door of a twenty-one-year-old hood-lum who had been tutored by mobsters Johnny Torrio and Frankie Yale. Capone's disquieting demeanor, combined with the "techni-cal advice" he learned from these insidious pedagogues, contributed to the molding of the brutal Capone, whose nickname, "Scarface," evoked fascination throughout the world. It is said were it not for Frank Yale, Al Capone would have never left Brooklyn. Without his primary educator, Johnny Torrio, he probably would have wound up like so many of his counterparts, just another tough guy who failed to survive what must be considered the most precarious period in the life of an ambitious "wannabe," his twenties.

Years earlier, Capone's oldest brother, Vincent, had made an attempt to introduce young Alphonse to life on a grander scale than evidenced in the grimy streets, tenements, and clubhouses of their crime-infested neighborhood. Vincent's fascination with the Old West and his love of horses prompted him to bring his eight-year-old brother, Alphonse, with him on a ferry ride across a stretch of water in Brooklyn called the "Narrows" at the point where the Verrazano-Narrows Bridge (once the world's longest expansion bridge) now spans the bay. He shared with little Alphonse his mythical kingdom on Staten Island, which happened to be the most peaceful and pastoral terrain in the New York City area at the turn of the century. Rural and not yet victimized by overcrowding or heavy industry, Staten Island was home to a large stable of horses engaged by a company to pull wagons loaded with blocks of ice chopped from Clove Lake. This provided refrigeration for the folks on Staten Island before electricity. Vincent Capone had befriended a stable groom who allowed the brothers an occasional romp through the meadows and hills of the island.

When he was around fifteen years of age, Vincent decided to sub-mit to Horace Greeley's edict to "go West, young man" and embarked on an adventure of his own. A family friend drove a melancholy young Alphonse by buggy to the Brooklyn shore, where he watched Vincent board the ferry for the last time.

Vincent settled in Homer, Nebraska, where he assumed the surname of one of his heroes, the silent film cowboy William S. Hart, and called himself Richard Hart. He kept his new identity secret from the rest of his family for almost two decades. In a real twist of fate, Richard Hart would eventually join the forces of good by becoming a deputy sheriff in Nebraska and was involved in busting moonshine operations in his part of the country while his younger brother was becoming a large purveyor of illegal beer and liquor to Chicago's thirsty population.

Gang Rosters

FRANK IOELE'S (FRANKIE YALE) BROOKLYN MOB

Boss:
Frankie Ioele (1915-1928)

Senior Advisor:
Batista Balsamo (1868-1940)

Soldiers and Hitmen:

Willie "Two Knife" Alterie
George "Gino" Ballati
    Anthony "Tony The Chief"
Bonasera
Joe "Rackets" Capolla
Vincent "Jimmy Sham
    Brown" Caponi
Anthony "Little Augie Pisano"
    Carfano
Vincent "Jimmy" Crissali
Anthony Desso

Miguel "Mickey" DiMessio
Anthony "Mr. T" Ercole
Joey "Squats" Esposito
Phil Mangano
Vincenzo Mangano
Giuseppe "Momo" Municharo
Jimmy "Nap" Napoli
Johnny "Bath Beach" Oddo
Benedetto "Crazy Benny" Pazzo
Salvatore "Sammy" Pollaccio
Joseph Profaci

Associate Members:

Fiuri "Fury" Agoglia
Sylvestor "Silvie" Agoglia
Alberto Anastasia
Gido Bianco
Frank Brancato (Cleveland
    Bound 1921)
Alphonse "Al Brown" Capone
    (Chicago Bound 1919)
Frank Capone
Ralph Capone
Vincent "Jimmy Files" DeAmato
Joseph "Frenchie Collins"
Carlino

Rocco Fischetti
Charlie Fischetti
Giuseppe Florina
    (Alias Speranza)
Johnny "Silk Stockings" Guistra
Rocco Morganti
Frank Nitto
Tullio "Crater Face" Piccone
Joey "Big Beef" Polusi
Anthony "Tony Spring" Romeo
Vincent "Jimmy" Santoro
Constantino Scanavino
Jack "Stick Em Up" Stabile

Yale commanded an army of over one hundred armed hitmen and associates. His criminal empire became a Brooklyn super power due in great measure to his viciousness in the Italian underworld. He also was very sympathetic toward the poor in his neighborhood and became known as the "Prince of Pals" throughout the entire Italian underworld.

BROOKLYN'S NOTORIOUS AND LONG ESTABLISHED WHITE HAND GANG

Boss:
Dennis "Dinny" Meehan (1910 – 1920)
Murdered March 31st 1920 by Rival Italian mobsters

William "Wild Bill" Lovett (1920 – 1923)
Murdered at direction of the Frankie Yale mob on Halloween, 1923

Richard "Pegleg" Lonergan (1923 – 1925)
Slain December 26th, 1925 by Alphonse Capone and his Brooklyn compatriots

Soldiers and Associates:

Gary Barry
Joseph Behan
Peter Behan
Ricco Branche
Jimmy "The Bug" Callahan
Cinders Connolly
Nun Connors
Johnny Crowley
Charlie "Cute Charlie" Donnelly
Kevin "Smiley" Donovan
Cornelius "Needles" Ferry
Arthur "Criss Cross" Finnegan
Patrick Foley
Mikey Gilligan
Aaron Harms
Jimmy Hart
Frank Healy

Banty Hines
Joseph "Ragtime" Howard
Edward Hughes
Edward "Kid Eddie" Lynch
William "Billy the Kid" Lynch
Patrick "Happy" Malone
Chris Maroney
Matthew "Matty" Martin
Pegleg McCarthy
Charleston Eddie McFarland
Edward McGuire
Timothy, Alias "The Postman"
Quilty
Skidder Reinhardt
Frank "Ashcan" Smitty
Johnny Travers
Willie "Willyboy" Walsh

Meehan, Lovett and Lonergan commanded an army of more than one hundred armed soldiers and hitmen. They were an underworld super power and defended the Brooklyn waterfront in a five year gangland feud with the Frankie Yale mob.

1

Touch Us If You Dare!

TOMMASSO, WHERE'SA MY *bacile?*" muttered the rotund, five foot, four inch tall Maria Adamo as her seventeen-year-old approached. Knowing his mother always did her wash at this time of day, the youngster figured out just what she was looking for.

"I don't know, Mama, I haven't seen the washbasin. Maybe you left it in the yard," he replied, with a sheepish look on his face. He wouldn't dare let on that he'd seen one of his brothers carrying it in the hallway earlier that morning. The thirty-eight-year-old mother of five boys and two small daughters was remarkably youthful-looking despite her many childbirths, but this morning the usually patient, mild-mannered lady was more than a little agitated. She threw her arms in the air and began mumbling a repetitive round of profanity, concluding with *putana diavalo* (whore of the devil) as she walked outside the doorway and circled the yard once again. Maria, dressed in a loose-fitting beige dress covered with a spotless white apron that she had sewn for herself, was becoming resigned to the fact that someone had stolen her new metal washtub.

"Im'a keep it right here, where it stay alla time," Maria complained, while pointing to a nail protruding from a wooden beam close to the door that led to the yard.

The Adamos' apartment consisted of two separate levels, the basement and the parlor floor of a rented, three-family house at 125 Navy Street where she resided with her large brood and her husband, Francesco, a short, husky dock worker who walked with a limp, his abnormal gait the result of an injury sustained four years prior while toiling on Brooklyn's Pearl Street piers.

Tommasso "Tommy" Adamo left his bewildered mother and took a stroll up the block in search of his younger brothers, thinking they might have taken the rather large basin for one reason or another. Just as he expected, Tommasso found them at the corner of Navy and Tillary Streets. Sixteen-year-old Gerardo, thirteen-year-old Johnny Boy, and the youngest of the Adamo boys, eleven-year-old Francesco—known as Junior—were hanging out with their clique, called the "Navy Street Boys." It was May 12, 1907.

This youthful brotherhood consisted of the previously mentioned Adamo brothers and several other local toughs, including the Capone brothers: Ralph, almost fifteen; twelve-year-old Salvatore (known as Frankie); and the youngest of the group, chubby Alphonse, who was just past the tender age of eight. Alphonse was taller and heavier than most of the other kids his age. He looked like a boy of eleven and the older guys accepted him in the gang as sort of a mascot.

The unchallenged leader of this group of roughnecks was nineteen-year-old Frank Nitto, a tough cookie who was squat (five feet, five inches in height), good with his fists, and much more dangerous when he wielded a weapon. Frank Nitto would gain notoriety later in life as Frank "The Enforcer" Nitti. It was Frank's strong leadership, combined with his boldness during rumbles, that helped make the Navy Street Boys truly feared among other youth gangs of that era. Not only on their own turf but also throughout the borough of Brooklyn, all one had to do was mention "I'm with Navy Street" and that alone caused other youngsters to cower and make tracks. The supercharged fraternity, consisting of mostly Italian Americans, were "cliqued up" with some of the toughest street gangs around and the time for a little teamwork was fast approaching.

Some of the others who were destined to play a role in the impending rumble on the side of the Italians were Frank's brother, Lally, James "Filezee" DeAmato, Rocco "Rocky" Mangano, "Tough" Tony Caputo, and around a dozen others.

"Did any of you see Mama's wash basin?" Tommasso asked as he approached the gang. He directed the question to his youngest brother, Junior, who was seated, cross-legged on the wooden steps of the house where Tony Caputo lived. "She's going nuts looking for it because she wants to wash some of Papa's work clothes."

Junior Adamo bore a blank expression and remained tight-lipped as the hoodlum commander, Frank Nitto, who was leaning against a corner lamppost with his right shoulder, hesitated for a moment, then lit a cigarette, which hung from his lips, and took a drag. Sucking the smoke deep into his lungs, Nitto held it for a moment, and then exhaled the nicotine fog into the gentle breeze.

"She'll get it back in good shape as soon as we finish using it. When the shit's over!" Nitto barked, and then softened his tone reassuringly with, "You have my word on that, Tommy."

Tommasso sighed a little, but his anxiety was allayed when little Alphonse disclosed the fact that Frank told him to hide the basin under the stairs in the hallway of his house and furthermore, young Capone promised that he would protect the tub.

The oldest Adamo brother, arriving late on the scene, was not aware of the "war council" that he had unexpectedly interrupted. The gang was upset because one of the guys in their clique, Rocky Mangano, recently had a family member, an aunt, insulted by some local Irish hooligans. The young Irish toughs thought it was funny to sneak up behind this dark-haired lady, who in this particular neighborhood was undoubtedly Italian, and lift up her skirt to expose her bloomers.

This meant war to Frank Nitto, especially as more stories, real or imagined, were coming forth from the lips of the Navy Street Boys. They continued relating the many insults, some amounting to atrocities, being committed by the Irish.

"I heard that piece of crap Billy Walsh snuck up behind the owner of the Chinese laundry on York Street, Jimmy Lee Fong, and snipped off one of his pigtails—all the way up to his ear," Nitto exclaimed.

"Who's Jimmy Lee Fong?" Tommasso asked, as he brushed past his brother, Gerardo, in order to better hear Nitto's voice above the rattling and clip clopping of a horse-drawn ice wagon that was passing by. "Are you deaf or stupid or both?" Nitto roared, "Jimmy Fong is the owner of the Chinese laundry on York Street. He's also the guy whose father sometimes gives us free cookies and nuts. He's an all right guy, even though he's a chink."

Nitto's eyes grew large as he spoke. Not unlike a general issuing battle orders, he pointed a finger in the direction of his brother, Lally.

"I want you to take the trolley car, go to Third Avenue. See that guy named Vaaha Minelli, the guy we went to bat for that time in Prospect Park, remember him?" Lally nodded as his older brother continued the assignment. "Look for him at the Commodore Social Club and tell him to bring a few of the Garfield Boys along with him." Nitto then turned to address another of his pals saying, "Rocky, I want you to go right now. Take the Columbia Street trolley and get off at Pioneer Street. Go near the movie house and find 'Louie the Beef.' Ask him if he can get the Red Hook Pointers over here in a hurry.

"At about a quarter to seven tonight, we'll all get together near Ralphie's father's barbershop."

The gang's appetite for blood was growing more intense with every new threat that spewed from the mouth of their leader, Nitto, who finalized his inspiring dialogue by slamming one of his big fists into the palm of his open hand while he ordered his young cohorts.

"Bring bats, sticks, rocks, anything you can get your hands on," he urged, as his voice grew louder and the veins on his thick neck protruded to the point that one would think they'd explode.

"We'll march straight up Sand Street and stop right in front of Toomey's, then we'll challenge the bastards by hanging outside the joint and singing to them this tune: *We are the boys of Navy Street and touch us if you dare!"* Nitto suddenly whooped out a war cry like an Apache chief getting his warriors ready for the massacre, but with just one difference. His weird shriek was in his native tongue, Italian.

"*Ammazzola!*" (kill) he cried, taking a few steps back from the gathering. He began jabbing his muscular arms in every direction, throwing imaginary punches and kicks at the inescapable enemy.

• • •

TERESINA CAPONE CAME outside to throw away some garbage in the front of their apartment situated above her husband's barbershop. She decided to stay there for a moment to admire the brand-new lettering recently painted on the windows and the shiny barber pole on the sidewalk, which she polished every morning herself. The big, red characters on the glass said simply, BARBER SHOP. Under that, in smaller black lettering it read, HAIRCUTS AND SHAVES. The glass on the door of the tonsorial emporium was also newly inscribed with fancy script that read, "*Gabriele Capone—Proprietor.*"

Teresina strolled to the entrance of the shop and opened the door just enough to pop her head inside to remind her husband of the lateness of the day. Teresina always wore her salt-and-pepper-shaded hair tied up in a bun. She did this to placate Gabriele because he always told her he thought it was too long.

"Gabriele, do you know how late it is?" she asked in gentle Italian. "What time do you want your dinner?" She disliked bothering him when he was at work, but she thought her husband worked a little too hard in his effort to provide for their large brood.

"Teresina, please, can't you see I'm busy now?" The balding, five-foot, ten-inch barber and father of Al Capone (and five others) replied in his native Italian, "Please, *cara mia*, I want to finish cutting the hair of this young man because I feel he's going to give me a nice tip. Now go upstairs," he said, promising her that this would be the last customer for today. He also assured her that he'd be finished in fifteen minutes.

"Well then, I'm locking this door right now, before somebody else sees the door open and decides he needs a haircut too," she snapped, adding, "Let the young man out from the hallway."

"You wanna shorta haircutta?" Gabrielle asked the man in the barber chair, who appeared to be a sailor out of uniform, probably docked in the nearby Brooklyn Navy Yard.

"Not too short, but trim the sides even," the redheaded man with a southern accent replied. "I hate getting haircuts on my ship."

Responding in a thick Italian accent, Gabriele Capone offered, "I always try my besta to make'a the customa happy."

Later that evening, the first ones to assemble in front of the barbershop were the Capone and Nitto brothers, who witnessed the somewhat comical spectacle of young Al Capone in tattered, black cotton pants that were slipping down from his waistline, their cuffs draping over his scruffy shoes. He had found a rope and tied it through one handle of the washbasin, which he thrust squarely against his belly like a bass drum, while using one of his mother's wooden spoons as a drumstick.

The Italian youngsters were now armed with all sorts of weapons as dictated by Nitto and the increasingly large crowd commenced a march once around the block before going south toward Toomey's saloon. They soon picked up a chant initiated by Gerardo Adamo. "Fall in with our parade, get lost if you're afraid," they crooned, repeating this phrase over and over again until their lyrical display of solidarity began drawing youngsters from as far as three blocks away. They managed to recruit another twenty or so kids of various ages as a result. Those who joined the ranks averaged around fifteen years of age. Most were not necessarily looking for a fight, especially with the more mature Irish, but they welcomed the chance to stand up to the bullies, and being part of a parade seemed like fun. Quite a few others saw this as an opportunity to forge friendships with some of the "tough guys" who reigned over the cobblestone streets and alleys that lay in close proximity to the towers of the then twenty-six-year-old Brooklyn Bridge.

Some left the ranks long enough to tear wooden slats from picket fences to be used in the imminent battle as eight-year-old Alphonse Capone led the mob, banging a beat on the metal washbasin borrowed from Mrs. Adamo's backyard. The throng of the like-minded, tough street gangs walked sprightly as they began a new chant, the one suggested by Nitto, "*We are the Boys of Navy Street—Touch us if you dare!*"

The future "Enforcer" for the Mafia, Frank Nitto, had the gang break up into three separate groups, leaving but a small fraction of the mob to actually stand in front of the dingy joint in order to challenge the beer guzzlers to step outside. The remaining Italians filled the sidewalks on either side of Toomey's while the strange, comedic burlesque continued. *Banga-da-banga-boom, boom boom,* little Alphonse beat out his monotonous cadence on Mrs. Adamo's washbasin.

The customers inside the bar roared with hysterical laughter at the sight of the ragtag army and the indiscernible serenade they were repeating over and over. It was just too much for the beer drinkers to bear.

"Stupid wops, what are you training for? Coxey's Army? You chickenshit dagos, go home and eat some macaroni!" They shouted, jeered, and giggled at the rather small bunch of dumb Italians who were undoubtedly attempting to goad them.

Now the Italians began a new chant, "One-two-three-four, step outside the fuckin' door!"

The first one to bid the chant's challenge and step outside the entrance to Toomey's was the main troublemaker, Billy Walsh, a brown-haired youth, followed by his close friend, Mickey Daly, who was still carrying his half-empty bottle of beer. "Git the fuck outta here or else we'll break your stinky asses," Walsh shouted.

Frank Nitto's face turned beet red as he stepped in front of the drunken Irish youth, who looked to both sides of the street and suddenly noticed the tremendous crowd of Italians gathered. But Walsh's drunken stupor allowed him a sense of false bravado and his emotions were uncontrollable. His attempt to continue the bitter harangue was swiftly interrupted by Nitto, who hauled off with a table leg he had brought along with him. Swinging the heavy wooden object, he scored a direct hit on Walsh's noggin. Then he swung the thing again, whacking the right side of Mickey Daly's face. Both went down instantly, the blood flowing like Niagara from Walsh's deep head wound.

Meanwhile, Toomey's patrons bolted out from the bar to join the fray. The time of the attack had assured Nitto that the place would be full of potential victims, who now armed themselves with chairs, empty beer bottles, and baseball bats as they emptied the bar and struck back at the Navy Street Boys. But the Irish were terribly outnumbered and within just a few minutes the swarm of Italians swinging their lead pipes, sticks, and belts with bolts and nuts attached to the buckles were winning the day.

Little Alphonse slipped the rope tied from around his neck and bashed the tub into the head of one guy who was attempting to rise from the sidewalk. In all of the confusion and bloodied faces, the fallen man was still recognizable to Alphonse. It was Billy Walsh, the lowlife whose degenerate actions had been the catalyst for the uprising.

"This is for Rocky's aunt," he roared at Walsh, who attempted to roll his body into a ball while pleading for his life as Frank and his brother Lally struggled to separate him from his trousers. Yanking them from his squirming body, they tossed the blue jeans into Toomey's bar, which had already been stormed by the attacking force, causing tremendous damage to the interior and the loss of hundreds of dollars in beer and liquor.

Not a single beat cop was summoned to the early evening riot. If a policeman were in the vicinity, you could be certain he'd have hesitated before going anywhere near the scene of the carnage.

When the dust cleared, the emergency rooms of nearby Cumberland, Brooklyn, and Long Island College Hospitals were filled with the injured. Most of the Irish were being delivered to the overwhelmed Cumberland and Brooklyn Hospitals, while the Italians, who suffered far fewer casualties, were driven to the Long Island College Hospital in two private horse-drawn wagons driven by Mangano's uncle, Joe, and a friend. This was done in order to avoid further violence. Luckily no one was killed in the melee, but the main concerns of the medical attendants were patients with broken limbs and the many who required stitches. A few had to spend the night under close supervision, one of these being Billy "Kid" Walsh. Besides twenty-seven stitches to his head and a broken kneecap, this patient also needed something to repair his shattered ego.

The subsequent police investigation into the incident was stymied because all the participants in the skirmish declined comment.

Maria Adamo was happily surprised the next morning when she found her lost washbasin hanging in the hallway, near the yard in its usual place with only one small dent noticeable on it, and the ladies in the neighborhood never feared embarrassment on the street again. From that day forward, whenever Mr. Fong walked past Toomey's restored tavern, he was greeted with, "Good afternoon, Mr. Fong."

2

Shoeshines and Shopping Bags

ALPHONSO, COME OVER here," Gabriele Capone called to his fourth son. Although he was only eleven years old, Gabriele was proud of the fact that this one looked and acted much older than his years.

The child entered the room to find his father seated comfortably by the window of the new apartment Gabriele managed to move the family into early in 1910. The address was 21 Garfield Place, in an area called South Brooklyn.

Looking about the spacious room while admiring some of the new furniture, Gabriele seemed ready to reprimand his little boy. "Mama says you don't like working in the barber shop with me. Is that right?"

Gabriele was sitting in his spouse's old rocker, which he had painted shiny white, and the boy approached with his head down expecting to be scolded. But instead, Gabriele said, "Well, I have a surprise for you, Alphonso."

The boy was puzzled when he saw his papa reach down to the side of the chair and raise into view a square, red object that he could not identify. "What is that?" asked the child, as he drew closer for a better look.

"It's a shoeshine box," the man said with a smile as he placed it back down on the carpet near his feet. Alphonse picked the thing up. It felt much heavier than he expected, and while he studied it, he heard his father say, "I won't force you to work in the barbershop, but I will tell you this: When all your brothers reached the age of twelve, I always tried to encourage each one with an opportunity to make some money."

Lighting a cigar that he pulled from his shirt pocket, he made a motion for the child to sit on the couch. Alphonse responded quickly, carrying the brand-new shine box with him as he sat down.

The boy was very much interested as his Papa went on talking about his three older sons. "Ralph was working after school in my shop until he started the job in the book bindery when he was around fourteen. Your oldest brother, Vincenzo, he likes horses so much that I tried very hard until I found him that job working in the stables on Douglas Street. Did you know that I also made a shoeshine box for your brother Frank? But he was not inclined to work. He kept it for a while, then sold it to another kid for money to go to Coney Island. Frank is lazy and what he did was not too smart. Alphonso, never sell something that is a tool that can bring you steady money, *capisci?*"

"I understand, Papa, and I promise I'll never sell this one."

Gabriele's eyes widened as he asked his son, "Did you look inside of it?"

The box had a small hook and eye on one side and when the child opened the lid, he could see two brushes, some cans of shoe polish, and two buffing rags. "Put the box on your shoulder by the strap. That's the reason I put it there."

As he slung the leather strap over his left shoulder, the boy lifted the box and held it by his side.

"No, no," Gabriele said to his son. "You're right-handed, so keep the shoeshine box on your right shoulder. That way, you have better control of it and you won't go banging into something with it."

Little Alphonse walked over to a mirror that hung on the wall behind him and raised himself on his toes to inspect the image he projected as a shoeshine boy.

"Listen, son," Gabriele confessed, "when I was a boy in Italy I never wanted to go to work with my father, either. I tried it once, but all I ever heard from him during the work day were reminders of my boyish mischief, of things that happened the night before. So, I really can't begrudge you for feeling that way. But because you act much older than your age and you eat like a big boy, I'm treating you like one."

Gabriele leaned over in his chair, urging the child who was parading around the room with the box to stop immediately. The eleven-year-old had gotten a little carried away with the worldly advice being presented to him by his Papa, who the boy thought until now still treated him like a baby. After all, the only times he was allowed outside of the house at night was when he lied and said that he was going with one of his older brothers. He also knew that his brother Ralph was an active member of the Navy Street Boys, and the code the gang lived by, the sacred principle they had all adopted at a tender age was, "You never turn rat!"

"Alphonso, I know a place where you can make some good business with that shine box!" Gabriele remarked as the boy returned to sit on the couch.

"Near the Navy Yard, where the old house was?" the boy inquired.

"No, boy, I'm talking about a place that's got even more men's shoes that need to be cleaned. You must realize that most sailors, when they are ashore, are always in a hurry and yet they always seem to find plenty of time to shine their own shoes." Gabriele's advice made sense to Alphonse, who waited to hear his father's suggestion as to just where a good spot might be found.

Gabriele, it seems, had another good idea up his sleeve. "As a matter of fact," he said, "it's such a busy shopping area that on some days, you can even leave the shine box home, go there with only your willingness to work, and make some money."

Alphonse settled back in the couch and made himself comfortable as he inquired, "How can I do that, Papa?"

Gabriele Capone was busy trying to relight his cigar, which had gone out. Once lit, he started puffing on the crude stogie until it raised a white cloud above his head. Waving a hand through the smoke, he squinted and told his small son, "The spot I'm talking about is at the corner of Union Street and Columbia Street. Do you remember the place where I took you last week when I bought the *capozella* (lambs' heads)?"

"Oh, I know where you mean," Alphone said. "Where all the push-carts are. Is that it?" His father nodded affirmatively.

"On a Saturday or a Sunday that area is very good for a shoeshine boy. Any other day after school, you're better off selling paper bags on Union Street."

The boy remained sitting quietly on the couch with a puzzled look on his face while his father explained. "On the same side of the street where the pushcarts are, just a few stores away from the corner, you'll see a store with lots of egg crates outside. That's where you can buy shopping bags for a penny apiece and sell them in the crowd of shoppers for two cents each, *capisci* Alphonso?"

The child was mesmerized by the idea of making his own money after his father had explained to him about his inability to provide spending money for his brood. "You'll make enough money to get some of the things I can't possibly get you!" his father said. "If you turn the corner on Columbia Street and stake out a spot under the big clock, that's where you'll be kept busy shining shoes."

Gabriele reached into his trousers pocket and handed his little boy a nickel. "You take the trolley car on Union Street and get off at Columbia Street. You can see the clock from there, so you can't get lost! You'll have to use your earnings for the trolley ride back home. All right, Alphonso?"

The child willingly agreed to do everything his father advised, with the exception of how he should spend the five cents. Tomorrow was Saturday, he was already preparing mentally to start out in business for himself. Tonight, he figured, he would risk the five cents by investing in the poker game that took place on his friend Jerry's stoop.

If Gabriele thought his little boy would spend the nickel he was given for a trolley ride, he was sadly mistaken. Trolley rides had always been free for Alphonse. Ever since he was old enough to jump on the back of a streetcar and hang on to the window railings, they were free. Hitching a trolley was considered something you did for kicks. The older kids hitched rides when they had somewhere to go, but the boys his age often hitched rides to anywhere and nowhere in particular. Making transfers by jumping from one streetcar to another, they would sometimes wind up getting themselves lost in another part of town.

Alphonse Capone tried his luck, leaning against the base of the eighteen-foot-high clock that stood near the corner of Union Street and Columbia streets for at least half an hour before he finally heard someone else besides himself say, "Shine."

The man wore a pair of high workman's shoes, black, the laces frayed and knotted in places. He also had on a pair of the whitest stockings the boy had ever seen. Although this man did not appear to be very rich judging by the old shoes that he wore, he was certainly spotless in his appearance.

"Please, son," he said, "try not to get any polish on my stockings, heh? The last time I got a shine from one of you kids, both my stockings and the cuffs of my trousers were soiled."

"Well, you didn't get that shine from me," the boy exclaimed.

"No," the man said, "I remember the kid who messed me up that day. I never paid the little shit either."

Capone was as careful as possible to act in a professional manner as prescribed by his Papa. He followed the steps he was told were necessary to bring luster to a dull pair of shoes and when the job was completed, he was rewarded with a three cent tip.

The sight of a shine boy doing his thing on a customer's shoes always seemed to attract other shine boys to that particular spot, as if gold had been discovered there. Most of the time, they would become disappointed and walk to another of their favorite spots, usually within a radius of just a few blocks.

Young Alphonse started a conversation with one of his competitors, a pale-looking kid of around thirteen with a fancy shoeshine box riveted in places with small rhinestone studs, giving him what he considered a very professional appearance. He learned from the boy that some of the kids had steady customers who looked for *their* shine boy once a week to stop by their home or place of business to work on their shoes.

"How much money can a guy make in a day around here?" the inquisitive Capone asked.

"I usually don't go home until I've made one dollar, but there are days when I've made as much as three dollars, working 'till around six o'clock. Not today, that's for sure!" he added. "There's too many of us down here today, so I think I'll try another one of my spots."

In an effort to learn some other places where he could later go in order to pick up business, Alphonse watched the boy walk to the corner and turn down President Street. Capone trailed slowly behind, hoping the kid wouldn't know he was being followed.

Another customer, this one a well-dressed fellow in his late teens, was pointing down to his shoes, a beautiful pair of brown oxfords, with one hand while swinging a long key chain with the other. "Are you new around here?" he asked, "I don't think I've ever noticed you shining shoes on this block."

"This is my first day," Capone replied, while watching the man raise the cuff of his right leg and placing his foot on the shine box.

"Your first day? Oh no," he said, "I'm not gonna be no guinea pig." He removed his foot from the top of the box and was getting ready to leave when Alphonse clarified his statement with a lie.

"What I mean is . . . I'm just new around here. I usually work over by the Navy Yard."

"I dunno, you do look a little young to me," the customer said. "How old are you, anyway?"

"I'm thirteen," Capone lied. "I'll give you a good shine, believe me, mister."

"Oh, what the hell, go on," the customer said. "Just be careful, okay?"

Halfway through the shoeshine, Alphonse noticed the man seemed to be staring at a group of older men who stood talking on the corner.

"Do you know who those people are?" the customer mumbled.

"I just finished telling you mister, I'm new around here. I don't know anybody down here except another shoeshine kid. Why? Are they big shots or something?" he asked.

"The one with the brown overcoat and fedora is. His name is Balsamo and he's like . . . the boss around here." Alphonse turned his head to have a look while his customer quickly admonished him. "When you turn to look someplace else, stop your work, heh? Don't get polish on anything but my shoes, okay?" The boy nodded his head and went back to work.

"What do you mean the 'boss'?" the youngster inquired. "Everyone seems to tip their hats to him when they pass by. Is he the pope's brother, or what?"

"To the people in this neighborhood, he's held in such high regard that some call him the Mayor of Union Street," the customer answered.

After completing the first shoe, the boy paused for a moment, then asked, "What does he do for a living? Is he a killer?"

The small-time hood never stopped to realize the effect his words were having on little Alphonse, whose inclination to emulate those he considered to be rich big shots had his head spinning. He could see himself having all the respect and wealth that Balsamo enjoyed while his young mind was busy entertaining thoughts about his own future.

"To answer your question about what he does for a living, he owns a fish market," the customer said. "But that's not how he makes most of his money. Did you see all those pushcarts around the corner?"

"How could I miss them?" the youngster responded.

"Every week, without fail they pay *accamura* to him."

"Never heard of that! What does that mean?"

Alphonse had completed the shine, but the man stood talking for a while, fishing for money in his vest after putting his long key chain back in his pocket. "*Accamura* is insurance money. That's what."

The man tossed him a quarter, which prompted the boy to admit that he didn't have change for the two bits yet. He was kneeling down on a small pillow his mama had given him for his knees, with the shiny quarter in the palm of his hand. "You can keep the change," the customer said. "I made a good score last night! And I'm gonna do better tonight."

The young man continued bragging to young Capone of things he knew about the mob, enlightening the boy about *accamura*. Alphonse learned that it was insurance against a certain calamity striking a business establishment.

"Why are people afraid of him?" the boy inquired. "He better not try fucking around with me."

The customer scoffed at the youngster's remark and disclosed one of the man's sources of power. "Batista Balsamo's got plenty of muscle guys working for him and that's what makes him tick."

The customer asked him, "What's your name kid? I like the shine."

"Alphonse Capone" the youngster replied. "What's yours?"

"My friends call me Tommy Red," said the customer.

Before leaving the spot, Tommy Red waited for the boy to rise and, drawing a bit closer to him, he whispered in his ear, "By the way, Alphonse, remember, keep away from Batista Balsamo. He has been known to look at you one instant, then blow your head off without blinking an eye. To me, my little friend, that's a very dangerous man."

The young boy remained stunned by the revelations. To think, that one guy could interfere with another's business by threatening violent repercussions. It made him think of the man they called Don Pellegrino, the only customer that nobody ever saw pay his papa. Perhaps his own father was paying the same kind of insurance when he refused payment from this important-looking man for barber services rendered.

"Oh no, Don Pellegrino," his father would say, "*Il piacere e' mio* (the pleasure is mine)!"

Alphonse walked toward the corner, where the mayor was still in conference, in order to get a better look at the man's face.

"Shine mister?" he asked. Balsamo responded by raising a hand from his side and moving it back and forth as if he were whisking the boy away. Alphonse did turn away when another man, a short fellow with a stubbled chin, took a step toward him and chased him from hearing distance while the don turned his back and continued his conversation.

Young Capone had picked up something besides sixty-five cents that morning in 1910. His view of life was changed forever. A young, petty hood unknowingly had planted the seed of crime in the impressionable child's mind.

The ride back to Fourth Avenue took a little longer than usual because it was rush hour. The cross-traffic trying to get to the Brooklyn Bridge gave the youngster plenty of time to think.

The wheels in his head spun faster than the wheels of the trolley as he pictured himself, along with his gang, reaping benefits from the labor of working suckers. That's certainly what he'd report to the Garfield Juniors.

The following day, Alphonse found two of his cousins, Charlie Fischetti and Sylvester "Sylvie" Agoglia hanging around the corner of Twentieth Street and Fifth Avenue. They were joined by Jimmy "Filezee" DeAmato and Tony "Scraps" Scrapisetti and very soon, the band of would-be extortionists were hitching their way down the slope to Alphonse's "garden of wealth." The first shoeshine boy that they encountered on the strip was Jerry, the pale-faced kid with the rhinestone-embellished shine box.

Capone walked up to him, followed by Tony Scraps and Charlie, and proceeded in his attempt to offer the frightened kid "protection." He asked Jerry if he would let him examine his shoeshine box. When the first victim of their extortion scheme did so, Capone flung the strap over his shoulder and started to walk away. Poor Jerry looked around for someone that he could turn to for help, but couldn't find a single person he knew.

Eleven-year-old Al Capone strolled down to the corner with the kid's gleaming shoeshine box over his shoulder. However, the box was not what he was after. "You'll have to kick in ten cents, if you want to be a part of our club," he told Jerry, who realized they were serious. The nervous boy did just that when he found himself surrounded by five tough-looking hoodlums, one of them holding his beloved shine box hostage.

Jerry soon turned over the dime to Alphonse, asking, "Is this gonna be every week?" Alphonse handed the box back after receiving payment. Capone stared at the kid and replied, "No, this is gonna be every day. That's right Jerry, every time you come down here to shine shoes and you see one of us, you have to give up a dime. Get it?" The frightened boy nodded.

Excited by their first triumph, the gang searched the streets for more victims while deciding upon a name for their new clique.

They agreed on calling themselves the "South Brooklyn Rippers," because everyone in the world knew of London's "Jack the Ripper," who, with his sharp surgical tools, had dismembered six prostitutes in the Whitechapel murders. They figured the name was bound to strike terror in the hearts of their intended victims.

"There goes one now," shouted Fischetti, as the five boys moved down the street to have a little chat with another shoeshine boy. They split into groups; two of them followed directly behind, while the other three walked the far side of the street. They finally cut him off a couple of blocks from their starting point, near the corner of Carroll Street, and threatened him into giving up fifteen cents because, they figured, what the hell, it was so easy getting ten cents from the first guy, why not try for more?

This one, however, reacted differently. Tall and thin with a swollen eye, the tough-looking character put a hand in his pocket and was seemingly ready to oblige. Suddenly, he turned and started a dash through an empty lot. He then exited the far end of the lot through a hole in the wooden fence and disappeared.

They followed the general direction of his escape, which was behind a junk pile, and found the hole in the fence. Then, from a safe distance, the pack noticed their intended victim jogging half-way up the block, entering what looked like either a pool room or a social club.

"Shit!" screamed Charlie Fischetti. "Did you ever see a faster runner? What's the plan now?" he asked, rubbing one of his knees, which was bruised climbing over the junk.

"I don't think he's coming out for a while, so we'll go back to the corner," Alphonse replied. "There's lots of other shine boys around and we haven't even touched on the kids who sell shopping bags yet."

They turned the corner and were back on the main street, Columbia, again when they were surprised and alarmed to hear strange sounds coming at them from the area they had just left. Loud screams filled the quiet Sunday morning air: "Eeeeiiiii, get those bastards!" The Rippers turned to see a large mob, whose ages ranged from some barely in their teens to others who looked like fully grown men, coming at them like a crazed war party.

Some were swinging garrison belts, while others had pool cues or baseball bats in their hands; the gang carefully dodged the bottles and rocks being tossed their way by mixing in with the crowd of men, mostly longshoremen, who regularly gathered under the giant clock. The South Brooklyn Rippers ran at a frenzied pace while they made their way, in different directions, to the trolley tracks a little way up the line.

The gang was not completely reunited until Sylvie Agoglia and Tony Scraps jumped off the moving streetcar, relieved to be back in their own familiar territory of Fourth Avenue. They could laugh at the incident now; all except the bold Alphonse, that is, who wanted to try the same stunt again, the very next day.

Fischetti's encouraging words to Alphonse would be prophetic in the years to come. "Don't worry about nothing Alphonse," he said. "Someday people will pay dearly just to stay friends with the Rippers." While Tony Scrapisetti added, "This insurance idea that you picked up is a good one. It's just that we tried it without knowing about some of the things we gotta be ready for next time, that's all."

"We'll try it again soon, that's for sure!" was Capone's angry response.

3

Eyes in the Mirror

IT WAS EARLY November and thirteen-year-old Al Capone awoke to
the familiar chill that always permeated his family dwelling at this
time of year. He washed himself with cold water and downed a cup
of coffee while munching on his breakfast, which consisted of some
day-old Italian bread.

Teresina Capone was an early riser who always prepared lunch and
had it waiting for her brightest child, Alphonse. She sincerely believed
this particular child would go far in life if he'd only stay away from the
dregs in the neighborhood who were always trying to show him ways
to acquire "*sorda cenza fatigla*" (money without working for it). It
was true that young Alphonse often brought home some of the spoils
from his unscrupulous activities for the family to share in, but it still
offended her that one of her children would be a crook. She anguished
over this, lighting candles and praying that he'd not be lured into a
life of crime. Nevertheless Teresina accepted this flaw in his character
with great melancholy, often being overruled by Gabriele, who himself wielded little control over the oversized youngster.

Young Capone put the sandwich—two slices of bread, filled with
the remnants of the family's previous night's dinner, meat loaf—in a
pocket of his well-worn wool coat, put the garment on, and headed

out the door with every intention of attending school, PS 133, on Fourth Avenue and Butler Street in South Brooklyn.

One of his young friends, Gido Bianco, revealed in later years that the young thug actually enjoyed arithmetic and showed real ability in that area. Bianco claimed it was pure irony that the setting for the one subject Capone truly showed interest in, numbers, would be the locale for the incident that permanently curtailed Capone's formal education.

The previous day, Alphonse had another sandwich, this one consisting of some hard salami and cheese, robbed from right under his nose. He had stuffed it in the same pocket of the same heavy coat, which he hung in the same place, the wardrobe situated in the rear of the classroom, but when the teacher rang the bell signifying lunchtime, Capone retrieved his coat only to realize his sandwich was gone.

Bianco heard Capone cursing in both Italian and English as the youngster looked around the room, searching with wild eyes at the crowd of teens who were pouring out the door. Most of the kids were heading for the schoolyard in a hurry to devour the contents of their brown bags and yellow tins despite the crisp weather.

"If I find the one who robbed my lunch, he'll wish he was never born," Capone bellowed at Gido, vowing he'd catch the bastard.

"Could it have fallen out of your pocket on your way to school?" Gido inquired.

"No way," Capone replied assuredly. "I patted the damn thing down myself after I hung my coat up in the closet. Somebody's off eating my salami and cheese right now in some corner. The sonuvabitch!"

This day would be different, Capone thought to himself, vowing not to be made a fool of twice and go hungry again. This time he'd keep his sandwich under surveillance with all the zeal of a bulldog guarding his precious ham bone. He came to class early for the express purpose of being one of the first to enter the room. Quickly hanging his coat in the wardrobe, he shuffled slowly toward his assigned desk, never removing his eyes from the wardrobe. For ten minutes or more, Capone surreptitiously studied the actions of every boy as they removed their outer garments in the rear of the room and hung them inside the large, wooden wardrobe that spanned almost the entire back wall. He was hoping the bastard who stole his lunch the day before would have the nerve to think that one of the South Brooklyn Rippers, namely, Al Capone, was a real jerk and thus try to repeat the stunt that left him famished. But besides the hunger pangs what was really hurt beyond repair was Capone's ego.

From the vantage point of his desk situated on the outside row, about a third of the way up from the teacher's desk, Capone could turn himself slightly in his chair to see his red-and-white checkered coat still hanging undisturbed on its hook in the closet. He took his eyes away from it for just scant seconds at a time while continuing to scan each boy for some bit of evidence, some facial expression that would help spill the beans on the guilty party.

As time progressed, both Alphonse and his buddy, Gido Bianco, were thinking a repeat performance of the sandwich incident was unlikely, but they never relaxed enough to bury their heads in their studies. Things changed just few minutes before the end of the session when, while the teacher had his back turned to the class, a figure suddenly arose from the back of the room and slithered toward the wardrobe. Hunched over and looking every bit the culprit, the blond-headed youth reached into the pocket of Capone's coat, grabbed the sandwich, and was stuffing it down the front of his belted trousers when both Capone and Gido sprang into action.

The teacher, Mr. McGuire, was a soft-spoken person who loved his job enough to tolerate the commute from the Far Rockaway section of Queens on a daily basis. A middle-aged man of average height with white hair that he parted in the middle, McGuire was always dressed impeccably in a suit, white shirt, and tie, and always carried a briefcase in his travels. He had just turned to look at the clock on the wall when he caught sight of Al Capone jumping over the seat of his desk and making a dash for the rear of the room.

The teacher saw Alphonse grab the boy, who turned out to be Melville Miller, in a headlock and commence banging repeatedly on the unforunate lad's head and face in a one-sided slugfest that caught McGuire by complete surprise. Running swiftly to the scene, McGuire tried pulling the heavyweight off of the much skinnier, but taller, boy, who was taking a tremendous beating. Bianco claimed to have landed a few punches to the body of Miller himself when Alphonse turned abruptly from his victim and landed a knockout punch to Mr. McGuire's chin. The teacher fell backward, striking his head on the wooden floor, and the thief, young Miller, fell to his knees inside the closet, bleeding profusely from his face and mouth.

Capone grabbed the remnants of his sandwich while pushing Miller to the ground inside the compartment. Bianco stepped over the fallen teacher to retrieve his own coat and both youngsters hightailed it out of the schoolhouse, strolling briskly with righteous pride onto Fourth Avenue.

Shortly thereafter, the police were sent to the Capone residence, where Gabriele Capone falsely reported to them in his broken English that he hadn't seen his son for three days now and that the family feared the boy had run away from home.

An officer versed in Italian told Gabriele, "It would be for his own good if Alphonse would report to the station house as soon as possible." The police assured the Capones that because of the circumstances and the teacher's reluctance to press charges, Alphonse was facing no criminal charges. They were also guaranteed that if he turned himself in, his only punishment would be mandatory attendance in a reform school where he would receive "compassionate, corrective assistance and help." Teresina heard only the word "help" and that was enough for her. She ceaselessly begged her son to turn himself in, but that was not an option for the strong-willed tough guy who was beginning to find an intoxicating power in pounding out his particular brand of violence. To know young Al Capone one had to respect his temperament, and his ego.

Actually, it wasn't the police that did the hunting for Capone, but the truant officer for the South Brooklyn section of the borough that included PS 133, who was assigned the task. Accompanied by the beat cop who tipped him off that a boy fitting Al's description was frequenting one of the local pool rooms, Alvin Roseman, the plague of the neighborhood hooky players, confronted the youngster on the steps of the billiards parlor.

Perhaps if young Al Capone had been apprehended and forced to submit to the educational requirements of the city of New York by attending a school for troubled youth, his future might have turned out differently. But he slipped from their grasps that day, running inside the pool hall knowing there was a rear exit and utilizing it. From that day forward, Capone kept himself away from that area and stayed closer to the corner of Union Street and Fourth Avenue, where his good friend and sometime employer, mobster Johnny Torrio, maintained a clubhouse where the locals played cards, munched on light meals, and guzzled alcoholic beverages.

It was in that vicinity that Torrio spotted the truant officer who was about to enter Solomon Shapiro's clothing store on Fifth Avenue, hoping to find a nice shirt to wear with the brown suit he planned on wearing to his nephew's *bris* (circumcision) the following week.

"Hello, Mr. Roseman," he heard a voice behind him murmur.

The truant officer turned to see Johnny Torrio standing on the sidewalk behind him escorted by a large man, obviously a bodyguard, around thirty years of age, with blond hair and the rugged face of a gladiator. The well-known mobster was decked out in clothing the city official could never hope to afford.

"I'm sorry, I don't know your name, but I know I've seen you someplace before," Roseman replied, looking down to admire Torrio's black, patent leather shoes.

"I run the Torrio Association on Fourth Avenue," Torrio said. "It's a clubhouse, a nice place where some nice people meet to relax and socialize."

"I know where it is," Roseman said. "And now that you mention it, I have a friend, Joe Pappola, who goes there regularly."

"Sure, Mr. Roseman, Joe is also a good friend of mine," Torrio replied with a smile. "He loves playing poker and he's pretty lucky at it too, I might add."

"May I ask how you know my name?" the truant officer inquired, to which Johnny replied, "We have another mutual friend, a relative of mine. He's a nephew, one of my sister's children, named Alphonse Capone." Torrio was lying on behalf of the youngster. There was no family tie between the two.

"The kid claims that you're being a real ball breaker," Torrio added.

"Alphonse Capone?" Roseman shrieked. Tugging the collar of his shirt while shifting his weight from one leg to the other, the truant officer nervously asked, "Why would you entertain the idea of allowing that young man to skip school and miss out on acquiring an education?"

"You shouldn't worry about Al Capone," the crime figure declared. Drawing closer, he began to whisper in Roseman's ear. "If I were you, I'd worry about myself and my own well-being."

"Wh-wh-why . . . what are you talking about?" the perplexed man stuttered. "It's my job, my duty, to see the lad gets an education."

Suddenly, the threat he had just received began to register. Roseman's eyes opened wide and he gasped as he became aware of the large figure standing beside Torrio, who seemed to be blocking his entry into the clothing shop.

"But if you think someday he'll see the errors of his ways and return to school on his own," Roseman said, his tune changed, "then I guess that'd be enough reason for me to leave the issue to providence."

"Are you promising me that you're willing to leave Alphonse alone?" Torrio asked.

"Yes, I will definitely leave his future in your hands, Mr. Torrio."

Torrio dragged on his cigar and pointed in the truant officer's direction. Flicking the ashes he smiled and said, "Call me Johnny. Come up to my clubhouse soon. I really think you'll enjoy yourself there."

• • •

THE WOODEN STAIRS leading down to the cellar were rickety, and the narrow passageway forced young Al to turn his body sideways while he descended. He was carrying stick matches that were lit one after the other until he managed to reach and light the candle that lay on a badly chipped, wobbly porcelain table located in the middle of the shadow-filled room, which was otherwise bare except for some wooden boxes that served as chairs.

The candle flickered in the drafty, below-street-level clubhouse where the thirteen year-old-boy and three other youngsters who called themselves the South Brooklyn Rippers spent part of their day. It had been another eventful day for Capone.

The beefy lad had succeeded in getting his mentor, Johnny Torrio, to intimidate his truant officer, Mr. Roseman, who had begun the first steps necessary to place him in a reform school. That plan had been dropped, leaving Capone free to hang around the streets in the daylight hours if he so desired.

From the subterranean depths of their clubhouse beneath an abandoned building on Garfield Place, the small band of young hoodlums would often plan their nighttime raids on neighborhood shops. This day they were to divvy up the cash that was extracted from the register inside Tripp's Grocery Store.

"We're splitting according to who did the most work," Capone announced to the gang as seventy-something dollars were placed on the table. "I think I deserve two shares because it was my job. Any objections?"

Capone's tone was distinct and businesslike, as unemotional as a board chairman presiding over a corporate meeting. Only these "board members" were keenly aware of the dramatic change that would take place at the slightest objection. The gang had witnessed Capone's rage unleashed in tussles with other gangs on numerous occasions and saw the cold, gray eyes of Big Al, whose heavy breathing was right now accompanying a scan of their faces. They simply allowed his proposal to go unchallenged, submitting to the will of the much larger youngster while watching him dispense the shares.

"This money will help my father pay for the cost of my new baby sister," he boasted, as he lit one of the cigars stolen on a previous occasion. "You know," he declared, puffing on the cigar, "Maybe I'm too young to smoke these things in public, but one day I'll have a brand named after me." His cap, tilted to one side, seemed too small for his head.

One of his closest partners in crime was a skinny teen with a pointy nose named Anthony Scrapisetti, a.k.a Tony Scraps. This tough guy enjoyed being called "Scrappy." His unkempt brown hair covered his eyes and he continued a protracted effort to push it away. Scraps was one year older than Capone and had the tenacity to be the most trusted member of the small gang, which included Joseph Carlino, later to gain notoriety as "Frenchie Joe Collins," a fair-haired youngster with a fantastic ability for throwing a knife. There was a fifteen-year-old hoodlum, Butch Grimaldi, destined to be killed a few years down the road in a hallway of one of the tenement buildings on Navy Street during a dispute over a gambling debt.

The last member of Capone's earliest clique was Gido Bianco, whose real first name remains a mystery, a man whose formidable criminal career included an intimate association with Capone.

It was four PM and Officer Walter Sheaf would soon be going off duty. Capone was beginning to feel intimidated by this particular cop because people were telling him the cop had been asking questions concerning his whereabouts. This happened to be the same policeman who had accompanied truant officer Alvin Roseman on his rounds when they attempted to confront Capone in front of the pool hall. The cop was still miffed about Al's dashing away from him. Since that day, Sheaf kept an eye out for Capone, knowing his family still lived in the neighborhood.

A strange occurrence would cause Alphonse to regain the ability to venture out into the streets of his old stomping grounds with impunity. It was the murder of a man known as "John the Russian" committed on Sheaf's beat, that gave the budding criminal this renewed confidence.

It happened that both Capone and the cop were witness to this murder, which occurred on a dark and rain-swept street. Sheaf, wearing his uniform under his rain gear, was walking down the slope from the Sixth Avenue Precinct to a private club on Nevins Street where he often found refuge from inclement weather, while Alphonse was just exiting the ground-level door of a friend's house directly across from the scene of the crime.

Capone, with an umbrella in hand, was startled by the strange scene occurring across the street. He quickly closed the umbrella and ducked behind a parked sedan, not wanting to get involved in what appeared to be an act of violence. Just a few seconds later, Officer Sheaf walked past Monte's Venetian Room, a classy restaurant on Carroll Street, and also became witness to the aftermath of the grisly strangulation of John the Russian.

Al stood transfixed and in total shock. Peering through a window of the car, past the rain drops, he recognized the cop, who appeared to be ignoring the sight of two men dragging their victim to a waiting automobile parked at the curb with its headlights off and its motor running. One would assume a cop, faced with such an unusual situation, would certainly draw his pistol and proceed to arrest the evildoers, but Alphonse imagined the reason for Walter's indifference to the dubious activity meant the officer was somehow party to the crime. In reality, Patrolman Sheaf had no direct involvement in the strangulation murder. He was, like Capone, just a witness to the evil deed, but unlike any other officer in the precinct would have, Officer Sheaf turned tail and departed the scene.

Capone wouldn't learn until many years later, while working for Frankie Yale, that the hit was performed on Yale's orders and orchestrated by his boys, James "Sham Brown" Caponi and Samuel "Sammy" Pollaccio, while Tullio "Crater Face" Piccone drove the car to a remote spot and helped dump the body into the murky waters of the Gowanus Canal, just one block from Monte's famous eatery. Why the crooked cop distanced himself from the scene of the slaughter was revealed at that time. It turned out that Sheaf recognized the killers as belonging to Yale's crew, and because he was on the pad of the local crime boss, he simply walked away hoping to garner a nice bonus from Yale.

The results of that incident paid dividends for the youngster soon thereafter, when young Capone was becoming increasingly brazen appearing in public. He was standing outside his own house one day when Officer Sheaf came strolling down the street swinging his nightstick. Alphonse was dressed casually in a blue shirt, green pajama bottoms, and shoes without stockings. The burly cop crossed the street and approached the youngster, who seemed to be interested only in the magazine in his hands.

"Some pair of balls on this wise bastard," Sheaf said to himself. "He sees me and doesn't even care that I'm headed his way." Sheaf reached over the gate and tore the magazine from the hands of the teenage criminal while screaming aloud, "Why aren't you in school? It's eleven o'clock in the morning. Are you sick or something?"

Staring straight back at the policeman's glaring eyes, Capone's temper rose as the cop started to rip his magazine in half. He almost gave into the impulse to sneak punch the cop right in his chubby face but resisted the urge, offering instead a loaded question.

"What's the matter with you, Walter?" the young wise guy inquired. "Is your brain still damp from the other night?"

Capone's strange words caused the cop's face to twist in anger. He'd heard enough crap coming from the mouths of these little guttersnipes lately, and now this overgrown child was trying to give him the needle.

"How would you like me to take you in? Find out why you're not in school?" Sheaf answered in a gruff tone, while stretching an arm over the waist-high fence to yank at the youngster's left hand.

"Wait a minute, Walter," Capone pleaded while successfully avoiding the bluecoat's grasp, "why don't you give me a chance to talk?" Capone watched the enraged officer begin to circle the gate, waving his club over his head in hot pursuit, but the young hoodlum never budged an inch. "Give me a chance to talk," he said again.

Sheaf froze in his tracks, controlling his temper long enough to allow a horse-driven fruit wagon to pass the spot.

"Good morning to you, sir," Sheaf said, forcing a smile in acknowledgment of the peddler's wave. When the fruit cart turned the corner, Sheaf raised his wooden club over his head once again, feigning a blow to the pudgy head of the chatterbox, but instead of following through with the swing, he lowered his arm and jabbed at Capone's ribs. Using his club as a ram, the uniformed officer shoved the boy back until Alphonse had no choice but to flop his rear end onto the wooden steps. From this seated position, the nervy youngster managed to grab the railing with one hand while kicking his legs in a successful effort to deflect the officer's blow with the side of one of his shoes. Aware the irate cop was trying to strike at his ankles, Capone managed to lift himself quickly and recoiled to his feet to begin a grappling match with the superior weight of the tough cop, who had switched his club-wielding hand. This close-quarters struggle now left the cop at a disadvantage in battling the young brute. Sheaf could use just his left hand because his right hand was keeping firm hold of his pistol.

"Hey, Walter, what's wrong with you? I'm only a kid, for Christ's sake," Capone begged. While fastening a grip on the end of the policeman's club and looking him straight in the eyes, Alphonse then added this strange remark: "You should be thanking me, not hurting me, for keeping the old woman from snitching on you."

"What the hell are talking about, you goddamned bastard?" the cop yelled in his ear. "What the hell are you trying to tell me? Hurry up and speak or I'll make sure you go to jail."

"Loosen up some and I'll tell you, okay? But take it easy." The cop relaxed his grip on the youngster as the rage inside of him was becoming tempered by reason, but all Alphonse could see was that Sheaf's normally warm, blue eyes were two red orbs that protruded from his head in a crazy stare.

Continuing to yank on the boy's shirt, the anxious cop nearly flipped when he heard Capone say, "How come you walked away from that awful scene on Carroll Street last Wednesday?"

"You sonuvabitch," the cop muttered. "Talk low or I'll kill you . . . but not here and not now." Releasing his hold on the youngster, the policeman straightened out his uniform by pulling his gun belt up around his waist and commenced brushing himself off.

"Don't be upset, Walter," Capone said. "I'm no rat. You can be sure of that."

Sheaf interrupted Capone's next sentence in a loud tone of voice, saying, "Cut out this Walter shit . . . Call me Officer Sheaf. Do you hear?"

Capone reached to the ground to pick up the torn magazine and addressed the patrolman once again, this time in a hushed tone.

"As I was trying to tell you, I saw the two guys drag that guy into a gray sedan last Wednesday night. It was just past Monte's place and even though it was raining, I saw you there." Alphonse's hand went up in a halting motion as Sheaf feigned a lunge at him. Capone decided to show the respect demanded. "Wait, Officer Sheaf," he said, "you should really be thrilled that I was there to see you at the scene, not just the old lady."

Sheaf raised a finger in front of his face and retorted, "I think you're nuts if you tell anyone what you imagined you saw on Wednesday night. And furthermore, I think you're flirting with the angel of death, lad."

"I'm not looking to cause any trouble, officer, but I want you to know an aunt of the friend I was visiting that night was looking out her window and later told me she saw the whole thing, too."

"This is all baloney as far as I'm concerned," the lawman shot back. "Why would anyone believe a cock-and-bull tale such as that?"

"Well, imagine for a moment if the cock-and-bull story did get out," Capone said. "And how does it stop from getting out?" Al's eyes lit up. He knew he had the upper hand as he told the cop about his successful effort to keep the old lady quiet. "I'm sure Aunt Lilly got the picture I drew for her and she's forgetting she ever looked outside her window that night."

The boy walked to the gate to lift the latch in order to allow the ashen-faced officer to exit. Sheaf patted his holster to show his superiority, but his words were words of appeasement: "So, smart kid, you're telling me that I have something to be thankful to you for?"

"Let's just say I believe that one good turn deserves another and leave it at that, Officer Sheaf," he replied.

"By the way, kiddo, what do they call you on the street?"

"Some people call me 'Allie Boy,'" Capone said with a smirk.

. . .

THE SOUTH BROOKLYN Rippers decided to hook up with the Navy Street Boys when the hostilities started between the Garfield Boys and the Butler Street Dukes. That was the conversation taking place when dapper Johnny Torrio stepped into the candy store.

His dark, cashmere coat was gently stroked by one of the smaller kids while he passed through the group of young gang members who were gathered there. He was buying some cigars when he spotted Capone among the others. Overhearing the chatter, Torrio walked from the counter with his purchase in hand and called the boy aside.

"Listen Alphonso," he said, "that's all bullshit! Somebody goes looking for trouble, he's bound to find it." He placed an arm around Capone's shoulder and walked with him down to the corner of the block where he imparted this advice: "Most of those kids in there are punks who think belonging to a street gang makes them big men." Capone looked into the mobster's face and listened intently. After all, here was a successful person, respected by all and with enough cash to dress swell, ride around in a flashy car, and have all the best-looking girls in the neighborhood swooning over him.

"Alphonso, you know how dumb some of those cliques really are?" Torrio asked. "To brawl all the time is, in my opinion, the mark of a really stupid person."

Capone glanced back over his shoulder to see his Rippers evidently still talking about the imminent battle.

"The fight you guys were talking about in there, what started the fucking war anyway?" Torrio used his teeth to tear the end off his cigar. "You don't know, do you?" Torrio egged the boy on, hoping to coax him into a response. When Al did reply, the words were along the lines of what Torrio expected.

"You gotta protect what's yours, Johnny," the youngster declared while clenching his big fists. Turning to face him once more, the mobster placed a hand on the boy's shoulder.

"That's all well and good, Al," Torrio said. "But I'm willing to bet the dumb gang war is about something really stupid. Yeah, that's right, something real stupid." Torrio waved a hand through the air and continued his lecture. "They fight over dames, they fight over who dominates a confraternity dance at the church social hall. They want to fight about everything except the most important thing."

Capone figured out just what Johnny T was speaking about as Torrio moved in the direction of a garbage pail, deposited his cigar wrapper inside the can, straightened up, turned around, and pulled out a thick roll of dough.

"Alphonse," he said softly, "this is what all fighting should be for." Torrio's dark eyes gleamed with pride. "If half of those jerks worried about what they could afford to buy and less about who punched who outside the Prospect Hall, they'd be dangerous . . . and I'd have a lot more competition." Smoothing his hair down with a hand while depositing the cash back inside his pocket with the other, Torrio's words to Capone struck a chord.

"Most of those suckers work their asses off all day long for a few crummy bucks and call it 'making a living,'" Torrio continued. "And when they get together, all they want to do is fight. Does that really make sense to you?"

Capone pondered the wisdom imparted by the slick mobster on that fateful day, and decided to live his life by the adage: "You resort to violence only when cash profit is the purpose."

Until the time Frankie Yale replaced Torrio as his personal confidant, Capone's gang-banging ceased in all matters that offered no cash payout. Fusing the advice of his future boss, Yale, whose strong-arm tactics the youngster admired, with the clever strategies of Johnny Torrio, the world would soon be faced with a brutal and cunning individual—an oversized hoodlum with both brains and daring.

· · ·

THE CHICAGO SYNDICATE was calling Johnny Torrio out of town for jobs that entailed greater responsibility and he returned home only on occasion, when his personal attention was warranted.

While in Brooklyn, he began using the kid who was still in his early teens to run small jobs for him, which included the delivery of firearms in sealed paper bags and smuggling narcotics inside innocuous-looking cans of tomatoes. Capone was one of the few kids who never questioned the contents of the packages he was delivering. Because of this and the fact that he was bright, Torrio believed he could trust the big kid with assignments that required a bit more finesse.

On one particular occasion he summoned Capone to his club sending word that the youngster should be dressed in a suit and tie. When he arrived, Torrio looked Capone over and said, "I want you to go tell that fat pig Corino the baker to give you fifty dollars for me right now!" Torrio knew the boy would follow his orders to the letter, as he requested a non-violent technique be used in this collection.

"If he says he doesn't have the dough on him, scare him a little, but don't hurt him, Alphonse. Do you hear me?" Nodding in the affirmative, Al walked to the baker's place of business and found the shop closed and a funeral wreath hanging on the door. A sign below listed the name of the deceased: ANNA CORINO, AGE EIGHTY-SEVEN. The funeral director's name and his chapel were also listed.

He walked the five blocks to the funeral chapel and stole a glance while passing old man Tripp's grocery, noticing they were replacing the front door (for the third time since Capone moved into the neighborhood) with a covering of impregnable-looking steel plates that were being welded together and outfitted with a bright, chrome padlock. The tiny chapel had just opened and was devoid of mourners except for a heavyset man, dressed in black. Capone assumed this was his mark.

"Excuse me, Mr. Corino," the youngster said, "may I speak to you for a moment?"

The single mourner was startled by the sudden intrusion. He had been kneeling in front of the coffin and when he stood up to turn around, he exhibited eyes that were red and watery. The rotund man thought the lad might have been making the delivery of flowers he had ordered. Corino the baker gave his runny nose another wipe with his handkerchief and walked toward Capone.

"Terrible thing," Capone commented while shaking his head and looking down at the silver-haired lady in pink who lay in the casket. "I'm with Johnny T," he said in a hushed tone, adding, "he sent me to pick up the money for him."

"Oh shit!" the man yelped as he suddenly gasped for air. He stared at the ceiling and seemed barely able to control his trembling as he pointed to the deceased woman while crying out, "That's my mother in there. Do you realize that?"

Regaining some of his composure but feeling a sense of outrage, the baker pleaded, "Don't you people have any heart at all?"

"I don't know about that, mister," Capone said. "All I know is I was sent to pick up some money."

Corino was beside himself. The veins in his thick neck seemed ready to pop and sweat was pouring from his head while he screamed inside the lonely chapel, "He sends a kid? I gotta talk to Johnny T." Capone never flinched. Rather, like a junkyard dog staring down his prey, the youngster stood to one side and waited while some visitors entered the chapel and went straight to the coffin.

Capone followed Corino's retreat to the rear of the chapel, and while the heavyset man pulled his handkerchief out of his pocket to wipe the sweat from his face, the younger man pulled out a shiny, new revolver. The display was in a flash.

"This is going too far now," Corino spoke with a shaky voice. "I'll never do business with Johnny again. And this I swear."

"I don't know about that and I don't care about that," the snazzy-dressed youth exclaimed. "All I'm interested in is the money. Now!"

"All right, young fellow," Corino said. "I'll give you all the cash I have on me right now." The grieving baker began shuffling through his wallet, emptying it of cash, which amounted to thirty-seven dollars.

"That's all I happen to have with me, so whatcha gonna do, kill me? Go ahead if you want to," he said tearfully, "this world is getting to be a terrible place to live in anyway." Mindful of the snarling lips and the cold, metallic eyes on this monstrous young hoodlum, Corino turned his face away in fear as he handed over the money.

Frankie Yale was the one who suggested to Capone later on in life that he should practice eye control by looking into a mirror and teaching himself to contort his eyes in order to perfect the technique, the harrowing gaze the youngster became noted for. Alphonse spent long periods of time looking into a mirror until the desired effect, "the look," was achieved, and he used it often to frighten victims into submission without ever having to utter a word. Yale once told him, "Alphonso, your eyes will deliver the message. They'll tell someone, 'If you don't do what I want, I'll kill you on the spot!'"

Gido Bianco once heard Yale tell Capone, "Al, your eyes are so scary, they'll even cause General 'Black Jack' Pershing to quake in his boots."

Capone used the look, his "death stare," whenever he felt it was necessary. The best part was, it usually worked. But if by chance his practiced eyes failed to deliver their full impact, Alphonse Capone wouldn't hesitate in banging out an example of his violent rage.

"Stop your sniveling." the boy gangster advised Corino. "Just listen to what I have to say. Now, suppose I give you your money back and lay out the fifty for you. All you have to do is pay me back ten a week for six weeks, would that suit you?"

Corino reached out to receive the money he'd forked over just moments ago and began to count out ten dollars.

"No payment until next week," Capone stated, as the baker's face brightened and regained its color. "But don't let me down, do you hear me?"

"Sure thing and you have my word on that," Corino said. "With my mother gone and less doctor bills coming in, I'll have a bit more money for myself now."

Capone noticed the awkward stance of the baker and realized it was the result of the man wetting himself. His hands, no longer trembling, were still folded in prayer-like manner. Corino smiled and nodded a display of gratitude. He was relieved at the assurance there would be but one dead Corino this day. When Capone turned to leave the chapel with a pronounced swagger, one hand still inside his jacket pocket, he heard the baker remark:

"Thank you young man. I knew you were a nice fellow the moment I laid eyes on you." "See you next week, Mr. Corino," Capone replied.

4

A Yale Education

BROOKLYN'S COBBLESTONE STREETS were covered with an icy glaze on a chilly, windswept morning in early December 1914. Some children who were playing hide-and-seek on the sidewalk paused momentarily from their game to watch four teenagers toss several cartons from a thirty-foot flatbed truck parked at the curb.

The pilot of the rig, Thomas Mullins, was taking a short break, grabbing himself a fast cup of coffee at Mario's place on Fourth Avenue and Carroll Street, a popular breakfast and lunch joint. As he sipped his steamy brew, he was totally oblivious to the young plunderers already at work. Mullins was not only a gigantic man, but quite an intimidating one as well. His huge forearms, etched with gaudy tattoos of exploding bombshells, made customers who didn't know him uneasy when he removed his coat. Mullins's face was not easy to look at either. Having large brown eyes, a flat nose and thick, cracked lips that never smiled, his face carried a message to all who came into contact with him: They'd better not mess with him.

Mullins had just finished picking up a load of Hannon and Son's shoes at the Green Dock pier on Thirty-Fifth Street and was following his usual route that took him along Fourth Avenue toward Flatbush Avenue where he would make a left turn, proceeding over the Manhattan Bridge into the city to deliver the cartons of footwear.

YOUNG AL CAPONE

He had just finished paying for his coffee when one of the small kids that was playing in the street came to the door of the restaurant and anxiously urged the driver to come out. Mullins opened the door, stepping onto the cold pavement. For a split second, he froze at the sight. A gang of young punks were in the act of raiding his merchandise. He made a dash for the truck, shouting at the top of his lungs, "Put those cartons back you sons of bitches, or I'll break your fuckin' heads!"

Fifteen-year-old Al Capone scrambled from the side of the truck, still fumbling with one of the cartons while Joey Carlino screamed, "Let's get the hell out of here!" With that, Capone jumped down from the street side of the transport, trying to balance the box of exclusive footwear valued, at the time, at around fifteen dollars a pair.

Big Tommy Mullins grabbed for the closest teenage culprit, Charlie Fischetti, who happened to be a second cousin to the taller, stockier Capone. Charlie made a desperate attempt to break away while screeching in a high-pitched voice, "Let me go you fuckin' rat bastard!" Mullins wrapped his big, hairy hands around the youngster's plaid jacket, causing the hooligan to gasp for air as he struggled to tear himself free from the giant figure squeezing the life out of him.

Patrolman William "Whitey" Conners had just turned the corner and spotted the commotion. With the tails of his brass-buttoned coat flapping in the afternoon breeze, he sprinted toward the chaotic scene. Capone, Filezee DeAmato, and Frenchie Carlino jumped into the fray, trying to get the tough trucker to release their cohort from his stranglehold. They were too engrossed to notice that Officer Conners was approaching them with his Smith & Wesson .38 revolver in hand, ready to put a stop to the fight.

Capone, who had already removed his garrison belt from his waist while wrapping one end of it around his stubby fist, proceeded to land well-aimed blows with the belt's heavy buckle to the truck driver's head. Mullins released his hold of Fischetti's squirming body to clutch his own crimson-soaked forehead, from which blood streamed down his face in a crazy, zig-zag pattern.

"Everybody freeze!" The policeman's ear-splitting command thundered in the frigid air. Conners trained his pistol at the teenage boys yelling, "What's going on here?" It had been obvious to the cop that something was wrong when he first spied several loose cartons strewn along the curb of the street, and he couldn't help but notice the hulking Tommy Mullins bent over and clutching his bloodied skull with both hands.

By this time, a group of onlookers had assembled at the corner. Their curiosity was aroused by the halted traffic and the sight of a policeman with his gun drawn. Within minutes, the incident also attracted the attention of two neatly attired men who were standing a couple of short blocks away, on Fourth Avenue and Union Street.

Frankie Yale, dressed in his usual Beau Brummel best, had gotten wind of the fracas and started to walk slowly toward the scene. The mobster boss sported a dark brown, double-breasted suit and a white shirt with an elegant, fawn-colored silk tie that matched his light brown Chesterfield overcoat, adorned with a dark brown velvet collar. He wore the cashmere coat in the traditional underworld fashion, draped over his muscular frame. A dark brown fedora and a pair of dark brown pointed shoes completed Yale's luxurious wardrobe.

Yale was with his bodyguard and chauffeur, James "Sham Brown" Caponi (no relation to Al Capone). The six-foot-two Caponi, with his burly frame and receding hairline, was so completely devoted to his boss Frankie Yale it bordered on hero-worship. Sham Brown Caponi worked strong-arm, mostly extortion assignments on behalf of his boss and benefactor.

Within minutes, Yale and Caponi reached the corner where the action was taking place and spotted the youngsters, who were familiar to them from the neighborhood. Fifteen-year-old Al Capone, Filezee DeAmato, Fischetti, and Frenchie Collins were in the process of being reprimanded by this officer who was also starting to place cuffs on the wrists of Capone. "You guys are going in for attempted larceny, assault, and resisting arrest," said Officer Conners, who didn't have to wait long for assistance. It arrived in the person of a fellow beat cop, Edward Stratton, who had drawn his sidearm also.

"Now, wait a minute!" shouted Yale from the sidelines, "why don't you put those guns away before somebody really gets hurt."

"What the fuck are you talking about, mister?" piped Mullins, blood still dripping from the side of his head. "Can't you see somebody has been hurt already? Are you fuckin' blind or something?"

"Talk nice, will you friend," Yale responded. "You shouldn't be so impolite to someone who has a solution to the problem at hand."

The trucker's curiosity was aroused, especially as he noticed the first officer on the scene, Conners, nod a smiling greeting to the well-dressed strangers.

"Just what are you talking about, mister?" Mullins asked. He stepped over a carton to reach into the cab of his rig for a clean rag to help stem the flow of blood from his head. Yale walked toward the big man, speaking in a gentle tone. "Do you mind if I take a look?" he asked. "Maybe the gash requires a few stitches." The red-faced trucker obliged, nodding his head in Yale's direction. "I think you may need two or three stitches," Yale continued, "so I'm gonna offer you fifty dollars a stitch. How's that? I'll throw in another fifty for the emergency room. You tell your boss you slipped on some ice, do you hear?"

Tommy Mullins was startled at the man's offer, which he calculated at two hundred dollars. "Yeah," he said, "but I still want to get my hands on the one punk who was swinging the garrison belt."

"Look, I happen to know the kid's parents," Yale lied. "They have their hands full with him. When I tell his father what he did he'll punish him good. That I promise you. But I'm asking you to accept this money so these kids can avoid going to jail and having a police record."

"But the cops are right here," Mullins said. "How are you gonna . . . ."

"Don't worry about that. I know both of them well," Yale said, laying a pair of hundred dollar bills on the seat of Mullins's truck. Yale turned to see the youngsters' relieved faces as he stepped between the group of detained young lawbreakers and, with a wave of his hand, affected the removal of the cuffs that held them together.

"Now you boys help pick up the cartons," he ordered. Turning to the cops, Yale inquired, "What do you say, Whitey? Could you and your partner overlook this one? A thing like this could ruin a kid's life, being collared, you know, a dim future, jail and all that stuff."

The boys gathered around Yale like bees to honey, willing to wash his feet with showers of gratitude for getting them off the hook.

Turning back to Officer Conners, Yale smiled and patted his back with his left hand and extended his right palm for a friendly handshake. When the godfather withdrew his arm, Conners was overjoyed to discover a crisp fifty dollar bill in his mitt. Yale grabbed the cop's rubbery face with his thumb and index finger and gave it a gentle tug.

"You're a goddamned good cop Bill," Yale said. "A gentleman, if I may say so."

"My partner," whispered the cop, nodding his head in the direction of the smiling Officer Stratton.

"Are you kidding me?" Yale asked. "Of course I won't forget him. But let me go back behind the truck for a minute because I have to go into my pocket again. We don't want to be too obvious."

Mullins was directed to drive his rig to Holy Family Hospital a few blocks away at the corner of Hoyt and Dean Streets in downtown Brooklyn. The pain he felt was now tempered by the realization that the two hundred bucks would go a long way toward his buying the car of his dreams.

"What the fuck is wrong with you guys, heh?" Yale exploded, blasting the youngsters as they strode away from the scene. "Don't you dumb fucks realize that you don't shit where you eat? Somebody sees you that knows your face, even where you live, maybe. Why don't you guys go down by the docks to do this kind of shit?"

"Well . . ." Capone stammered, embarassed at getting caught in the act, "the opportunity presented itself and it looked real easy at the time.

"Listen, you little . . . what the fuck is your name anyway?"

"My name is Al, Mr. Yale. Al Capone," he replied, while Sham was ordering the gang to walk a few steps ahead and not crowd the sidewalk.

"I want you kids to know it cost me six hundred dollars to getcha off the hook," he said, inflating the total of the multiple bribes. Then, with a serious expression on his face, he reminded them, "You guys owe me big time." He shifted his gaze to Sham and offered the man a grin as he said to the youngsters, "Yes, you guys owe me for this favor. Don't think I'll forget it, either."

5

The Cigar Box

THE TROLLEY THAT brought Capone to Coney Island clanged its bell to signal the hour as it wormed its way through the teeming street traffic of busy Stillwell Avenue. Crowds had already started to gather in front of Feltman's food concession as the youngster walked past the sea of smiling faces.

This warm-weather paradise in Brooklyn was alive with the sounds of laughter and screaming children. Exciting amusements and music produced by brass bands tuning up filled the salty morning air while policemen on horseback prepared for another sweltering day of crowd control.

Capone could not resist the temptation of downing a few "red hots" along the way, though they barely satisfied his large appetite.

Arriving at the Harvard Inn, Capone noticed the beautiful mirrored pillars that stood outside its entrance and the stained glass windows, circular in design, depicting garden scenes. This place, part-owned by Johnny Torrio, was a popular "dine and dance" joint featuring good music, a nice dance floor, and some of the prettiest young ladies in town. As a matter of fact, Capone was surprised to be greeted by one of them at the front door. For a moment, her size made him think she was a child reaching up to slide the bolt on the door. She smiled warmly when he entered, noticing that his eyes seemed to be enjoying the exposure of her full breasts provided by her low-cut, satin dress. The petite beauty let a soft hand brush the youngster's cheek as the smell of her cheap perfume entered his nostrils, setting his young, Italian blood on fire. Capone made a bold move, attempting to feel the girl's breasts, but she pulled away from him quickly, giggling at the youngster's impudence.

"This way, big kid," she chimed, ushering him past some oak casks a worker was busy placing behind a long bar. His eyes were trained on her gentle, swaying buttocks and her shapely legs encased in white, rolled-down stockings. He thought to himself, "What I wouldn't do to get some of this."

His face was red as a beet when they reached the office. Johnny Torrio, seated at a table, noticed the boy's agitated state and remarked, "What's wrong with you, Alphonso? Didn't you ever see a girl before?"

Settling himself in a chair across from Torrio, Capone removed his cap and replied, "Plenty, John, but not too many like her." Capone's answer prompted the girl to resume giggling.

The youngster directed his conversation to the man who was seated behind the desk, but his eyes remained fixed on the girl's nipples, which poked through the thin, silky material of her dress.

"Annie honey," Torrio interrupted, "would you close the door and leave us alone for a while?" She responded immediately with another big smile and turned her beautiful ass in Capone's direction once again. Young Al brushed the sweat from his forehead with the back of one hand, completely frustrated and bewitched by this young, sexy lady.

"You like her, don't you?" Torrio said, smiling, a cigar dangling from his lips. "She's called Shorty Annie, and she's the best hump I've had in a long time!"

"No shit?" the boy asked, "she's really good, eh?"

"She's nineteen years old, from Cicero," Torrio said, flicking cigar ashes into a brass tray. "That's in Chicago. I brought her back with me on my last trip."

Capone thought of how lucky the man was, to be able to have a broad like Shorty Annie spread for him. Capone thought of the homely girls that he was screwing at Sally's, a Brooklyn whorehouse, lately and realized the difference was having the cash to be able to afford real class.

"Forget about her for a while, will you, Alphonse?" Torrio's face grew serious. "I asked you to come this morning because I've got a good deal for you." Torrio opened the lid of a cigar box that lay in front of him on the table, revealing that it was filled with cash.

"You see this?" the dapper Torrio asked. "This represents an important part of your new job."

Capone listened intently while trying to figure out whether the cigar box contained large bills or only petty cash. He just knew it held a lot of bills.

Closing the lid, Torrio pushed the box toward young Al. Then he shoved a piece of paper with some numbers on it toward the puzzled teen.

"Look at the numbers written down on this slip," Torrio said, his well-manicured fingers tracing down to the numbers that were circled at the bottom. Torrio then produced some rubber bands and tossed them to Capone, saying, "The job is an easy one, but an important one."

The youngster drew close to the table, placing his hands on the cigar box, which contained more dough than he'd ever seen at one time in his life.

"What's today's date?" he inquired of the boy.

"Why, today is Friday the twenty-first," the youngster responded.

"Right! So far, you pass the test." Capone was surprised by the mobster's grin. "Today is Friday and I want you come here every Friday while I'm in Chicago. Every Friday evening you come here, pick up this box, sit at this table, and count the money inside of it."

Torrio raised himself from his chair saying, "I know you can count money because you worked a little with Tringali, the bookie, and he told me so."

Capone looked down at the cigar box while Torrio offered him some beer. "See this place?" Torrio asked. "It's a little different later on, when we're open for business. Frankie Yale is my partner and he runs the place, but I need you to take this money from here to my cousin's house once a week."

Torrio reached across the table and placed his hands gently on top of the thick hands of Capone's while looking into his gray eyes. "Alphonso," Torrio said, "I'm trusting you to operate like a clock for me. Do you hear?" Al nodded.

"The money you find in the box should always be even with the amount that's circled at the bottom of the slip," Torrio continued. "Charlie, my bartender, will give you the ledger slip. The box itself you'll pick up downstairs in the cellar. I'll show you the exact spot when we finish here."

Capone's round face beamed with pride, the idea of being trusted with Johnny Torrio's money warmed his heart as he sat with his hands folded on the table in front of him.

Torrio encouraged the boy to drink another glass of beer, which he poured from a small keg he kept on ice in the office.

"What happens if the money I count doesn't equal what's circled on the slip?" inquired Capone.

Torrio's eyes fixed on the boy. "If the difference is sizable, say, more than twenty dollars, be sure to tell my man, Charlie," Torrio said. "He's going to be here every time you come around for the box and he'll tell you what to do."

Torrio reached down to his knees where a button was located on the side of the table and Capone heard a buzzer sounding in the distance, a signal that brought the bartender to the office. He was a paunchy, graying individual with a handlebar mustache and a bald head. Carrying a towel, the man flung it over a shoulder when Johnny Torrio introduced him to his "nephew" Alphonse.

Capone was ordered to listen to Charlie if a shortage was ever discovered and to follow the bartender's instructions.

"Charlie is the only one that you ever talk to about the box, ever," Torrio said. "Got that straight?" He emphasized his statement by placing the palms of his hands on the table in front of Al and looking him right in the eyes. Capone stared back.

"What do I do with the box after I count it and the money inside is okay?" Capone asked. Torrio sat back in his chair, took a small sip of beer, and wiped his lips with the bartender's towel.

"That's all, Charlie," Torrio said. "You can go back to work."

"Don't worry about a thing, lad," Charlie said before leaving the room. "I'll help you all I can."

When the door closed behind Charlie, Torrio turned serious. "Al, only when you're sure the amount is correct, you put the rubber bands around the box so it doesn't accidentally open on you. Keep the slip in your pocket . . . and I suggest you slip the box inside your shirt or your jacket."

Capone nodded his head to show his understanding so far.

"Go back the same way you got here and bring the box straight to my cousin Perry's house on Union Street. You got that?" Torrio asked, giving him the exact address.

Torrio was sitting with his feet up on the desk with his hands clasped together in front of his chest as he searched the boy's face for a reaction to the orders. Assured by Capone's silent smile, the mobster pushed himself back, got up from his chair, and walked toward the youngster.

"You have to be at my cousin's no later than six every Friday night," Torrio said. "Ya got that?" Alphonse nodded his head while Torrio continued the instructions.

"My cousin leaves his house every evening shortly after six to pick up his son from work, so get there on time, Alphonse." Placing a hand on Capone's hefty shoulder, Torrio looked him in the face and informed him that Perry would be giving him his pay for the job each week. "Of course feel free to accept work from Frankie or Don Paolo as long as I'm in Chicago," Torrio said, "but you have to carry out this job for me every Friday until you see me again . . . Agreed?"

"Without a doubt," Capone replied with a wide grin. "I really want to thank you for this opportunity and the trust you're placing in me . . . all that dough."

"I want you to know I'm very proud of you, Alphonse," Torrio said. "I mean on your appearance, staying away from those small-time hoodlums and all."

Capone gloried in the words coming from one of the most successful people he knew, the person he wanted to emulate. Al smiled once again and replied, "Thanks John, you're the guy who made me see the light. I think maybe I'm about ready to make some real money now."

After the pleasantries were exchanged, Torrio led the teen into a private dining room where they previewed some of the food being prepared for the customers of Coney Island's Harvard Inn. Torrio was truly amazed at young Al's appetite. After consuming what amounted to almost a whole chicken, he followed that with two heaping plates filled with lasagna and finally completed the meal by wiping his dish clean with half a loaf of Italian bread. When the last morsel was swallowed Capone let out a burp, then innocently exclaimed, "What ever happened to that girl?"

That sudden inquiry caused Torrio to break out in a fit of laughter that made Capone scratch his head, wondering what was so funny. The rosy-cheeked youth was beginning to get a little perturbed because the laughter continued on until even Charlie the bartender joined in.

Alphonse never appreciated being the butt of a joke, and anyone attempting to make a laughing stock out of him never tried it twice.

Wiping away tears from his eyes, Torrio noticed the serious expression on the boy's face. "Hold on, Alphonso," he said. "Don't get angry. It wasn't what you said that was funny. It was your timing."

"What did I say that was so funny?" Capone answered. "All I asked was where the girl was."

"That's just what I'm talking about," said Torrio, who by this time had ceased laughing only to start again when Capone repeated the question. He patted Capone's hand, but it was no consolation for the overgrown boy as he began to rise in order to leave the table—or else do something he might later regret.

Torrio began to plead that Capone not feel insulted.

"Alphonse, I tell everybody you're my nephew and I really do feel like you're family," Torrio said. "I'd cut my throat before making a fool out of you, believe me." Capone's face was blood-red as he tried to slide out of the booth but found his path blocked by his idol. "Please, Al," he pleaded, "nobody was laughing at you. The funny thing was your appetite, that's all."

"You saying I ate too much? You kept pushing the fucking food in front of me," he grumbled, pointing to the table. "What was I supposed to do? I was hungry!"

"No, Alphonso, I guess it was just something . . . I mean I guess it was your youth that I found humorous, that's all."

"Something about my youth?" he responded in a huff. "Tell me what the fuck you're talking about or get out of my way, John." Capone's eyes started an icy stare that worried the older gangster, actually causing him to feel intimidated by the headstrong teenager. Using the art of diplomacy, which was second nature to him, Torrio persuaded young Capone to return to his chair by grabbing hold of his shoulder and gently pushing him back into his seat. His voice came in a soft tone.

"Alphonse," he said, "I remember when I was your age. My stomach was always my first concern, too. It was that we sat here eating for twenty minutes and you never once mentioned the girl. After you filled up on food, I heard a burp, and in the next breath you asked 'Where's the whore?' There was no offense meant, Alphonse. It just reminded me of my own youth. Don't you understand? As soon as one appetite is satisfied, another is born."

He tried his best to make the youngster laugh with him but found the tactic fruitless, so instead he thought he'd change the subject and make the boy happy at the same time. Torrio had learned something about Al Capone that stuck with him all though his crime-ridden life.

Never ridicule the youngster, nor speak to him in a manner that could possibly serve to deflate his ego. Instead, give him what he wants by clever negotiation. Johnny thought to himself, he wants the girl? I'll give him the girl. But not until after I leave.

"Alphonso, listen to me," Torrio said. "The girl is not going back with me when I leave for Chicago. So, if you really want to hump her yourself, you come back next week. Come a little earlier. Then, I'll let her take good care of you."

"Do you mean it would be okay with you, John?"

"Why sure, like I said before. When you work for me you're like family. She's such a hot tomato I don't expect her to be loyal. Besides, I think she likes you."

"She thinks I'm a kid," Capone responded.

"What the hell are you talking about?" Torrio said. "I told you I would set it up for you, didn't I? So, relax and be patient. Then you'll show her how much of a kid you are next week. Right, Alphonso?"

Finally finding something to laugh at, the young Capone repeated Johnny's statement. Grabbing his crotch, the youngster said, "Yeah I'll show that Shorty Annie how much of a kid I am."

The trolley ride home seemed much longer than usual. Maybe it was because Shorty Annie remained on his mind—the shape on the girl, the way that she walked, even the way she giggled. All he was left with was the scent of her perfume in his nostrils and the bulge inside his trousers.

• • •

WHEN THE BIG day finally arrived, young Capone boarded the trolley car headed for Coney Island. It was raining heavily and travel was slower than usual, but he'd allowed himself plenty of time by leaving the corner of Fifth Avenue and Ninth Street at eight AM He antici- pated a quick frolic in bed with Shorty Annie. After that, he'd go down to the cellar to pick up the cigar box.

Arriving at the Harvard Inn, he found the front door locked and the place looking deserted. The clatter of the nearby Cyclone roller coaster warming up for the new day drowned out his loud banging at the door. Capone eventually heard a whistle. Then, backing away from the building, he spotted Shorty Annie's head in the window above the street. She pointed down toward a side entrance, indicating that Capone should enter through it.

Young Al walked around the building and found the side door unlocked. He climbed the steps and was surprised to learn that a well-furnished apartment existed above the dance hall.

She was waiting for him by the upstairs door with a sad look on her face. "What's wrong with you?" he asked, noticing that her demeanor was quite different from the previous week.

"I've got my period," she said dejectedly. "I was hoping for us to have a real nice time too." Al's face dropped.

"Shit!" he exclaimed. "Of all the luck."

"But don't worry big kid," she said, "I'll keep you good company and when it's gone, I'll be all yours."

"What the hell is that supposed to mean?" he fired back.

"I mean, maybe I can stay with you awhile and maybe find a way to satisfy you." Annie gave the youngster a wink while she puckered her lips.

The excited young man was persistent.

"I got work to do in a little while," he said. "It's got to be now." Capone grabbed at the tease, ready to force himself on her, if that was the only way he could have her. But she was too quick and slipped out of his grasp.

"Hold it a minute," she said. "Right now, I'm not in the mood for anything, but give me a chance to get washed and dressed, okay?"

He pretended to go along with her and turned his face away, but suddenly Capone made another lunge in her direction and cursed when he once again failed.

This time, the agile girl made it to the bathroom, locking the door behind her.

"Make yourself a drink," he heard her say from behind the door. Drink was not the thing on the youngster's mind as he rattled the doorknob and tried pulling the door open.

"Don't be too rough—you'll break Johnny's door," she screamed.

Disgusted, Capone turned away and walked into the bedroom.

Some of Torrio's clothes were hanging in a closet and the youngster ran his fingers over the fine material of a dinner jacket. A pair of expensive-looking shoes lay on the floor next to the window.

This Torrio really knew how to be good to himself, he thought, as he sat down on the edge of the bed. Someday he hoped to be in a position just like his boss, to be able to afford a nest like this one, right above a very busy cash register.

He noticed some flimsy garments laying on a chair and lifted a pair of her pink scanties. They transmitted the same intoxicating aroma to his head and served to stir his passions anew.

Young Capone waited about ten minutes for her to come out of the bathroom. When she finally did, she was wearing a robe. Capone envisioned her silky thighs inside the robe and the large, firm breasts that first caught his eye. This time, she walked straight to the bed and sat down alongside of him.

"Guess what?" she squealed, as Capone grabbed her around the waist. "I think maybe by tonight it'll be gone. I've had my period for three days now, and it finally looks like it's going away."

"Tonight? What's wrong with right now?" he exclaimed. "I don't mind, if you don't." He started to unbuckle his pants.

"Listen, big boy," she said. "I'm not at all in the mood when I'm like this. You'll have to wait."

Capone started to grow impatient with her rebuke and his angry temper flared out of control.

"Why you filthy, low-life bitch!" he yelled. "I came here so early in the morning for this?" He got up from the bed, throwing the covers to the floor as Annie cringed with fear.

"I want to please you, Al. I promise that I will. But it has to be later tonight. Okay?" Capone looked at the watch on the dresser. It was already nine-thirty and he was obligated to carry out his assignment for Torrio by the end of the day.

"So tell me, what do you want to do?" he inquired, still not giving up on his piece of tail completely.

"Why, I can hang around with you for the day, then we can come back tonight and have us a real party," she said. "Besides, Johnny told me some things about you that I find very exciting."

"I got business to attend to and you'll get in the way."

"No, I won't get in the way. I'll wait until you finish whatever you have to do. Oh, please Al, I'll be bored to death hanging around this place all day." He tried pushing her back onto the bed, but the girl rolled out from under him and retreated back to the bathroom.

"I'll be out in a flash," he heard her say.

He waited for her, sitting on the edge of the bed, resigned to accept the girl's promise to give him anything he wanted in due time. It was getting late and if he wanted to keep his boss happy, he would have to go down to the cellar soon to pick up the cigar box. He figured he could wait until after he made his delivery and then bring her over to one of the Five Point's clubhouses, which was nearby.

She came out of the bathroom fully dressed. A real knockout, he said to himself, licking his lips at the same time. He felt like a fool. He knew that he wanted her body so much that he had reached the point of letting this whore get the better of him. They left together and walked around the corner to the front, where Charlie was busy polishing the mirrors behind the bar.

Annie was wearing a shawl, which suggested to the bartender that she was going someplace with Al. He grew concerned when he saw her pull a chair from under one of the tables and proceed to make herself comfortable. Involving this dizzy dame in a serious business matter wasn't a smart thing to do, he thought, as he stepped down from the ladder to question the boy.

"Aren't you supposed to do something for Johnny?" he asked Capone.

The youngster's trip to the office in the rear of the building was reversed and he turned back to face the bartender with a snarl in his voice. "Johnny said I was to take orders from you in case there was an error, that's all," Capone said. "I don't want to hear any bullshit out of you for something that's none of your fuckin' business."

Charlie froze in his spot and his knees started to wobble. He quickly began to stammer an apology to Capone, submitting himself to the notion that perhaps it was none of his business after all.

Capone walked to the office with a hesitant Charlie Neuman following behind, still carrying his sponge. The boy went downstairs to retrieve the box from the cellar while Charlie, following the boss's orders, sat himself down to oversee the kid's tally.

"Twenty-two hundred and fifty dollars," Capone said. "That's what's here." His count was checked with the amount scrawled at the bottom of the slip handed to him by the bartender.

"It's all here!" Capone declared. "We can close the box." Charlie nodded his approval as the youngster concealed the cash on his person.

By the time Capone and Annie left the club, the day had turned muggy. The air was filled with the aroma of hot buttered corn and sweet candy while the normal crowds of weekday pleasure-seekers were just beginning to fill the narrow streets of the Bowery, a famous back alley in Coney Island located between Surf Avenue and the Boardwalk. The steamy weather caused people to remove their hats and other loose apparel as they waited in line to enter the place billed as the "fun factory," Steeplechase Park.

They walked across busy Surf Avenue with Shorty Annie clinging to the muscular arm of her new friend, whose quick stride kept her in mid-air for most of the trip. Boarding the streetcar, she climbed the steps first and was not really surprised when she felt his hands trace the outline of her buttocks. She turned around to see a lecherous smile on his face and decided against scolding him for being so nasty in public. Instead, she made up her mind to accept the younger man for what he was. Capone was brash and vulgar and had no manners to speak of, yet there was something about him that interested her.

Taking seats in an unoccupied section toward the rear of the trolley, she sat with her hands in her lap and stared him in the face.

"How come you don't say much, Mr. Al Capone?" she asked. The boy pulled the cigar box from inside his waist and placed it on his lap.

"So you know my name," he said. "Well, in that case, maybe I should know your full name too. What is it?"

"My name is Ann Snodgrass," she snapped, "and I come from a good family that lives in Illinois." Her response broke him up.

"Snot what?" he laughed. "Do you mean to tell me that's your real name?" She cast her eyes away from him, content to look out the open window. After a few minutes of silently enduring the look on his face, she turned to him and whispered in his ear. "Well, I don't think Alphonse is so hot either," she said. He looked away pretending that he didn't hear her. "I'll just call you Al from now on," she said, squirming around in her seat until her curvaceous body pressed against his.

With a gentle touch, she placed a hand under the cigar box and let it rest in his groin area while her soft fingers began a search for the buttons on his fly. She thought he'd like that.

"What's inside the box, Al?" she asked as she inserted her hand inside his pants and began to manipulate his throbbing member.

Capone leaned back in his seat, enjoying the girl's action while ignoring her question. Burning with passion, he made a rough attempt to lift her skirt, to feel her smooth skin and hot thighs in his hands, but she stopped him cold. "Don't get crazy on me now," she said, "we're on a streetcar and it's daytime. Be still, let me do it to you—I don't feel like getting arrested." The girl kept a straight face, covering his exposed parts with her shawl while servicing him with her hand.

Capone, meanwhile, had moved the cigar box out of the way for comfort, placing it at his feet while the rhythm of Annie's skillful hand soon brought him to a climax.

Before he had a chance to recover from his bliss, she grabbed the box and darted out the rear of the slow-moving trolley, jumping down onto the cobblestone streets of McDonald Avenue.

The less-than-agile Capone yelled curses at the fleeing girl and tried following her with his pants still undone, but lost her when she turned a corner, dissapearing somewhere in the dark and gloomy streets of the Kensington section of Brooklyn.

His anger spilled over to an innocent stranger who Capone figured had a good chance to spot the girl as she turned the corner.

"Do you mean to say you're standing right here and you don't see anybody running past you?" Capone yelled at the stranger. His patience was growing short with this man. Maybe he was clammed-up simply because he saw a guy chasing after a woman and his instinct was to protect the woman. The man was a foreigner, about forty, and he stood perplexed at the verbal assault that was being directed at him by young Capone.

Although the man understood little English, he certainly did understand the word "kill" that Capone used in his tirade against him and ran off screaming for the police.

Capone searched some stores in the vicinity, but gave up in a short while, resigning himself to the fact that the bitch had gotten away with his box. Now he barely had time enough to buy a box of Celia Corona Suprema cigars, so that he could empty the box and use it as a replacement.

Catching a taxicab to ensure the timely delivery of the money, the youngster fumed in the backseat of the cab, pissed-off at the girl, but mostly at himself, because he didn't fuck her while he had the opportunity. He realized he'd never get another chance, because if and when he ever saw her again, he would surely kill her.

When he finished reloading the cash into the new cigar box, he cursed her again, that bitch. She never expected to get away with pulling a dirty trick on Al Capone, did she?

The cabbie pulled to the curb on Union Street while the red-faced youngster reached over the seat and dumped most of the twenty-five cigars onto the front seat beside the driver.

"Why thank you, Johnny," the driver exclaimed with a broad smile on his face. "Are you in the tobacco business or something?"

"Not really," Capone replied. Watching the man's happy face, Capone whispered, "I just needed the empty box."

He wondered what that little tart's face looked like when she removed the rubber bands and opened the lid of the box to find *no cash*, but only one of Charlie's damp rags inside.

6

Going for Baccala

THREE YOUNG MEMBERS of the Five Points gang congregated under a lamppost that stood on the corner of Fourth Avenue and Union Street, bragging to each other about their particular choice of spring attire. Charlie Fischetti was asking his seventeen-year-old cousin Alphonse for an appraisal of his new hat. "How does it look on me now?" he asked.

"Just a little bit more to the right and you've got it," quipped the husky ringleader.

Capone's loose-fitting blue cardigan sweater served to exaggerate the slight downward slope of his shoulders, giving him a gorilla-like appearance as he stood on the sidewalk with his hands at his sides.

The third crew member present was Anthony Scrapisetti, whose spring wardrobe also reflected the latest styles of 1916. Tony Scraps reached into a pocket of his beige summer slacks and yanked out a gold chain, which held his dead father's gold railroad timepiece.

"Hey, do know what time it is, you guys?" He smacked his lips together. "It's almost one o'clock, time to eat. What do you say, boys?"

Capone raised a hand to pat his plump belly under his sweater and rubbed it vigorously. "Let's stay close to home," he said, "because I promised my mother that I would try to bring home some *baccala* (cod fish) for her to cook for dinner tomorrow."

Scraps suggested they go downtown to Paolo's focacceria for Sicilian cuisine. "We can be there in only ten minutes," he said with a smile. "After lunch, we can go right there on Union Street to get the stuff your mother wants."

Charlie Fischetti was not inclined to go along and offered an alternate suggestion. "Whaddya say we go to Coney Island, get us a couple of red hots? There's plenty of fish stores along the way."

"Siciliano, that's the way to go," Alphonse growled, delivering a faint slap to Fischetti's face. "You think I'm stupid, Charlie? You wanna drag Scraps and me to Coney Island for what?"

Capone taunted his cousin Charlie, a familiar look on his face. It was the friendlier version of a peculiar expression, which made it difficult to discern whether Capone's gray eyes intended a halfhearted smile, or if the look was meant as one of disdain.

"I know why you want to go to Coney Island, Charlie," Capone said. "For the babes, right? Well, not today. I think we're going for *vasteddi* (Sicilian sandwiches). If you wanna come along, you're welcome. If not, fuck you, Charlie."

Capone noticed a familiar figure ambling across the street. It was Jimmy Boy DiVico, another member of the young crew who was agreeable to the idea of going to Paul Mancino's for some Sicilian food, prepared in the Parlermo tradition.

Scrapisetti darted across the wide thoroughfare and slowed down to a trot while crossing the cobblestones of narrow Union Street. His light blue shirt fluttering in the warm breeze, Scrappy sprang onto the safety of the blue slated sidewalk. He walked a few paces to a black iron pole that was used to support the overhead cables that supplied electrical current to the public street cars, or as the British called them, "trawley cars."

Scrappy Tony pressed the side of his head, his ear in particular, against the cool pole and put a hand over his other ear to block out all sounds except that which vibrated inside the pole.

This streetcar, on the Union Street run, followed the tracks from world-renowned Prospect Park down the slope toward its last stop close to the docks on the Brooklyn side of the East River. Scraps listened with the experience he gained as a small child. At one time, the boy was able to estimate the arrival of a trolley car by kneeling down in the gutter and putting an ear to one of the steel tracks. That's what the smaller kids would do. But when somebody was wearing nice, clean clothes, an ear to the pole was good enough.

The faint, whirring sound emanating from the metal wheels was carried across the voltage cables, alerting Scrappy Tony to the proximity of the streetcar. "Come on guys, the trolley must be around by Sixth Avenue now," he declared. "It'll be here in a few minutes."

They boarded the streetcar, paying the nickel fare as grown gentlemen who could still remember when the only way to travel in the city was to hitch a ride on the outside of the trolley car. In those days they were always prepared to jump off the car quickly and run away at the sight of a blue coat, or perhaps a conductor who would deliberately stop the coach to chase the kids off.

The motorman opened the two accordian-type doors that folded inward, creating a clacking sound as they hit the sides of the passenger entrance. Inside the trolley, the foursome relaxed on seats made of woven rattan strips with horsehair-cushioned padding. En route, they engaged in conversation about women and flirted with some of the young ladies who strolled Union Street dressed in their light spring apparel.

"Oh my God," said Charlie Fischetti, pointing out one particular girl. "Did you see the big tits on that bitch?"

"Yeah, but her face was full of warts or something!" replied seventeen-year-old Jimmy Boy DiVico. "So ugly, I wonder if her own father could eat at the same table with her."

"That's the trouble with you guys," snapped Fischetti. "All you care about is the face. Give me that babe in the sack with the lamps low and I'll have a much better time than you do with that Clara, or whatever her name is that you're so hot about."

"Don't talk about Clara like that," Jimmy Boy retorted. "She's way out of your class."

"Cut the shit!" Capone cracked. "You guys are like a couple of kids, arguing about something stupid like that. I'm certain somebody is humping that girl, warts and all."

"How would you know that, Al?" Fischetti inquired.

"Yeah Al, how do you know she isn't a virgin?" DiVico chimed in.

"Because, you dumb fucks, she's pregnant. Couldn't you tell by her clothes?" Capone mocked the two of them. "Jimmy Boy," Al said, "you were looking mostly at her face while Charlie here saw only the big tits. Neither one of you noticed that her belly was sticking out about a mile from under her dress."

They all joined in the cheerful humor created by Alphonse's sharp eyes and his dramatic ability to dispense a Solomon-like resolution to yet another one of their silly arguments.

Getting down from the trolley, they walked one short block from Sackett Street to the restaurant opposite the pushcart-lined Union Street, where fresh fruit and vegetables were sold by vendors yelling to the passing parade of customers in their mother tongue. "Here it is, the best around. Get it while you can. Cheap today. Fresh today."

The side of the street was where the affable Paul Mancino operated his tiny focacceria, which specialized in mouth-watering sandwiches made famous by him with recipes brought over from the old country. Mancino busied himself behind the counter, whipping up his delicious *panelle* made from crushed chick peas formed into rectangular shapes and deep fried in a large black kettle filled with hot oil.

The most sought-after sandwich treat in the place was vasteddi, made from, of all things, cow's lungs (*suffrita*). The tender meat was piled inside of a soft, seeded roll and topped with ricotta cheese and thin strips of Pecorino Romano cheese.

The shop's patrons included, at times, judges, politicians, and crooked hats (gangsters). They all rubbed elbows with longshoremen from the nearby docks, who accounted for Mancino's main source of business.

Mancino never held a wine or beer license, but that didn't deter him from offering alcohol to his steady customers. He served wine— good homemade vino manufactured for him in the cool cellar of his neighborhood brownstone—surreptitiously in empty soda bottles, in order to avoid a fine.

The boys headed for a table in the back of the small dining room as the waiter made some finishing swipes at the top of it with a damp cloth. The chairs were made of steel wire rods twisted into a heart-shaped design on the backrest, with the seat portion comprised of plywood covered over by a thin layer of leather.

The waiter, a tall, thin man with thick, black hair, wore a heavy plaid woolen shirt, despite the balmy temperature. He spoke to them in English in a corny attempt at acting cool. Standing in front of the boys he said, "Okay, guys, what can I bring you today besides vino?"

They saw this as a compliment, considering they were all in their teens and obviously underage. Capone ordered first, saying, "Gimme two vasteddi sandwiches and a side dish of panelle." Scratching his chin, he added, "Oh, first, I want some of the sliced *pulpo* (octopus) salad with the black olives."

"And to drink?"

"Bring me some of that red wine," replied Capone, "and be sure to bring my salad first. Okay?" The waiter took the rest of the order and within a few minutes the boys were gorging themselves while making small talk in between bites.

"Goddam fly," said Tony Scraps, hearing a buzzing around his ear. He tried swatting it with a hand, but the pest continued a flight pattern that exclusively dominated the portion of the table closest to the wall, where Scrapisetti sat. The uncomfortable feeling increased as the critter landed on the table where the rest of his meal lay. This time he swung both of his hands at the persistent fly. Finally believing he was successful in chasing the annoying pest away, Scraps relaxed, regained his composure, and tried to enjoy his meal.

But soon Scraps heard the insect's familiar buzz yet again. Cursing the fly's family in Italian, Scrapisetti wondered why it decided to single out his food alone for its filthy mission. He watched as the winged creature landed right on top of the food in his dish.

Everyone except poor Tony Scraps was in hysterics; Charlie Fischetti laughed so much at his friend's plight that some of the sandwich he was chewing spewed from his mouth in a gagging fit that splattered the contents across the tiled floor of the restaurant.

"Waiter, over here," Scraps cried out, ordering the man to remove the untouched (except by the fly) sandwich that lay in his dish. By now, the fly was headed for parts unknown, and when the waiter approached, he looked down at the table and at the young man who had called him, asking, "*Ce che?*"(what's wrong?).

"Oh nothing," Scraps said. "Just a fucking fly was taking a stroll on my sandwich, that's all. I can't eat that now. Bring me another one, please."

By this time, the proprietor came to the table to find out what the trouble was.

"A goddamned fly was on my panelle, that's what's wrong!" Scraps bellowed.

Mancino just stood there, observing the group for a moment, then his five-foot-seven-inch frame, paunchy stomach, and receding hairline squeezed past the crowd while he shook a finger at his waiter, scolding him in Italian for serving wine to the youngsters. His usually pleasant manner was a little shaken on account of the boisterous activity he thought might be annoying some of his other patrons. Mancino's eyes scanned the area.

"I don't see any fly. You sure?"

"Well you didn't expect him to wait around for you, do you?" Scraps snapped back, frustrated by not being able to enjoy his food in peace.

"As you can see, I have a nice clean place here," Mancino said. "And if a fly comes in . . . it could happen once in a while. It happens in your own home, doesn't it?"

"Oh, no it doesn't," Capone butted in. "Where he lives, the flies would never go, because they think it's too filthy."

Everyone had a good laugh except Scrapisetti, who was still sulking when he accepted another freshly made sandwich.

The boys' laughter continued until it eventually affected the owner, too. Mancino stood behind a brass cash register that was mounted on the counter midway in the store, where they waited for him to tally up their bill.

"*Arrivederci, tutto* (good-bye, all)!" Mancino shouted as the boys were leaving. His mild snicker was caused by something the youngsters were not even aware of. As they were walking out the door, Mancino could swear that he saw a fly following close behind Scrapisetti's curly head.

The boys then headed for the *stocco* and baccala market, where they found a large crowd picking items from in front of the store. One-gallon tins of olive oil and cans of tomatoes as well as strung cloves of red garlic were being offered to the sidewalk shoppers from boxes set up one on top of the other.

"Tomorrow is Friday," Capone reminded them. "That's why the place is so busy."

"Why don't you come back tomorrow?" asked Fischetti, moving out of the path of a man who looked like he was on a desperate mission.

"Listen, Charlie," Capone responded, a little irritated. "We're here now, so I'm going inside to get the baccala, even if it takes all day."

The store was drenched with the smell of dried fish and herbs, olives, and various other old-world products that when blended together and formed the unique aroma typical of a *stocco* baccala store. Straw baskets full of light beige snails lay uncovered by the crowded entrance.

Capone eyed the pieces of fish in a tiled basin filled with constantly running water in which the *stocco* (fillets) and baccala strips were soaking to remove the preservative salt.

Among the twenty or so customers in the store, Charlie Fischetti took special notice of one in particular, the man who rushed past him in his eagerness to enter the place first. Roughly five feet, seven inches in height, his name, they learned later on, was Giuseppe Sposito, a local man with the devious preoccupation of going into crowded places in order to brush his body against the female customers. This was not his only obsession by a long shot, however. Sposito's favorite vice occurred each evening with the fading sunlight.

Sposito lived on the top floor in one of a row of flat-roofed, four-story buildings on Union Street; when nighttime arrived, he would turn into a real "prince of darkness."

Dressing himself like a commando, his practice was to wear dark navy or black clothes, a black baseball cap, and a pair of pier-stolen binoculars around his neck.

Climbing the iron fire escape in the rear of his family's apartment to the roof of his building, Sposito had unlimited access to his neighbors' roofs and windows, which provided him access to intimate details of the goings-on within their apartments.

Sometimes he would position himself on one of the fire escapes, inches away from a window, watching a neighborhood girl undressing or showering. If he was real lucky, he would be able to catch one of these young ladies having sex with a mate or a boyfriend. On more than one occasion, the rooftop prowler was able to pluck the bloomers of a female neighbor from her backyard clothesline and he began collecting them. They remained in his room as mementos of his life's greatest accomplishments, treasures that only a depraved mind such as his could appreciate, or even comprehend.

Charlie Fischetti's attention was drawn once again to this strange-looking man. He also noticed a real beauty, a young lady with long, black hair who was standing in front of the man. Sposito was trying his best to act nonchalant, but the fact that he no longer seemed to be in a hurry, coupled with the weird expression he had on his face, gave him away.

She moved about the store's tight quarters holding a bundle of freshly dried oregano in her dainty hands, paying no attention to the man who was following close behind her.

Scrapisetti noticed the doll, too. With a nudge applied to Charlie's ribs, he whispered into his buddy's ear, "Look at that beauty over there."

"Yeah, she's a knockout all right," Fischetti agreed, "but get a gander of what's following her around." Scraps and Charlie stopped in front of the big window and began looking through the glass with growing interest.

Jimmy Boy, who had been standing on the sidewalk, edged closer to his friends, while Alphonse was the only one of their gang who was actually inside the store. He was nudging his way through the crowd, trying to get the baccala for his mother, vying for the attention of the store owner. This kept young Capone from noticing the drama that was unfolding on the other side of the store.

The three boys could plainly see Sposito trying to squeeze past a customer who had suddenly cut him off, mumbling to himself, desperate to resume direct contact with the object of his lust.

Her name was Rosa Cambria and she wore a light-colored dress in the latest fashion, which was much shorter than anything her mother would wear. It allowed her shapely ankles and a bit of her legs to be exposed to view, but Giuseppe Sposito's eyes were instead glued to Rosa's bulging ass.

She stood in front of the ceramic pool with its brass fixture protruding out of the center. Like a fountain, it sprinkled a constant shower into the pool, where pieces and long lengths of raw, salted fish were being soaked. Sposito snaked his arm around another customer and brushed the palm of his hand against her heart-shaped butt. Rosa was a little surprised at herself for thinking such a thing could happen in this store and shrugged it off as perhaps being caused by one of the children who were being tugged at by their mothers. Sposito was encouraged, but he kept his eyes away from his mark, trying to appear innocent. If asked by the owner of the store what it was that he wanted, Sposito was prepared to buy five cents worth of lupino beans (salted beans, soaked and sometimes eaten as a treat).

Jimmy Boy DiVico stood alongside his friends and found it hard to understand what they found so interesting.

"Boy, you guys are really sick," he said. "It's like you never saw a pretty girl before! Do you want to know something? I think Clara has a much prettier face than that babe inside the store."

"Shut up, will you Jimmy?" Fischetti snapped. He grabbed DiVico's chin and turned his friend's head around toward the action. "That scumbag has been trying his best to dry hump the babe ever since he rushed into the store. Try not to stare at him because Scraps and me want to see how far he'll go."

Rosa stabbed at a smaller piece of the codfish with a finger, then decided to utilize the prongs that lay nearby to raise it from the water to test it for firmness the way she had been taught to do by her mother. Sposito used this as an opportunity to reach out to the object of his perverted lust, this time allowing his fingers to offer a light pinch.

Rosa's doubts had been erased. There was indeed a degenerate present among the customers who remained straight-faced. All of them seemed to be engrossed in trying to draw the attention of the single server in the store. All with the possible exception of one man who seemed disinterested and in no particular hurry. She believed Sposito was the culprit, but to be absolutely sure, Rosa decided to trap the bastard.

Allowing a big smile to appear on her face, she tried to mask the volcanic, Sicilian rage that was shaking her whole body. She said to herself: If this lowlife wants it that bad, then I'll give him something to really enjoy—for a few seconds anyway!

Her smile, combined with her new posture in which she stuck out her voluptuous ass even more, was too much for the pig-snouted Sposito to resist. *She likes it!* he told himself, noticing her consenting smile. He allowed himself to think that this woman actually wanted him.

Pretending to be reaching for a certain tin of tomatoes on a shelf in front of where Rosa stood, Sposito pressed his body closer to the girl, who remained peering into the shallow depths of the pool.

After carefully studying the pieces of raw codfish, Rosa selected one and when she felt she was in the right position, she reached down with both hands and pulled out one of the larger, newly soaked fish. Spinning her body around quickly, Rosa swung it like a baseball bat and whacked the hard, wet fish into the left cheek of the deranged man.

Sposito screamed in horror and pain. The impact caused him to drop to his knees while other customers, feeling the splatter of liquid thrown around the store, scrambled to avoid becoming involved in the violent incident.

"Hit him again lady!" Fischetti screamed. "We saw the whole thing."

Rosa Cambria had every intention of doing just that. She swung the fish by the tail once again at the sneak. This time the blow struck the top of his head as she yelled at him, "You *disgraziado* bastard. Do you think you can fool around with me or any other woman around here like that?"

Sposito tried to make it to the door in a crouch, only to be stopped by another customer, a female, who pushed him back inside the store where he tripped over a barrel of salted capers and tumbled to the ground once again. Sposito lay face up on the sawdust floor and waited for his eyes to regain proper focus. Capone and some others then lifted the demented man to his feet while Sposito feigned an inability to stand on his own.

"What would you like done with him, senorina?" asked Alphonse.

"I'll go across the street, where there's a telephone to get the police! Okay?" said another one of the men who witnessed the incident.

In the few seconds it took for her decide whether or not she would want to appear in court, or even if she wanted to go through the trouble of going to the Hamilton Avenue police station to swear out a complaint, Sposito suddenly bolted the store.

His remarkable recovery caught everyone by surprise, but his escape was not without a painful farewell tossed his way by the youngsters. Scrapisetti, Fischetti, and DiVico rained cans of tomato paste and handfuls of hard-shell snails at his back and head. One particular toss by Jimmy Boy hit the fleeing, disgraced man square in the face when he turned around to see if he was being chased.

"I hope that fixes your fuckin' pig nose!" DiVico screamed at the creep.

When Vincenzo Cacioppo, the shopkeeper, cleaned up the mess, he asked aloud, "Who's gonna pay for these dented cans and the snails?"

Capone stepped in, saying to Cacioppo, in Italian, "My dear sir, this will be paid for by the increased sales you will undoubtedly receive from the neighborhood people when they hear about the *stocco* and baccala store where the people stick up for a woman no matter how young or demure she may be."

The flattering remark caused young Rosa to smile at Capone, who had pulled the owner aside. "You should report what happened here to your mayor, Batista Balsamo," Capone told Cacioppo. "Maybe he'll inform you that you should be paying us for the services we provided." Capone's eyes stared at Cacioppo, causing the man to feel guilty of even considering his damaged and lost merchandise.

Taking the hint, the store owner asked Capone, "*Che cosa posso fare per lei?*" (What can I do for you?)

"I came in here to pick up three pounds of baccala for my mother," Capone responded.

Cacioppo proceeded to wrap about five pounds of his fresh baccala in waxed paper, place it in a brown paper bag, and hand it to Capone. He thanked the owner and walked out of the store with his gang at his side.

"*Il piacere e stato mio* (the pleasure has been mine)!" the owner called.

7

To Catch a Star

LOOKING MORE LIKE a bank teller than the leader of a vicious mob, Don Paolo Antonio Vaccarelli stood at the door of the Five Points associated clubhouse at the corners of Carroll and Smith streets in the Gowanus section of Brooklyn as the band of young hoodlums came streaming in.

"Where's Alphonso?" he asked, shaking hands with each one of the young men as they passed him. The aspiring new members, in addition to young Capone, were Anthony "Tony Scraps" Scrapisetti, James "Jimmy Boy" DiVico, James "Filezee" DeAmato, Joe "Frenchie" Carlino, Gido Bianco, and Tommasso "Tommy Butch" Grimaldi, along with a few others whose identities remain unknown as far as gangland history is concerned.

Capone entered carrying a case of whiskey on one of his broad shoulders and placed it at the feet of Don Paolo.

"This comes with the compliments of the proprietor of the White Horse Tavern," he said, while extending a hand to his new boss. The older man shook Capone's hand and smiled, but his face soon turned serious as he closed the door behind the youngster. Don Paolo was visibly upset.

"Oh no!" he said emphatically, waving a hand in front of his face. He was refusing to accept the gift of the wooden case containing twelve bottles of fine Canadian whiskey saying, "I cannot accept this, Alphonso. I want you to keep this booze for yourself. Take it with you when you leave. It's yours." The serious look remained on the old man's face as he patted Capone on the back. "You alone were responsible for bringing the White Horse account into our club, along with all the other new ones," Don Paolo said. "You deserve to do what you want with that case."

"Well, if that's how you feel, Don Paolo, there's only one thing to do," Capone declared. "Let's have a drink right now." He picked the case up and walked it over to an empty chair that stood by the club's solitary pool table and said, "Filezee, open this thing up for me, willya?" Capone's pudgy face beamed with pride as he watched his young partner-in-crime hurry toward the kitchen area and return with glass tumblers in hand. Butch Grimaldi handed a drink to Al, who'd gotten comfortably seated while awaiting the boss's return from his usual routine as doorkeeper of the clubhouse. This amounted to sliding the bolt lock on the front door and pulling down the shade.

Don Paolo stood at only around five feet, four inches tall and had a rather dull look about him, but despite his appearance, he was well-respected by all who knew him and actually feared by some.

The conversation quickly turned to the waterfront deal every member of the club was tuned into. "Those Irish pimps hold all the cards when it comes to the real dough," the oldest member of the club said. "On the docks it's a bunch of old farts who depend on the muscle of a few guys to keep harmony."

The don raised his glass to offer a toast: "*La fortuna degli Irish non e abbastanza per la palle della nostra banda.*" (May the luck of the Irish be not enough for the balls of the Five Point Club.)

Everyone in the place responded with a loud, "Saluddi, Don Paolo."

The newest members, which included Capone, were aware of the steady trickle of cash being generated by their gang's activities down on the docks. Even the few members who contributed little to the effort benefited financially. As a matter of fact, it was Joe Carlino's job that allowed Don Paolo to get the gang's foot in the door. Known on the docks as Frenchie, Joe Carlino was treated kindly because of his ability to get narcotics for the personal use of some of the big shots on the piers. It was his association with a certain pier manager that allowed Carlino to get work for many of his fellow gang members. They worked as extra labor, longshoremen, maintenance workers, and at other positions involved with the pier.

Looking much older than his sixteen years, Joey had become a saboteur for the Italian mob. His clean-cut looks gave him the semblance of being a "nice kid," and Carlino played it to the hilt. He sat in one of the three armchairs the club offered with his long, spider-like legs stretched out, sipping on his glass of Canadian whiskey, enjoying the praise being heaped upon him by Don Paolo for his "diligence and ability to confound the waterfront's security."

"Some good people are saying the stevedore company may be willing to pay a couple of grand to the guys who can put a stop to whoever is responsible for destroying so much cargo on their pier," Don Paolo said. Looking straight at Carlino, he continued. "As a matter of fact, they think they have a good idea who's doing the damage. They've tried using their friends, the police—even the White Hand mob can't help them." Don Paolo's eyes widened as he put forward his budding idea.

"They seem to feel it's the agents of some new, fanatical workers group intent on putting them out of business." Don Paolo walked over to where Carlino was slouched in his chair and placed a hand on the teen's shoulder. "Joey," he said, "I think pretty soon you'll be able to quit setting fires and fucking up the cargo." His slim hand came away from Carlino and his face brightened. "We got us a patsy! It's a dumb Spanish guy they believe is sparking the damage." This came as great news to Carlino, who felt relieved not only because he worried about getting caught with matches in his pocket but because he was grateful that he had accomplished what he had set out to do.

Don Paolo explained the situation a little further to his young charges.

"It seems they got the guy shadowed. Everywhere he goes there's an Irish, *Mano Bianco*, right behind him. Although they continually follow him, they never catch him doing a damn thing wrong. But they still believe it's him who's giving the orders."

Tony Scrapisetti raised his voice to offer a question. "Don Paolo, how come the spud eaters don't just kill the guy and be done with it?" Scrappy Tony's voice was deep and gravelly, not what one expected from his rather thin and delicate face.

"It looks like the guy in question is hot into politics and he's related to a judge in New Jersey," Don Paolo responded with a smile. "For that reason, they're scared to lay a hand on him."

The Five Points boss pointed a finger at Tommy Butch and said, "When the deal is ready to close, you, Alphonse, and Filezee are gonna lay out for this clam digger and send him to the bottom of the river. When Frenchie stops doing his thing and the word comes down that the destruction on their pier has ceased, we'll take credit for making things right." The instructions to his underlings continued with specific orders. "We'll do it on a Friday night, after the patsy gets his pay, so those who still believe in fairies will think he got robbed and murdered for his pay."

"And of course, his judge in New Jersey will think the Irish mob did the job under contract with the stevedore company," Scraps cut in. "Clever, Don Paolo."

"I don't really care what his relative, an uncle, I believe, thinks," Don Paolo said.

Capone pulled two bottles from the case and placed them on the couch beside Frenchie Joe, saying in earnest, "Take these home and enjoy them with your lady friend, Frenchie, but remember, as Don Paolo has advised, if that company doesn't come up with the dough after next Friday, you may need your matches again."

Carlino laughed as he took hold of the bottles. He looked toward the old man who displayed a broad smile at Capone's generosity, knowing him better than most. Don Paolo was learning that the big youngster was quick to reward, but quicker yet to avenge a dirty deed that was done against him.

When the serious business was finished, Capone drew Scraps aside, saying, "I'd like you to do me a favor tomorrow without the world knowing about it." His eyes became sinister-looking and glued to one spot on the ceiling as he spoke. "I want you to go to Tersie's drugstore, see Pete Lynch. He works there," Capone said. "I understand that guy comes from Cicero, Illinois. Find out if by chance he can drop a line on a little dame that Johnny Torrio was humping. She said her name was Ann Snodgrass and she came from the same town."

· · ·

THE LAST PEOPLE in the world that Frenchie Collins wanted to offend while working on the docks were the dangerous criminals known as the "White Hand." Composed mainly of Irish toughs, this syndicate held each and every pier facility on the New York–New Jersey water-front in their tight grip and jealously controled all the lucrative action. Being the "protectors" of the busiest harbor in the world, they were the logical ones to summon in an emergency.

"I came on duty at four PM I was making my rounds and I smelled smoke. It's a good thing I have a good snoot, too," Artie Walsh, one of the pier watchmen, boasted as he held his nose with two fingers. The man's uniform was wet, a result of his running through the pier, filling pails of water taken from a nearby toilet and dousing the fire to help contain it until the city fire department arrived. "I'm just happy it never reached the hazardous cargo area, otherwise we'd have a real mess on our hands," he said.

Walsh had already reported what he knew about the suspicious fire to the police, the fire department, the U.S. Customs Service, the stevedore manager and now, Gary Barry and Frank "Ashcan" Smitty, who were there on behalf of their crime boss, Dinny Meehan.

"This was a close one," exclaimed Tim Hanley, the longshoreman timekeeper who carried a clipboard in his hand and a pencil behind an ear. "Being so far down the end of the dock, it could have easily gotten out of hand."

"The fire was intentionally set, so says the fire chief, and if Artie wasn't doing his job, we'd have lost plenty of dough right here," remarked another watchman, who came on the scene too late to be of any help.

"It's a good thing we didn't take much damage. We won't have to miss a single sailing date, not to mention the lost revenue for the working stiffs on this pier," Barry exclaimed, patting the pier guard on his back for a job well done.

"What I'd like to know is who the hell gets his kicks from setting fires?" the timekeeper asked.

"How many people do you have working here today, Hanley?" the more outspoken of the two gangsters, Barry, evidently the one in charge, wanted to know.

"I can tell you exactly how many workers the Bull Lines employed today. But that's the longshore roster only, which doesn't take into account the other crafts involved in the day's activities," replied Hanley, who removed the pencil from his ear and tapped it on his clipboard.

"As you know, there's dozens of others working inside the shed on any given day," he reminded Barry, "including government customs workers, carpenters, cargo weighers, cargo samplers, coopers, livery drivers, and their helpers . . . and I might add, most of them are practically strangers to us."

"C'mon, c'mon, how many do you figure had business in the area?" the redheaded Barry snapped.

"Well, the stevedore company, Bull Lines, actually paid two hundred and seven people today . . . that's including me." Hanley scratched his head with the pencil. "My estimate of the people who had the right to be inside the shed is around two hundred, but those who had business in the general area would be around fifty or so."

The timekeeper's eyes scanned the two mob associates' faces and saw only bewilderment and frustration. Ashcan Smitty's disappointment was evident as he turned to his partner with a puzzled look.

"Four or five hundred human beings had the opportunity to set this fire and we're supposed to find him?" Smitty asked.

"Don't worry, we'll catch the bastard," Barry said. He glanced at the timekeeper, then shifted his gaze to the sullen-looking watchman. "This is probably the same guy who's setting all the fires, and he's bound to make one fatal mistake. That's for sure. Then, we'll burn *his* ass!"

Ashcan's attention seemed fixated on the second pier guard, who had arrived on the scene after the fire trucks showed up, and called Barry aside to confer with him privately.

"Say, Barry," he whispered, "wasn't this same guard down at the Green Dock last week when that fire erupted in the special cargo section of the pier?"

Barry responded with a smile and a snicker. "Ashcan, you are dead wrong in your thinking," he said. "Some of these guards are assigned to different piers on any given day."

"Well that's nothing for you to laugh at", Smitty responded. "After all, didn't Dinny tell us to do some snooping?"

"If you feel like questioning him, Ashcan, go right ahead," Barry said, with an air of superiority.

Ashcan Smitty stood only five feet, two inches tall and was not particularly bright. Known for his audacity, not his brains, this White Hand gangster got his nickname from a youthful incident where he got caught stealing an ashcan and beat up the neighbor who caught him in the act.

"Excuse me, what's your name?" he asked of the watchman. Outfitted in a blue uniform, the thin, blond, younger man looked for all intents and purposes like a city cop, but without the sidearm. He was surprised and a little insulted at being questioned concerning these fires and didn't hesitate to let Ashcan know it.

"My name is Michael Dolan," the guard said. "I'm the son of Patrick Dolan, who happens to be a first cousin to Dinny Meehan . . . your boss, I think." "Well now, don't be getting huffy on me, lad," Ashcan said, taken aback. "I'm only trying to do a job here." Ashcan noticed Barry was snickering as the young guard reinforced Barry's contention that his security services were no longer required on the

Green Dock so his company, which was separate from the stevedore company, assigned him to work here at the Bull Lines pier.

"I'm surprised you don't recognize Mike Dolan," Barry offered. "He's always down at the Green Clover," a popular West Side gin mill.

"Well maybe it's the clothes," Ashcan said sheepishly, "no offense, Dolan." Considering his reputation vindicated, the youthful watchman responded graciously, "None taken."

Ashcan's failure to recognize a local was nonetheless overruled by his stubborn pride. Turning back to his partner he mentioned in a soft tone, out of Dolan's hearing, "You can't blame me for trying. After all, the guy was in two of the places where fires were started."

Gary Barry turned to face the head of the dock where firemen were still actively rolling up their hoses and putting their equipment away. Behind him was the scorched cargo, the remnants of what once were bags of Colombian coffee beans. Blackened and drenched with water, some fifty sacks of damaged, raw coffee beans stood as mute testimony to the destructive power of the arsonist.

"I want to see a list of every man who worked here today," Barry declared.

"Do you really think it could be a Bull Line employee?" the time-keeper asked, as he presented a list of names and company tag numbers written on three pages of red-lined paper.

"I have the authority to take and inspect your roster, every damn name on it," Barry replied. "I want to see how many of these men happened to be working at some of the places that this same problem came about."

"Does Arnie Chick know about this?" Hanley asked. "After all, he owns the company."

"Don't worry," Barry assured the timekeeper. "I'm having you copy these names for me as soon as possible. Me and Ashcan will wait for you in Chick's office, so I'd appreciate it if you'd get started right now."

Hanley was still holding the clipboard against his chest as he started the long walk to the head of the dock where his office was situated.

Feeling totally disgusted at being forced to copy each and every name on his timesheets, Hanley felt even worse when he heard the shorter guy, Ashcan Smitty, come out with a wisecrack.

"Hey Hanley," he shouted, "next time stick a piece of carbon paper underneath."

. . .

SEVENTEEN-YEAR-OLD AL CAPONE was much wiser than his years in 1916. Schooled by some of the shrewdest criminals to ever set foot on American soil, his stature in his gang was notable to say the least, and his ability to follow orders paved the way for his later insistence on loyalty and blind allegiance from his own underlings.

He spoke in Italian to Don Paolo so the don could understand every word.

"I think it's smart to wait a couple of weeks, Don Paolo. Give your man inside a chance to try again." Capone was referring to the heat that was being put on his good friend, Joe "Frenchie Collins" Carlino. "The truth is, Frenchie has already been questioned in regard to the fires. He'll never admit to this because he feels he's too slick to ever get caught in the act, but he knows the Irish have the word out on the street and that sooner or later somebody's gonna finger him as belonging to us."

The leader of the Five Points gang, Don Paolo Vaccarelli (alias Paul Kelly), pondered the situation while soaking his feet in a foot bath. Between working the cash register and acting as wine steward in his own restaurant, Don Paolo was tired, but he nonetheless realized he still had work ahead of him that night.

"You're right," Don Paolo said. "Frenchie should stay away from the clubhouse until this is over." Lifting one leg out of the basin, he rubbed the toes with a towel. "There's no reason to be stupid about it and rush things."

The older man, who could be ruthless when necessary, was feeling somewhat sympathetic concerning the damage carried out on one particular pier, the Green Dock. "I know we're going to close the deal any day," he said, "but I feel terrible about the cost of all this. I used to take my nephew, Vincent, fishing on the end of that dock when he was little. Some of the biggest fish in Brooklyn are still being caught in the Buttermilk Channel."

He was pulling on a pair of white cotton socks as he voiced his relief that the arson did no structural damage to the pier itself.

"Thank God the fire department got there so quickly," Don Paolo said. "We just want to send a message to these companies, but we have no desire to put any of them out of business. That is, so long as they see things our way."

"Don Paolo, you said it yourself. There's bound to be losses on our side when we venture into the Bay Ridge area to do our thing," Capone said. He was dressed in what he considered real sharp clothing that evening. From the snazzy fedora on his head all the way down to the expensive, white spats that covered his shoes, the brutish youngster looked almost handsome, and much older than his seventeen years. Having just entered the clubhouse, he removed his hat, tie, and tight shirt collar. Breathing a sigh of relief, he continued discussing the immediate future with his boss. "Don Paolo, give me a crack at shuffling the cash down there and I promise you in a few months I'll have most of the gambling action sewn up, even in some of the joints run by the Irish."

"You've already got your own book, Alphonso," the don responded. "Let's talk about stepping onto their turf and hustling in that area another time. Right now, I want you handy while the stevedore companies continue moving in our direction. Frankie's got some of his people driving the Irish to the wall now," he added. "Any day now, the shit's going to be on."

As Capone handed Don Paolo his cut of the money he was counting, the two men had their business dealing interrupted by the sound of breaking glass. Capone, being closest to the door, walked briskly and peered out the curtains that covered the window while Don Paolo, in his stocking feet, followed close behind. Seeing nothing unusual happening on the early evening street, the older man strolled back to the table, but Al decided the sound required further investigation. When he opened the door, he could hear the crunch of glass scraping along the ground.

"Don Paolo, *sguardo questo!*" he shouted. "Look at this!" The shoeless man came to the door once again where Capone was observing a trail of liquid that stained the face of the door.

"Somebody tossed a bottle of beer at the window. Lucky for us they missed the glass," Capone said, observing the broken bottle that lay on the sidewalk where a puddle formed. The youngster looked in all directions. "There's nobody around," he said. "It looks to me someone tossed it from a moving vehicle."

"Well, the driver would have more than enough time to turn the corner," the don speculated. "Didn't I just finish saying those bastards would start the shit real soon?" They both agreed the thrower had faulty aim and caused no damage to the club.

Don Paolo went to the rear of the onetime pool hall to retrieve a broom and a shovel, which he handed to his subordinate. As Capone began cleaning up the glass, Don Paolo remarked, "Why in hell would they throw bottles at the clubhouse? One would think they'd find a better way of showing their displeasure."

"I really don't think this is the work of the White Hand," Capone commented. "Rather, some young Irish, probably kids with too much hooch in their gullets." Capone took one last gander outside before closing the door behind him. "I was telling you just a while ago the word is out that we're moving into their treasured docks. Even their kid brothers are aware of it."

"Maybe I'll send Frenchie upstate to the Catskills to work at my cousin's place for a couple of weeks," Don Paolo said. "But in the morning, I intend to put more pressure on those companies."

"Excuse me if it seems I'm trying to second-guess you, Don Paolo," Capone said, "but do you think that's a wise thing to do? If you get reported to the authorities, the Irish will come after you with the coppers in front of them. All they have to do is pick up the telephone and they'll be waiting for you."

"You misunderstand me, Alphonso, I'm not going to intimidate them personally. Oh no! The fucking warning is going to come from socialist-minded Brooklyn dock workers who sympathize with those dockers in San Francisco. It's a fact that they have serious rioting on some piers in California, and the socialists are even causing unrest right here in the Wall Street area. Who can contradict the rumors that the bullshit is spreading to the waterfront?"

"I'm sorry, Don Paolo, but you lost me," Capone said. "What rumors? What unrest?"

The old man's eyes widened and he circled his index finger through the air. "The wheels in my head are turning, Alphonso, and I think I've come up with a good one. I'm going to sit down and compose a letter. Of course it'll be in Italian, but I want you to bring it down to Union Street where my good friend, John Tucillo, has his printing shop. He'll translate it into English and print it up for me . . . and he'll keep mum about it too."

Capone was mystified at the request. "Okay, Don Paolo. Tell me what you want printed."

"Sit down and keep an open mind, Alphonso. I think this just might work."

The don pulled a chair from the table that had a bottle of wine and some drinking glasses on it. Drawing two glasses toward himself, he poured red wine into both, then pushed one toward Capone. "This is to my brilliant brainstorm," he boasted, offering a toast. "This letter I'm composing will be in the form of a small bulletin, you know, on the order of those things they pass out on the street corners."

"You're speaking of the advertisements they hand out?"

"Exactly Alphonse. I want a couple of thousand of the things printed so we can flood the Bush Docks with them. We'll turn them loose before daylight in front of the piers on our list for winning over."

"I'm catching on now, Don Paolo," Capone said. "You mean like a *news letter*. But what will these things say?"

"I want to print up things that'll make the Stevedore companies and the steamship companies conjure up images of their labor force organizing for more money and getting ready to strike."

Capone was awestruck at the idea. Here he was watching a master tactician at work, one who was even dreaming up a name for the propaganda sheet. "We can call it the 'Docker's News' or the 'Voice of the Waterfront,'" he said, with a lilt in his voice. "And for now, we'll concentrate on distributing it in front of the Green Dock piers, the Bush piers, and every other pier that's on our list."

Capone took a sip of wine. "I trust you to write things that'll knock the socks off their garters," he said. Clever as a fox, Don Paolo would be the moving force behind Capone's yearning to procure his own territory. Hopefully it would be one of the richer areas now under the thumb of the White Hand gang.

"Alphonse, I want you to get Filezee, Butch, and another guy to use as a driver because I think the time is here to bring this thing to a head. Bring them here tomorrow. We've got to sit down and talk."

Capone was smiling now. "Time to bring it to a head," he repeated as he watched the old man put his shoes on. He was happy and genuinely grateful to this master criminal. Demonstrating his affection while helping his boss put on his dark, blue raincoat, Capone said "Don Paolo, I really would like to thank you. It's your prestige in the club that allows me to attend such important meetings." He talked while he put the final touches on his own apparel, gently patting his gray fedora as they got ready to leave together.

"You know Alphonse, I liked you from the start," Don Paolo said. "Man to man and pulling no punches, that's the way I deal with people and I see and admire that trait in you."

Turning off the gas lamps, they locked the door and began a short walk to Kenmare and Mulberry Streets where they were scheduled to meet another member of the Five Points gang named Joe Masseria. The pudgy, docile-looking Masseria laid claim to the murders of dozens of rivals in his young life. He controlled the gambling operations on the Lower East Side of Manhattan and was the major enforcer for Vaccarelli.

He was waiting for them in the back seat of his 1915 Cadillac sedan and waved enthusiastically when he saw the don carrying the package. Opening the rear door while bidding the two men to enter, Masseria slid across the leather seat while his eyes remained fixed on the package wrapped in brown paper. He clutched the parcel from Don Paolo's grasp with both hands and sighed. "Aha, pasta *con sarde* (sardines), my favorite," he cried out as gleefully as a child receiving a much-desired gift at Christmas. Masseria licked his lips while bending over to get a whiff of the contents of the package. He gingerly placed it on the shelf space behind his head.

Speaking in English, Masseria expressed his pleasure to Capone. "Nobody but nobody makes this dish the way Paul makes it. When we get to the Harvard Inn, I'll have the cook heat it up for me and . . . oh boy, this pasta, a couple glasses of wine, and I'll be ready for anything." His silly laugh and chubby face made him seem harmless, but nobody in that auto forgot his deadly nature for one second, broken English and all. Capone had come to respect Masseria for the good deeds he'd performed for other members of the Five Points gang. He was fast becoming known as the most powerful man in their mob, which amounted to more than a thousand loose-knit members. Masseria's influence in political and judicial circles had immensely overshadowed the Tammany Hall connections of the older Don Paolo, whose power, but not respect, was on a steady decline.

"I was watching the face of that flatfoot who seemed fascinated at us getting into your car," said Capone. "I wonder what's going through his mind."

"You have sharp eyes, Alphonso, because neither me or my driver noticed a cop in the area," Masseria said. Turning around and peering through the rear window, he was still unable to locate the officer.

"Look by the doorway of the fruit store. Can you spot him now?" Capone pointed to the uniformed cop as the car pulled away from the curb.

"I hate it when those bastards hide like that," Don Paolo remarked as he sat with his hands folded in his lap, "in doorways, behind parked cars. Those hungry fucks are just waiting like vultures for someone to break a traffic law so they can shake him down."

"That's because shaking down the regular folks is the only way some of those creeps in blue know how to make a buck," Masseria chimed in. Masseria then introduced his chauffer, Albert Altieri, to the two men. A muscular young man in his early twenties, Altieri would serve Masseria faithfully until being gunned down a few years later. His voice was mellow and his manner seemed to be one of quiet assurance. As he turned the auto onto Chambers Street, which led to the entrance of the Brooklyn Bridge, he looked into the rearview mirror, and addressed a question to Capone.

"Say, Alphonse," Altieri offered, "what were you thinking when you spotted that flatfoot gawking at us back there?" Distracted by the sight of a lovely blonde crossing windy Park Row, Capone's response was delayed as he pointed out the girl, whose skirts were being tossed about and lifted by the breeze.

"To be honest about it, Albert," Capone said, "I was just wondering what was going through his mind seeing us dressed to kill and entering this swell car." "I'll bet he was wondering what the hell Don Paolo had in the bag."

"I *wish* he'd have stopped me to take a gander in this bag," Don Paolo replied. "He probably would have been disappointed to learn my bag wasn't filled with cash."

"Whaddaya talking about?" Masseria boomed, "what's in that bag is better than cash." He reached over and slapped the youngster's knee and noticed Capone's lips turn up at the corners in what passed for a smile. *Nothing is better than money*, Capone thought to himself—*except what money can buy.*

"Hey big fellow," Masseria remarked to Capone, "you look like you enjoy good food. Am I right?" Capone thought he'd offer an amusing reply to the man who everyone claimed was a good person to have on your side.

"Don Giuseppe," he said, "my brother, who they call Ralphie Bottles, says I pay twice as much for food as they pay for all the horses at Belmont Park in a season." Masseria broke out laughing as he settled back in his seat.

They were driving to Brooklyn, to a place that was becoming more and more familiar to young Capone. They were headed to Coney Island and the Harvard Inn, which was now completely owned by Frankie Yale.

Capone gazed out the window as Altieri steered the car over the famous bridge. He could see the lights coming from the busy docks with their cargo booms all aglow and thought of the murky docks and the money they generated as jewels that sparkled in the open palm of the White Hand gang.

The long ride from Manhattan came to a halt behind the cabaret's rear door where a crowd of revelers were attempting to gain entrance. A bouncer was trying to convince them the place was closed for alterations to the public.

"What are you trying to tell me?" one of the men in the boisterous party yelped to the two employees assigned to guard the door while Capone led the two older men past the onlookers with Altieri covering the rear. "Alterations?" the man complained. "Who're these four guys? The carpenter crew?"

A Yale hired hand, five-foot-six Anthony Carfano (alias "Little Augie") turned to face the much taller, obstinate intruder and warned him in a hushed but angry tone of voice, "Hey mister, if we do allow you inside, we'll make sure the carpenters take a saw to your fucking legs. Now get the fuck out of here right now or else be one sorry son of a bitch."

The other sentry posted there happened to be Frankie Yale's private bodyguard, Sham Brown, who moved in the direction of the back-stepping crowd, which began to disperse. One of them yelled, "Fuck this joint anyway. Joe's has Jimmy Durante, and they say he puts on a great show."

The long bar was closed and its bright-colored, stained-glass windows were dark. The gas lanterns that hung from the decorative, metal ceiling provided the large dance hall with just enough light for someone to see where they were going as the four men split up. Young Capone and Albert Altieri remained by the dimly lit bar while their seniors were directed to a staircase and the elegant cellar-turned-finished-basement below. The two men who had guarded the rear entrance were now busy finalizing the necessary security precautions, checking to be sure that every door was locked and all the shades were drawn.

Little Augie and Sham Brown walked to a table that was set up in front of the bar where some bread, cheese, fried chicken, and other finger foods were spread for the younger members of the Five Point "club." Capone and Altieri were invited to indulge, and they didn't have to ask Capone twice. Not having eaten for several hours, his giant stomach was grumbling and he had been complaining ever since he sat in the car with the aroma of Masseria's dish of pasta con sarde in his nostrils.

Just the fact that he was asked to serve Don Paolo on these occasions was a step toward attaining his dream of eventually being a boss himself, of someday sharing in the wealth and the power he knew they would soon be mining from the gold fields known as the Brooklyn waterfront.

Sham Brown was Yale's right-hand man, whom Capone knew from their old neighborhood. He remembered Sham as a rough type with a short temper who loved to brawl. He more than met Frankie Yale's requirement for an employee: "One must have nerve to serve."

The other muscle belonging to Yale was Anthony Carfano, who went by the name "Little Augie Pisano." This slightly built gangster in his early twenties had an ugly, hooked nose and was as deadly as a cobra when the chips were down. Though only five feet, six inches tall, his stature was more than enough for those who thought they could get away with avoiding paying dues to Frankie Yale.

At these sorts of functions, young Capone acted amicably and courteously, as did the other hopefuls in attendance who realized the privilege of being invited called for extending good manners to other members of the club. They had all learned an important lesson at some point in their young lives, a simple fact of mob life. There are but two distinct groups of people in the underworld: those who can help you on the road ahead and those who would destroy you.

Capone learned this lesson the first time he was in this place. Feeling slighted by Johnny Torrio, he got angry and almost walked out on the man who would eventually vouch for him to Frankie Yale and Don Paolo Vaccarelli. Since that day, he learned to show respect to everyone in the course of business, especially fellow members of the Five Points gang. "Never allow your emotions to cloud your business or you'll wind up a self-righteous guy *with no business!*" was Torrio's advice. It made sense to someone like Capone, who was never a bully to begin with. That's not to say he found it easy to keep his enormous ego in check. It was a constant battle he fought with himself, and he didn't acquire the flamboyant personality his name now evokes until later in life, after proving to his peers that his ability and fearless determination was second to none. As an adult, Capone never resorted to violence unless necessary.

Most of the conversation coming from the crew at Capone's table was lighthearted banter concerning their conquests of the opposite sex and information on some of the loose women in town. Eventually the talk turned to more serious matters.

"Masseria goes nowhere without his licensed 380 semi-automatic Browning and he's not scared to use it," said the well-built Altieri, showing off his own piece, a .32 caliber Colt revolver. The chatter around the table continued in that fashion, each man extolling the virtues of his own choice of weapon; downstairs the conversation had a somewhat different spin.

In attendance below were Ciro Morello, alias Ciro Terranova (known as "the Artichoke King"); Frankie Yale; Charles "Lucky" Luciano, who was a stand-in for his partner, Arnold Rothstein; Batista

Balsamo; Joe Masseria, and Don Paolo Vaccerelli. They waited for the bartender to close the door behind them and after a few minutes of exchanging greetings and some small talk, they settled down at a long, marble-topped table. Don Paolo remained standing to offer a toast. Raising his glass over his head, he proclaimed, "*Bene Salute tutto,* may this evening bring warmth to the heart, light to the mind, and *money to the pocket!*" Taking a sip from his glass, Don Paolo remained standing, as was the custom. Being the founder and senior official of the Five Points brotherhood, it was his obligation to announce the reason for the gathering. He stood at attention with his arms at his sides as he scanned the faces of the inner council of the Five Points gang.

"We are here tonight to discuss our interests, which happen to conflict with those of the White Hands and, in particular, our efforts at making inroads down on the docks," Don Paolo said, and turned to Balsamo to prod the oldest member of the brotherhood to speak.

"Zio, would you be kind enough to comment on the steps we are taking to avoid an all-out war with the Irish?" A shrewd businessman, Balsamo was affectionately referred to as the "mayor" of Union Street. Many consider him to be the first godfather of Brooklyn. His blue eyes and brown hair belied the expected picture of someone born in a small town just outside of Palermo, Sicily. Reaching for his glass, which had just been refilled by Yale, Balsamo took a sip of the wine made especially for the Harvard Inn by Vito "Happy" Randazzo. He smacked his lips together in an appreciative manner and smiled.

"The idea you told me about just a few minutes ago is going to work just fine, Don Paolo," Batista remarked. "I truly believe the way you're handling the pier thing is the right way to shake up the stale situation down there and playing up the 'radical angle,' which you'll explain to everyone here, will positively serve to break the grip of that Dinny Meehan on the docks."

Joe Masseria, destined in a few short years to be known to all as "Joe the Boss," realized that Balsamo had finished talking and thought he'd exercise a little of the power he was feeling as the most productive member of the club.

"*Scuza*, Zio," Masseria said. "It's my friends in the newspaper guild that are keeping the pressure on the shipping companies by publishing so many stories about the labor problems occurring right now in San Francisco." Masseria's eyes were dark and squinted slits as he sat there gnawing on another lobster tail, filling the large dish in front of him with discarded pieces of shell. He had devoured the pasta prepared for him by Don Paolo as soon as he was seated and ordered the cook to bring more food via the dumbwaiter, even though the others had already finished eating.

"Fights among the unionized longshoremen and scabs are reaching the point on the West Coast where some of our New York companies are convinced that labor troubles are bound to erupt here also," Masseria continued. He wiped his stubby fingers with his already soiled napkin and tossed it aside, using the cotton tablecloth to dry his lips. He gulped down another short glass of wine and continued speaking. "They are scared shitless!" he said with an air of certainty. "So scared that the management of White Star Lines has today made overtures on behalf of themselves and a few other companies to address the problems by employing us!"

Masseria's eyes went around the table and settled on Balsamo, waiting to hear the old man's reaction.

"Bono, Giuseppi," Balsamo exclaimed, "but don't think for a minute the one who's called 'Wild Bill' or that other Irish, Dinny Meehan, is not going to be wise to the transaction. They have spies on the docks and when they get wind of it, they're going to let the shit fly."

"Si, Zio Batista," Masseria replied, "but as Paulie planned it, they won't even know what's happening until it's too late."

Lucky Luciano realized it was incumbent on him to offer his opinion concerning the matter before them.

"As you all know, I'm here on behalf of myself and my partner, Arnold Rothstein, the best Jew since Moses came down from the mountain." Luciano hid a snicker behind a red napkin in his hand and waited for the laughter to stop. "Rothstein couldn't be here because he's on his way back from our nation's capital. He's sent word to me that he's made inroads with some officials in the Labor Department. He also suggested that when he hits New York, he'd like to speak to Ciro about an idea of his in regard to the perishable cargo that comes into and leaves the port of New York."

"I think I know what he wants," replied Terranova, a cherished friend of Don Paolo. Only in his early twenties, Ciro had already earned himself the nickname "Artichoke King" because he controled the sale of every single bushel of the thistle-like vegetable throughout the metropolitan area.

"I happen to know that Rothstein has been buttering up one of the chief inspectors that controls the checking of everything that enters my Hunt's Point market," Terranova said. "That's where most of New York's fruits and vegetables are inspected by the government." Luciano's eyes widened.

Terranova now realized what Rothstein had been up to when he took the chief inspector, who had the powers to either pass or quarantine the merchandise, out to lunch one afternoon. He had tipped his hand, but this was of no concern to Terranova except, if he had known what Rothstein was up to at the time, he would have been more than glad to pick up the check. The Five Points fraternity always pulled together in times of mutual benefit, and this was one of those times.

Luciano responded by admitting he was unfamiliar with the specifics of the deal, but promised that upon Rothstein's return he would go straight to Terranova to discuss the details with him.

"Allow me to explain what I think Rothstein has in mind," Terranova declared. "If an examination of—just for example—a Canadian shipper's onions shows signs of vermin infestation, that means an entire boatload of onions could be condemned by our government inspectors and consigned to the trash heap . . . or thrown overboard."

Don Paolo's head shot up as Balsamo let out a roar of laughter.

"I can just hear you now, Paolo," Balsamo said, "asking your boys to go down into the hatches of the filthiest English freighters in the port to gather all the rat shit they can find so they can sprinkle it among the produce being imported by those *disgraziato* shippers that refuse to kick in."

"Don't laugh, Zio Batista," Terranova bellowed. "You want to know something? That's a fucking great idea."

Balsamo's humorous state was spreading around, prompting Don Paolo to rap on the table with a spoon. When quiet returned, Terranova's voice, still holding back a chuckle, tried getting serious again as he attempted to put the finishing touches on his report.

"These kinds of things can be developed in the future, I'm sure," Terranova said. "When Rothstein gets back, we'll talk about it. But concerning what's happening right now, I've arranged for seven truckloads of oranges and grapefruit to be diverted, that spells 'hijacked,' in the middle of their runs to the Hunt's Point Market. After my boys steal the fruit, we sell it to greedy retailers who offer it to the public at cut-rate prices, like a few cents off the regular prices." Terranova's face beamed as he continued disclosing his accomplishments in the overall plan.

"The importers are screaming that the price of their produce is being undercut and, as a result, they're finding their sales at an all-time low," Terranova continued. "Fucking well serves them right for not consulting with me first." He raised a finger in the air and began spinning it in a circular motion. "The shippers must realize that the only way they'll find themselves in the black ink again is if they acknowledge they have a good friend in Ciro Terranova, a very loyal member of the Five Points brotherhood."

Don Paolo sat relaxed and content with the progress reports. With a cigar in hand, he stared straight ahead at Frankie Yale, waiting for him to speak. The temporary silence was broken by Balsamo's courteous interruption.

"Frank," Balsamo said, "I know you're worried regarding your own position in all this, but as everyone knows, the Brooklyn piers belong to you. Because of that, you will lead the troops when the shit starts. And the consensus at this table is that you'll be up to the job."

Balsamo reached across the table to offer Frankie Yale an Italian cigar, which the dapper man readily accepted. Placing the cigar in his mouth, Yale let his square jaw exhibit a look of contentment and remarked, "Zio Batista, you're probably the only one I know who still smokes these." Yale stood up to use the flame from one of the brass lanterns that hung over the table. "Just like lighting up a dirty rope," he remarked. "That's not to say I don't find these cigars good. The powerful aroma reminds me of when I was young and used to sneak my smoking in the outhouse." Yale settled back in his chair and puffed away on the "Italian stinker." He looked around at the amused faces of his colleagues and said, "Do you want to know something? These cigars have a flavor that's missing in the expensive ones."

"Thank God for that," Don Paolo cracked, blowing the smoke from his Havana to the ceiling. The diamond ring on his pinkie sparkled in the light of the overhead lantern and Frankie Yale, sharp as a tack, began affirming his appreciation for the gang's efforts.

"I don't mean to jump the gun, but when we do take over the Brooklyn waterfront, that's over sixty wharves from the Greenpoint docks all the way to the Army terminal on Sixtieth Street. I will allow each and every one of you, my good friends, to share in the spoils," Yale said, his face growing serious. "My main concern is the strength of the White Hand down around Pearl Street and the Furman Street docks. Red Hook too. They're tough nuts to crack and I know there's bound to be blood spilled when we move in on them."

"Frank," Don Paolo said, "when that day arrives, all of us here pledge to you the manpower needed to get the job done." He pointed a finger in Yale's direction saying, "You'll be the general in charge of any trouble. Just know we've got some good, young soldiers on our side, Frank. Some youngsters with balls!"

The meeting broke up shortly thereafter, with Yale summoning some of his kitchen help to clean up the mess and extinguish the lamps. When he got upstairs, the first thing he did was seek out Capone, who was in the rear of the dance hall shooting pool with Altieri while Sham Brown and Little Augie were listening to some of Charlie's jokes near the bar. Tables had been pushed together and pots of hot coffee, anisette, and pastries awaited the dons who, finished with their business, prepared to enjoy the companionship of those who they had much in common with in a relaxed atmosphere. Capone laid his cue stick down when summoned to Yale's office and promptly used his handkerchief to wipe the blue chalk from his fingers before accepting Yale's outstretched hand. Offering an apology to the sharp dresser for his soiled hands, he walked with him into the office, which Capone had become familiar with a few years prior when he took on delivery of the money box job for Johnny Torrio. Around that time, Torrio had made his permanent home in Chicago, turning the Harvard Inn completely over to Yale.

"Sit down, Alphonso," he said. "I want to talk to you about something important. After that, we can go back to join the crowd." Yale sat down as well, and with his hands folded in his lap asked the youngster, "Al, how old are you now? And no lying. I want the truth."

"I got no reason to bullshit you, Mr. Yale. I'll be eighteen on January the seventeenth."

The custom-fitted suit and the silk tie Yale wore were a stark contrast to the rough-cut, stiff fabric of the suit Capone wore that evening and he felt self-conscious of his own knitted tie in the presence of the nattily dressed Frankie Yale.

"What would you say if I offered you a job?" Yale asked. "Sort of a combination bartender and doorman right here in the Harvard Inn."

Capone jumped at the offer, but admitted he had no experience behind a bar mixing drinks. "But if someone teaches me," he said, "I think I could learn, Mr. Yale."

"Listen to me, Alphonso, and get it straight," Yale said. "I don't like being around any *ruffiano* bastards (brown noses), so do me a favor and call me Frank, okay? And by the way, Torrio led me to believe that you're a bright, young guy, so how can you accept a job without knowing how much it pays?"

Capone stared at Yale and replied, "Ever since that day when I was a dumb kid doing that job on that truck driver, and got caught by the cops, I remember your words while we walked away from the scene. You said it cost you six hundred dollars between paying off the trucker and the coppers, so I figure I still owe you. Besides, Sham and Little Augie were telling me that you're the best guy to work for."

"That's because I enjoy rewarding loyalty and a person that does a good job for me," Yale replied. "If I make money, my people make money. The pay is seventy dollars a week and forget about owing me anything. As I recall, there were three other guys involved. Am I right?"

"Yes, Mr. Yale . . . I mean Frank. Sorry about the slip. I promise it won't happen again." He cursed himself under his breath as Yale rose from his chair. Standing alongside his new boss, Capone realized he was taller than Frankie Yale and still growing. Yale reached around Al's shoulder and walked him to the door.

"Be here tomorrow night, seven thirty," Yale told him. "And wear a suit and tie."

Working at the Harvard Inn turned out to be more strenuous than Capone anticipated, especially the chore that Yale referred to as "walking the clock," which entailed being on his feet for most of the night. This job required two bouncers casually strolling in opposite directions around the large dance hall. Each circled in opposite directions in a never-ending search for customers trying to smuggle their own bottles into the place. This was absolutely forbidden and Yale had signs posted at the entrance, the toilets, and all around the place warning customers not to bring liquor into the Harvard Inn. When the bouncers spotted someone with booze purchased on the outside, they would bring the luckless person into a special room with an exit leading to a back street. If the person refused to plunk down an amount of cash that was arbitrarily demanded by Yale, they usually found themselves in the alley between concession stands close to a Coney Island street called "The Bowery." As a matter of fact, over the course of a ten-year span, 1915–1925, more than twenty-five unsolved murders were reported inside or in close proximity of the Harvard Inn.

Capone found his calling when he had the opportunity to work the front entrance. That's where he shined. His pleasant manner served him well and Yale especially liked the way he dealt with people. Even the more bothersome of the big-spending customers learned to respect the big kid. Yale put Capone in that position as often as possible without hurting the feelings of his senior strong arm, Sham Brown. At the front door, Capone could make a few dollars in tips, as well as have a good reason to speak to the young ladies who entered the club. That was a perk young Capone relished.

One particular night in 1917, during Holy Week (preceding Easter Sunday), Yale kept the Harvard Inn dark because of poor business. He stayed busy by attending one of the craps games he organized and held on a weekly basis in an apartment over a garage used by a coal distributor to park his wagons. The garage, located on Third Avenue near Fourteenth Street in South Brooklyn, a predominately industrial section of town, was filled with livery stables and foundry shops.

The clanging of steel being hammered by a late-working blacksmith filled the night air as the four men, Frankie Yale, Al Capone, Sham Brown, and Gido Bianco, climbed the stairs leading to the floor above the garage where Yale's craps game was already in progress. Yale rapped a coded signal on the door, an eye peeped out from a tiny crack in the partition, and the door swung open.

The eye belonged to another Yale associate, Tino "Flame" Flamma.

"How's it going, Flame? Who's winning my dough?" Yale asked Flamma, a slender man with a corncob pipe clenched between his teeth and a black derby hat pitched to one side of his head.

Ushering his boss through a long foyer to the back room of the apartment, Flame whispered, "We've got a guy here who's cracking our legs every time he rolls the dice." With that, Yale threw off his black coat into the waiting arms of Flame. That kind of news was unsettling to Yale, especially when he learned how much the guy was ahead. Yale and company were usually assured of a handsome profit, and this night was turning out to be an exception.

The guy on the hot roll was a newcomer named Anthony Perrata, a ship-jumper who had taken advantage of a job he managed to land on a Norwegian freighter and slipped ashore a month earlier when the vessel docked at Hoboken, New Jersey.

"He really got the luck up his ass," said Flame, who insisted he never invited the guy into the game, but that Perrata learned of the location from Jerry "Beans" Rinaldi, an ironworker who was a cousin of the lucky man. "He's even staying at Rinaldi's house," Flame reported.

"Are you telling me it was that shit-eating Beansy who sent this fuck here to take the game over?" Yale asked incredulously.

"Sometimes it happens, boss. When you're hot you're hot!" Flame said.

Yale and Capone rubber-necked the game for a few minutes, then Yale grabbed Capone by the arm and walked him into another room where Sham Brown and Gido Bianco were relaxing with some glasses of white wine in hand.

"This clown's not going home a winner tonight," Yale remarked, bringing a look of surprise to all three faces.

"It doesn't matter to me, one way or the other," said Sham Brown, "but it's known all over town that a Frankie Yale game is an honest game. Why the change, boss?"

"I don't have to explain this to anybody," Yale said. "But if you really want to know, Sham, I'll tell you." He pulled up a wooden chair and sat down with his trio of goons. "The reason I want this guy to lose is because one of the guys in that game happens to be a good friend of my brother-in-law. I can see this guy is losing bad and the rat bastard that Beansy Rinaldi sent here is winning.

"The guy I'm talking about has the blue shirt with the black vest on. The poor guy recently lost a child, a beautiful little boy. Run over by a garbage wagon and he's been going crazy ever since." Yale's eyes were glazed as he related to his men how the incident had turned a nice, young man with dreams of becoming a doctor into a lazy, drunken bum: "He was so smart in high school that he won a scholarship to a good medical college, but he dropped out of life when he lost his boy."

"What do you want to do, Frank?" Capone inquired. "Taking the money back will be a snap. Is that what you want done?"

"Let's see the outcome of the game first," Yale replied. "But if this monkey ends up winning big, I want you to wait for him downstairs and reclaim the dough for me, okay?"

Capone's interest in the game intensified with each pass of the dice this slick-haired illegal immigrant threw until he actually found himself rooting for the man to win in order take this "boat job" over.

Yale left the premises in order to fulfill his promise to take his mother to the late mass being held at St. Rosalie's Church on Fourteenth Avenue and Sixty-Second Street. He left Sham in charge of things.

"That's it," whispered Sham Brown when he saw Perrata packing up his loot.

The miserable cheapskate won around fifteen hundred dollars and had the nerve to leave without offering even a few bucks to Flame, who represented the house. Flame stood by the door hoping for a tip, thinking he was entitled to something because he ran back and forth all night, bringing the guy beer after beer. *What a cheap fuck*, he thought to himself.

Sham thought of a way to keep Perrata there while the crowd of around eight players were heading for the door. He succeeded in hooking the immigrant into a conversation (in Italian) by inquiring if he was interested in an idea that would provide him with a way to remain in America.

"If you marry an American girl, you can stay in this country and file for citizenship papers right away," Sham explained to the foreigner. "It's done all the time," he assured him.

Once gaining Perrata's attention, Sham Brown kept it until the last player left the building.

"We've got a list of women right here in Brooklyn who are anxious to marry anyone who will pay them," he explained, "and the best part is, you don't even have to live with the woman if you don't want to. It's all done on paper."

"You say it no costa lotta money?" Perrata inquired in broken English.

"The total cost is probably just a little more than a hundred dollars," Sham explained.

"I give you the money right now. You do this thing for me." Perrata exclaimed.

Sham had been ordered by Frankie Yale to stay with the guy until Tino Flame cleaned up the room. Sham and Gido were to keep Flame from learning that one of his players was being robbed of his winnings.

Capone had them counted. Twelve men had already exited to the street, so he figured the footsteps coming down the creaky steps were those of his victim, Tony Perrata. Capone was hiding in the rear of the dark hallway and after being absolutely certain that it was Perrata, he pounced out and confronted the man head on, blocking the door to the street. His partner in crime, Gido Bianco, had just extinguished the gas lamp on the wall that provided light to the upper hallway, and Capone had adjusted the downstairs lamp to just a faint glow. Perrata was faced with the choice of racing, sightless, back up the dark stairs to the safety of the apartment, or confronting the large, shadowy figure that blocked his exit to the street.

"Getta outta my way, or I fucka you up!" he yelled while attempting to squeeze past Capone, only to find himself thrown to the cold, newspaper-lined floor. Perrata, on his back, placed a hand in his pocket and gripped his bankroll, which he knew was his attacker's objective. He tried getting up, only to be knocked down to the floor again by a heavy foot to his chest. This time, the alien managed a little body roll that culminated in a half-sitting position with his back against the wall. Perrata could see his assailant stooping over him, attempting to pull at his pocketed hand, which Capone felt was welded inside his trousers.

"Give me the money or you're dead!" Capone blared while loosening up on his victim's hand. He suddenly lifted the man by the collar of his coat and pinned Perrata to the wall with his own body. In the dim light, the man could see Capone's face.

"Maddona mia, look who it is," Perrata exclaimed excitedly. "I know you from the dance hall in Coney Island. Now, lemme go or you gonna be in bigga trouble."

"You're the one in big trouble, stupid," Capone said. "So turn the money over or get yourself killed." With that, Capone whipped out his revolver, a .38 caliber Smith & Wesson, and held it to the man's throat. But instead of complying with the forceful demand, the foolhardy foreigner began a defiant tirade of curses.

"You sonnafabitcha *muso porca* (pig face)! You no scare me witha that gun. Why you no sticka it uppa the assa you mama?" Capone's temper was at the boiling point, but Perrata continued the harangue. "You hear whatta I say? You disgraziatto bastard." Capone stepped back to release his prisoner and fired one shot into the man's chest.

The blast brought Sham and Gido running into the darkened hallway, followed close behind by Tino the Flame. Turning the valve on the gas lamp, they could see Capone standing at the bottom of the stairs, with one hand on the railing and his other hand pressed against the wall. Still straddling the body of his victim, he looked straight up at his cohorts and said, "Sorry, Sham. The fucking jerk asked for it."

Flame was beside himself. He was the one who dealt with the proprietor of this building and the owner of the coal-distribution company that occupied the space below. For this reason, Flame was shaking like a leaf, almost tripping over the body in response to Sham's urgent command to lock the front door.

"Don't worry about the noise," Capone declared, "Shots are heard around here all the time. When folks want to try out a new gun, they head down here to shoot at a few stable rats."

"Right, Alphonse," Sham Brown piped, "only this ship jumper's no stable rat."

"What are we gonna do with him?" Flame inquired of the others.

"What else can we do?" Capone replied. "We gotta clean up the walls a little, pick this fuck off the floor and dump him someplace." While Sham proceeded to turn the lamps to their maximum brightness, Capone and Gido dragged the body to the darkest part of the hallway urging Flame to round up all the old rags he could find to wipe the blood off the walls and floor.

"What do you think will happen, Al, when the boss finds out about this?" asked Sham.

"He's gotta understand, this guy had it coming," Capone said. "He really and truly asked for it."

"Sham cupped his stubby chin with a hand and replied, "That's not what I'm talking about, Alphonse. I was talking about Tino the Flame. Frank didn't want him to know anything about us rolling the guy for his dough." Capone responded by revealing to Sham that he's known Flame since they were kids and that he will understand, "especially when I offer him a couple of C notes for his pocket."

Sham's eyebrows went up. "Well," he said, "Frank is expecting something like fifteen hundred from the job, so where are the other two for Flame coming from?"

"From here in this belt." Capone replied, displaying a second bundle of cash that he'd found tucked away on the dead man's waist.

"This guy had nowhere else to stash his dough?" asked the older mobster. "How much do you think he had in there?"

"He won around fifteen hundred, right?" Capone asked. "Well, he had around sixteen hundred in his pants pocket and I found something like seven hundred more in his money belt. I'll split up the extra dough with you and Gido—that is if you'll help me get rid of the stiff."

Flame returned with an old mop, some newspapers, a small, floppy rug, and a woolen blanket from the bedroom.

"We need to water it down some," said Capone, adding, "I saw an empty jug in the kitchen. Hopefully there's no holes in the damned thing." He yelled upstairs to Gido to fill it with water and to bring it down while they kept busy drying the pool of blood that had collected at the foot of the stairs. Using newspapers and the cloth Flame had ripped from the dusty drapes that hung on the rear windows, they soon had Perrata wrapped up in a bundle, looking like a mummy and ready for transport. Capone had already squared things with Flame, who agreed to be the wheel man for the delicate task of dumping the body.

Tino drove without headlights to the front of the building, where he got out of the car with trembling legs and stood on the sidewalk, giving his fellow conspirators a signal that the coast was clear. Upon placing the body in the trunk of the car, a dog began to bark at the late-night activity.

"That fucking mutt better stop barking or I'll put a slug in it too," Capone said.

"Never mind the dog, Al," Sham exclaimed. "Let's just get the fuck outta here as soon as possible."

Capone, acting like he never heard the man's plea, walked to the wooden fence where the excited dog was located and fired a round at the canine, whose loud barking turned into a whimper and then, dead silence. Jumping into the back seat of the sedan, Capone was still pocketing his gun when he declared, "I hate loud mouths!"

Flame drove the car to a desolate spot at the foot of Degraw Street near Nevins Street where an opening in the tall grass led to the Gowanus Canal, a commercially utilized waterway with a notorious reputation. Over the years, the clouded waters of the canal had yielded the skeletal remains of innumerable murder victims, and Tony Perrata would soon be just another unidentified John Doe.

"Nobody will ever miss him," Capone said as they dumped Perrata's lifeless body into the canal. "Not even his cousin, who will be told we never saw him again after he left Yale's craps game with a sizable bankroll."

The next day when he reported for work, Capone immediately went into Yale's office and broke the news concerning the incident to his boss. Sham Brown was already there and after Yale heard the news, he called for Gido Bianco to be present also. The two low-level associates nodded their heads, attesting to the accuracy of the tale Capone produced. "Why did you have to kill the fucker?" Yale screamed. "I never specified I wanted the guy hit. It was supposed to be a stickup for his dough, plain and simple." Capone appeared hurt by the scolding. He stood in front of his boss, willing to take discipline and rebuke from the one person in the world he truly feared.

"I had to do it, Frank," Capone pleaded with a downcast head. "He belittled me and goaded me. He even cursed my mother. I'm sorry boss, but he got what he wanted, the miserable, suicidal prick."

Walking over to where Sham was seated in a lounge chair with his legs crossed, Yale began blasting him also. "Do you mean to tell me you allowed this kid to do the job alone last night?"

Sham looked at Capone and said, "Boss, Alphonso said he wanted to handle the guy by himself. What was I to do?"

Capone jumped into the conversation. "Listen, Frank," he said, "if you want to blame me, you can. If you want to dock me some money, feel free to do so. But leave Sham, Gido, and everyone out of it, please. It was my doing and mine alone." Capone proceeded to explain his strategy of that evening's work.

"Frankie, you ordered Sham to stay upstairs, to keep Flame from getting wind of the assignment. He was not supposed to know we were gonna roll the ginzo, right?" Yale nodded his head in the affirmative.

Capone walked closer to Yale as he testified, "It was my idea to station Gido in the upstairs landing, to handle the gas lamp and to keep the guy downstairs where I could handle him without Flame's knowledge. I know what I did was wrong and I regret it, Frank. But believe me, I felt I had no choice, the guy was suicidal, I tell ya."

"But this fucks up my relationship with my Flame, who does a good job setting up and running these games for me," Yale said. Always thinking of his bottom line, he was worried Flame would quit him now, not wanting to be a part of a crooked game.

"Oh no, Frank," Capone replied. "Flame isn't even aware of what happened, because he fell asleep in a chair before the work even began. Right, Sham? Gido?"

"That's right, boss," Sham spoke up. "I stayed talking with Perrata until the crowd left, and I know for a fact that Flame slept through the whole thing, gunshot and all. The old fuck missed the whole thing. After the incident I left him sleeping upstairs and Gido stayed with him while I helped Al get rid of that Perrata guy." Lucky for Capone and the others, the boss seemed satisfied with their explanation.

"Where's the dough?" Yale asked, sticking his hand out. Capone reached into his jacket pocket and fished out the sum of fifteen hundred dollars, which he promptly handed to his boss. "What happened to the rest of it?" Yale demanded. "You don't think I'm stupid, do you?"

Did Yale have a crystal ball? Capone wondered to himself. How on Earth could Frank know about the money Perrata had stashed in his money belt? The youngster searched his partners' faces for a clue, but he found none. Yale opened his billfold, placed the cash inside, and held the thing open.

"I'm talking about Perrata's stake. If the guy won fifteen hundred it's gotta be he went into the game with some kind of stake. Where is it?"

Breathing a sigh of relief, Capone remarked, "I'm sorry about that, Frank. I forgot to mention that Flame said the guy had a very small stake. He started playing at a low level and worked himself up by making pass after pass. You can check that out with Flame." Capone wiped his brow with his handkerchief as he related another brazen lie. "We didn't think you would mind, Frank. The three of us kept one hundred dollars apiece so we could get new duds, because we got blood stains on our good clothes and we had to burn them."

"Well, I do mind," snapped Yale. "And it's coming out of your pay, Alphonse. I'm sorry but that's the way it is." Capone tried looking disappointed, but deep inside he felt relieved and found it difficult to control his laughter and joy.

"Now get to work, the three of you. We're not running a kids' school here. Go pick up Augie and make your rounds of the midway. Or did you guys forget it's collection day?"

The three men promptly obliged, each more than willing to leave the premises as quickly as possible.

From the window of his office, Yale watched them walking away from the club and realized this youngster, Capone, had balls indeed. With the right supervision, he could see him as a valuable asset to his organization in the troubling days ahead.

95 Navy Street. Al Capone was born on the top floor of this house.
Municipal Archives of the City of New York

St. Michael the Archangel Church, where Al
Capone was baptized, at the corner of Lawrence
and Tillary streets.
Brooklyn Roman Catholic Diocese.

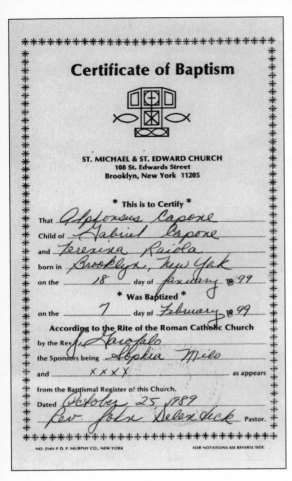

Certificate of Baptism

ST. MICHAEL & ST. EDWARD CHURCH
108 St. Edwards Street
Brooklyn, New York 11205

* This is to Certify *

That _Alphonsus Capone_

Child of _Gabriel Capone_

and _Teresina Raiola_

born in _Brooklyn, New York_

on the _18_ day of _January_ 18 _99_

* Was Baptized *

on the _7_ day of _February_ 18 _99_

According to the Rite of the Roman Catholic Church

by the Rev _J. Garofalo_

the Sponsors being _Sophia Milo_

and _X X X X_ as appears

from the Baptismal Register of this Church.

Dated _October 25, 1989_

Rev. John Delendick Pastor.

NO. 214N F D. P. MURPHY CO., NEW YORK   FOR NOTATIONS SEE REVERSE SIDE

Official baptism
certificate of Alphonsus
Capone.
*Brooklyn Roman
Catholic Diocese*

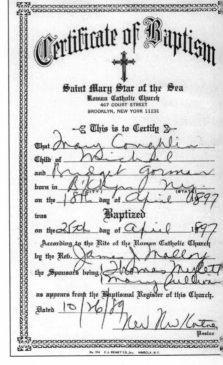

Certificate of Baptism

Saint Mary Star of the Sea
Roman Catholic Church
467 COURT STREET
BROOKLYN, NEW YORK 11231

This is to Certify

That _Mary Coughlin_

Child of _Michael_

and _Bridget Gorman_

born in _B'klyn, n.y._ (CITY) (STATE)

on the _18th_ day of _April_ 18 _97_

Baptized

on the _25th_ day of _April_ 18 _97_

According to the Rite of the Roman Catholic Church

by the Rev. _James J. Mallory_

the Sponsors being _Thomas Triplett_
Mary Sullivan

as appears from the Baptismal Register of this Church.

Dated _10/26/89_

Rev. Rev. Katine Pastor

No. 214 F.J. REMEY CO., Inc. MINEOLA, N.Y.

Mary Coughlin's (Al Capone's wife's)
baptismal certificate.
St. Mary Star of the Sea Church

69 Park Ave off Navy Street, Brooklyn, N.Y, where Gabriel Capone had his haircutting business and lived over the barber shop with his wife and children.
Municipal Archives of the City of New York

38 Garfield Place as it looks today. The Capone family home, Brooklyn, N.Y.
Photo by William Balsamo

21 Garfield Place as it looks today. Capone family home in 1911.
Photo by William Balsamo

P.S. 133, Capone's old school, as it looks today. He dropped out in the sixth grade and never attended another schoolday in the years that followed.

Photo by William Balsamo

Paolo's Sicilian Foccaceria where the teenaged Capone ate lunch with a cousin and a few friends on his way to buy Baccala for his mother Teresina.

Municipal Archives of the City of New York

This clock is the scene of Al Capone's shoe shine days at the age of 12.

It later became an underworld landmark among mobsters. The phrase was "I'll meet you under the clock." Extortion, kickbacks, and a few murder assignments were paid and issued under this Columbia Street clock.

Office of the Kings County District Attorney

Luna Park, Coney Island, in 1918.
Every amusement park, every stand, every ride, and every hot dog business had to pay *acamurra*—protection money to Frankie Yale and his mob. If you did not pay or you protested, the Yale mob would burn you down, thus the burning of Dreamland Amusement Park in 1911.
William Balsamo collection.

Francesco (Frankie Yale) Ioele. Junior five point gang leader, notorious killer and Al Capone's mentor. Photo taken in 1915.

Johnny Torrio, Capone's boss in Chicago.
Associated Press

Brooklyn water-
front as it looked
during the 1920s.
Looking east from
Manhattan.
*William Bal-
samo collection.*

Capone's Chicago home on South
Prairie Avenue.
Mark Levell collection

Al Capone removing his hat,
followed close behind by Vincenzo Gibaldi, better known as
Machine Gun Jack McGurn.
Pacific and Atlantic photo

Dennis (Dinny) Meehan, co-leader with (Wild Bill) Lovett of Brooklyn's infamous and deadly Whitehand gang.

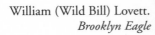

William (Wild Bill) Lovett.
Brooklyn Eagle

Irish Rose of the Brooklyn Waterfront, Anna Lonergan, sister of Richard (Peg Leg) Lonergan.
William Balsamo collection

A very dead (Wild Bill) Lovett.

Notice Lovett's hand is outstretched as if clutching a gun. He was in a drunken stupor before his killers struck and could not defend himself.

New York Daily News.

William Lovett's body was found in a Brooklyn warehouse. His service and record in the first world war won Lovett these military honors from Ridgefield Park V.F.W. at his grave.

New York Daily News

This picture shows Batista Balsamo, great uncle to William and John Balsamo. Born in 1868 in Palermo, Sicily, he was a low key gangster extraordinaire.
Family photo

Jan 1921 - Funeral of Salvatore Balsamo, younger brother of Domenico Balsamo. Domenico is the grandfather of the authors. In the crowd are the Mangano brothers, Philip and Vincent, and Charles (Lucky) Luciano.
Family photo

Salvatore Frank Capone's funeral, 1924. Shot down by police in Cicero, Illinois.

Alphonse Capone in late spring, 1925.
Brooklyn Public Library Photo Archives

Eyes in the mirror. This image is the best depiction of Capone's death stare.
William Balsamo collection.

Adonis Social Club, December 26th, 1925. Scene of triple homicide. Blood stains on the sidewalk show the exact spot (Peg Leg) Lonergan's dead corpse wound up seconds before dropping to the cold cement pavement. Inset are mug shots of Lonergan's bandaged head and Cornelius (Needles) Ferry.
Brooklyn Eagle

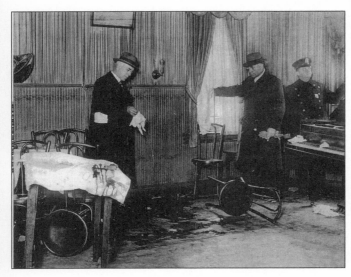

Adonis Social Club, December 26th, 1925.
New York Daily News

Funeral for Richard (Peg Leg) Lonergan, held at 738 Myrtle Avenue in Brooklyn.
New York Daily News

Richard (Peg Leg) Lonergan.
Brother-in-law to (Wild Bill)
Lovett, and his successor in the
Whitehand Gang.
New York Daily News

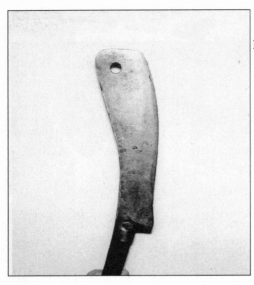

The actual meat cleaver used to murder Peg Leg Lonergan.
Photo by John Balsamo

In a group line-up days after the triple homicide known as the Peg Leg murders. Capone is at top right. His cousin, Sylvester (Silvy) Agoglia, is seated at center.
Office of the Kings County District Attorney

Ioele Family's Tombstone
Photo by William Balsamo

Frankie Yale, standing far left on May 22nd, 1928, a little over a month before his death on July 1st, 1928. Monsignor Cioffi standing middle. Ex-lawyer for Brooklyn D.A. Mr. Brancato on right.
Brooklyn Eagle

These are the actual weapons used against Frankie Yale July 1st, 1928. Yale was the first gangster in New York to die by a machine gunner.
William Balsamo collection.

Frank Galluccio, the Man who created Scarface.
Office of the King's County District Attorney

John Torrio
Mausoleum, Green-
wood cemetery,
Brooklyn, N.Y.
*Photo by
William Balsamo*

8

The Man Who Created Scarface

❝ CONTINUED HOT AND humid" was the forecast in the *Brooklyn Eagle*, the newspaper all of Brooklyn was reading in early August 1917. The heat spell was responsible for the deaths of 272 people and 278 horses in the city's most populated borough. The latter number created a severe public-health danger that could hardly be controlled by the eight wagons of New York City's Health Department assigned the job of removal of the dead nags. Even though it was not unusual to see animals lying dead in the streets, finding a horse in front of one's home or place of business caused many to lock up and leave because of the awful stench. Those who could afford to do so checked their families into the better hotels around town, those with electricity, in order to enjoy the blessed relief of an electric fan.

Earlier in that same week, more than 100,000 people spent the night sleeping on the beach at Coney Island, braving mosquitoes, chiggers, and sand fleas. Many were there because they had no other choice. The intense heat caused a stoppage of the elevated train lines when the crews of Brooklyn Rapid Transit, which serviced Coney Island, walked off the job because of the sweltering weather. Anyone who came to Coney Island by public service that day was stranded there, whether they liked it or not. Eventually, the telephone lines were also knocked out from heavy overuse, making it a terrible week for everyone except the owners of Coney Island's various concession stands.

Capone had his cab driver use Ocean Parkway, one of the direct roads that led to Coney Island. On the way there, he was not at all surprised to see many of the inhabitants of this wide thoroughfare, like the rest of the city, practically living on the sidewalks, trying to catch a breath of fresh air.

He sat in the taxicab, enjoying the light breeze that brushed his face, while the driver pointed out the massive housing structures being built along the way. Capone paid little attention to what the man was saying, as his mind was on the stifling weather and his job at Yale's place, the Harvard Inn. His job there was becoming too routine and he felt listless, although deep down he considered the opportunity to work for Yale a stepping stone to achieving his dream of one day putting his talents to work on his own behalf and for the benefit of his own pockets.

At times, his boss did things to make him feel like an apprentice, an upstart, an amateur without common sense. The incident in the hallway with Perrata and the fact he snuffed the guy out without Yale giving the okay was hard for Capone to live down. In the mind of Yale, Capone didn't follow orders that night and the gunplay should have been avoided. But Capone absorbed the rebukes and the boring assignments he thought were being dished out to him of late as a sort of punishment. Tonight he would be kept busy "walking the clock" alone because Yale had the rest of his crew off on various assignments, and Sham Brown had been appointed the job of handling the front door.

Upon his arrival in Coney Island, Capone had the cab driver turn down a side street in order to avoid the heavy traffic of Surf Avenue. This "poor man's Riviera" was a paradise for those seeking relief from the oppressive heat and the clean, sandy beaches offered thousands of city dwellers a cool place to lay down and spend the night. They arrived at Coney Island by auto, trolley car, and the recently completed BRT subway line. More and more they came, until one would think on a given day that the whole city was at Coney Island.

He allowed the cabby to drop him off on Neptune Avenue, around a block away from the dance hall, and walked the brightly lit street that was experiencing the usual traffic jam created by automobiles loaded with fun seekers circling the streets in search of parking.

Capone wore a light blue suit and a white shirt with collar and cuffs. He also wore a new, beige, straw hat on his sweaty head in a vain attempt to shield his noggin from the blazing August sun.

"Goddam it!" he said to himself. "I thought it would be at least a few degrees cooler down here." Most times, the breeze coming off the ocean did make it more comfortable to be in Coney Island, but on this fateful evening he was perspiring even more than he had during the day. Perhaps it was due to the crowded sidewalks and the steam generated by the concession stands strung along the way, or maybe it was the countless electric bulbs that covered just about every inch of space that wasn't walkable.

Capone removed his hat and wiped his brow with the back of his hand, carefully avoiding a puddle of stagnant water near the curb as he crossed the main drag, Surf Avenue. Capone's bloated, overweight condition partially accounted for the irritable mood he was in and while he walked, he renewed his vow to cut back on the beer.

The Harvard Inn was still closed to the public when Alphonse entered the rear door and hurried past the hot kitchen to one of the coolest spots in the club, underneath a large, overhead fan located near the pool room. Looking around the dance hall, he was surprised to find a small group of patrons already in the semi-darkened club being served drinks. Realizing they couldn't be guests of the owner, he walked to the bar and inquired with the bartender.

"What's going on here, Charlie?" Capone asked. "I understand that Frank won't be around tonight."

"They're friends of Albert Altieri," the mustached bartender explained. "They said Altieri said it'd be okay. You remember Albert, don't you?"

111

Shaking his head from side to side, Capone countered, "Yeah, I remember him, but that doesn't make it right. Just because somebody mentions somebody else's name is no reason to offer them special treatment."

"Oh, what's the difference, Al?" Charlie retorted. "We're due to open in around twenty minutes and they seem like nice people."

Capone was prepared to let this one slide when he noticed one of the two young ladies in the party appear to be leaving the table to go to the powder room. His eyes nearly popped out of their sockets as he watched the wiggle of the twin cheeks beneath her yellow dress as she walked toward the foyer where the restrooms were located.

"Nice girl," Capone cracked. "Do you know who she is, Charlie?"

Capone's question and the way his gray eyes seemed to come alive told Charlie that young Capone was very interested in this filly.

"I couldn't tell you a thing about her Al," Charlie replied, "except that she's not much of a drinker. Can't say the same for the guy, though. He's downing booze like we're giving it away for free. Uh-oh, there he goes again. He's ordering another boilermaker."

"How come they're sitting so far in the back of the place?" Capone asked. "Wouldn't it be much easier on the servers if they sat closer to the bar?"

"I asked that of Tessie already, but she claims the taller girl pleaded with her to be seated close to the fire exit," Charlie said. "People are strange, you know. Maybe she was in a fire once. Maybe her mother taught her to sit close to the fire escape, I dunno. In this business, you get all kinds of requests."

Alphonse kept his peepers on the door to the ladies' room, waiting for it to open again, for the pretty girl to cross the empty dance floor on her way back to the table. He pretended to be making a slight adjustment to the curtain near the foyer and raised his head when she approached him.

"And how are you this evening?" he asked her, in a very smooth and polite tone of voice. She swept past the skulking Capone without responding to his advance nor making the slightest bit of eye contact with the big fellow, who felt like a fool. He cursed himself under his breath for using this approach.

His objective was to establish a claim on her before the place was officially open and other young studs would arrive to offer competition. Because it was early, there were only two of the six servers working on that side of the rectangular dance floor. One, a female named Tessie, was in charge of the Harvard Inn's six food and beverage servers; the other, a young male called "Spider," Tessie's oldest son, was working the food orders.

The hard-drinking man was Frank Galluccio, a fairly handsome man who stood only five feet, two inches tall. But tonight, due to the large amount of rye whiskey followed by the beer he'd consumed, his head was in the clouds. His normally neat appearance was compromised by the fact that his shirt was out of his trousers and the knot on his tie was halfway down his chest. This man, who turned out to be a low-level associate of Lucky Luciano, showed genuine compassion later in life by helping pay the rent for friends and neighbors who were down on their luck. But tonight he was drinking up a storm.

The band called the "HyLights" soon arrived with their leader, Hyman Tornoch, who was dressed in a black tuxedo. Capone huddled with the thin, white haired man, reminding him to play some of his favorite tunes, which included "Yes Sir, That's My Baby," and "Melancholy Baby." Moments later, the rest of the band filled the stage, unpacked their instruments, and began warming up by playing portions of some of the numbers they would perform later that evening.

The young ladies accompanying Galluccio motioned Spider to their table to take their food order, with the idea of getting some down their soused friend's alcohol-laden stomach. Capone, meanwhile, was busy pumping Tessie for a line on the object of his desire.

"Best I can tell, Al, is the guy's date is the tall, skinny one," Tessie said. "I know that because he's constantly grabbing her hand and trying to place it in his lap under the table."

Capone soon noticed Galluccio, who was feeling the need to empty his bladder, boost himself up from his chair and head for the foyer. This induced Capone to try a different tack. After all, he figured, the beauty must be a third wheel, probably just a friend of the couple. So he followed behind the unsteady saunter of the drunk who was heading for the toilet in hopes of striking up a friendly conversation with the man. Alphonse thought it'd be a nice way to wrangle an intoduction to the young lady.

When Capone entered the men's room, Galluccio was standing in front of the tall urinal, pissing away like an Arabian racehorse. He was unaware of Capone's presence.

"How're you doing this evening, friend?" Capone asked Galluccio as he turned to button his fly. "I hope you're having a nice time."

Galluccio, who seemed to be having trouble fastening the top button on his trousers answered in a gruff tone. "I don't see how anyone can have a good time when the freakin' music in here stinks," he said.

"They're just tuning up, sir, give them a chance. I think you'll find them pretty good," Capone responded.

The young boozer brushed past the smooth-talking Capone before another word was spoken between them. *So much for that approach,* Capone thought.

A little while later, after he'd consumed some food, Galluccio did in fact hear the band play a fast number that he was fond of. Pulling on the arm of his date, he headed for the dance floor, which was already occupied by another couple jumping to the rhythms of "Tiger Rag."

Galluccio showed surprising agility dancing despite his drunken stupor, and Capone decided to take advantage of this opportunity to speak to the attractive young lady left alone at the table. He sat himself down in the chair Galluccio vacated and tried to engage her in conversation.

"Do you like ragtime?" Capone asked. She exhibited a vacant look, blinked, and turned her face to blow a puff of smoke from her cigarette.

"Really fellow, I'm not going to sit here and recite my musical preferences to you," she said, "so please leave before they get back."

"I know you like music because I've noticed you tapping your lovely feet under the table," Capone said. Watching her light-brown hair shimmer in the glow of the overhead lantern, he continued with his line. "It's been such a hot day and the ocean is so beautiful at night. I'll bet you wouldn't mind taking a little stroll on the beach with me later on. I manage this place," he lied as a wry smile spread across his face, "but I know they can run the joint without me for a little bit."

"That number is nearly over, fellow," she snapped. "Would you be kind enough to leave now?"

Capone's failure to impress her at this point was no reason for him to admit defeat. He would leave her side like any gentleman would after being rejected, but his character included such tremendous ego that he believed himself invincible. What Capone wanted he always got, and his strong desire for this sweet thing, as preposterous as it seemed to the bartender at the time, meant that he was sure he would have her.

A bit later, Capone noticed one of the young guys who regularly frequented the club stop at their table. Galluccio half smiled and came up from his drink long enough to offer his stamp of approval, mainly because of the young man's clean-cut appearance. Walking the object of Capone's lust to the dance floor, the man placed an arm around her waist, and drawing her close, he looked considerably depressed when the young girl pushed him back to what she thought was a respectable distance. The band was playing a slow tune while Capone stood close to the entrance of the kitchen, his eyes aware of every delicate movement of tender flesh beneath her soft-yellow dress as she danced.

Fuck Altieri, he thought to himself. And fuck this so-called friend of his, too. Albert Altieri had beaten him out of some sorely needed cash shooting pool one night not too long ago and this was enough to cause disdain for both of them in Capone's scheme of things.

It seemed that gulping down some food had somehow renewed Galluccio's stamina. Although he was still attempting to break the house record for boilermakers consumed in one sitting, his presence of mind was better than at any time in the evening. Capone thought otherwise, though. He was of the mistaken opinion that this puny little guy in the company of his lovely prize was soon ready to fall down of his own accord. Because of that and the man's size, Capone had absolutely no fear of Galluccio.

He waited near the edge of the dance floor until the musical number was over and the couple walked past him. When they drew close to where he was standing, he leaned over to the girl and murmured low, "I'd still like to take you on that walk to the beach."

Capone then had a conference with the band leader, requesting he play a special tune for a personal friend. This time, the tempo was spirited, as the HyLights blared out the first few notes of a song that went, "By the sea, by the sea, by the beautiful sea . . ."

The girl's name turned out to be Lena. She returned to inform Frank Galluccio, who turned out to be her brother, what had transpired on her way back from the dance floor. He was slow to figure it out, but when he saw the round face of Capone standing nearby, with his eyes beaming while moving his thick lips in sync with the lines of the song, "Oh how happy we'll be," Galluccio figured he'd taken enough crap from this overgrown wise guy.

Galluccio told his female companions to pretend they were going to the ladies' room, which happened to be close to the rear exit; if any trouble were to start, they were to slip out the door and wait for him among the crowd that always gathered in front of the funhouse. Lena urged her brother, Frank, to ignore the insulting brute and to bring them home because it was getting late, but Galluccio, who thought he should never have to stand for bullshit in a place that was recommended to him by "good people," decided to play it out.

Eventually, the reluctant girls gave in to their escort's command and began strolling toward the powder room. It was in the foyer that led to the ladies' room that Capone's shameful words to the young girl became the final straw. He stepped in between the two of them, startling them for a moment, then whispering to Lena in his raspy voice,

"I'll tell you one thing, you do have a lovely ass, and I mean that as a compliment."

Galluccio, drunk as he was, still managed to follow their exit with presence of mind until the rising anger inside him had reached its boiling point. When he saw his sister's face turn beet red from something Capone said to her, Galluccio stood, ready to step in menacingly towards the big fellow, but instead decided to hold his ground.

Meanwhile, Capone still hoped he could win Lena's brother over by buying him some drinks and dishing out some friendly chatter, never considering the insult he had just tendered toward the man's sister justification for the little man to begin a fight. He ordered Tessie to supply the table with drinks, compliments of the house, and in a few minutes she was placing another shot of rye whiskey and a mug of brew in front of the scowling Galluccio, who refused the drinks. Capone stood near the edge of the dance floor smiling, while Galluccio's hands were busy under the table.

"Come over here," the smaller man gestured with his left hand, while keeping his right hand hidden from view. Capone wasn't expecting Galluccio to start anything violent, but if the man wanted a fight, Capone was always ready for action. Galluccio sat there red-faced, but otherwise unemotional, with one hand under the table clutching an open pocketknife and the other hand behind his head holding onto the back of the chair. Meanwhile, Capone was weaving his large frame around some occupied tables headed in Galuccio's direction. He walked to the edge of the dance floor toward his destination with both hands outstretched and his palms up as a symbol of benign intent on his part. Before Capone could react, Galluccio was on his feet, tossing the chair he held in his hand along the floor in the bigger man's direction. Capone got his legs entangled as he tried jumping out of the way of it, lost his balance, and fell face down onto the sawdust-covered floor.

Although Galluccio didn't appear very muscular, he was wiry and quick nevertheless, because the instant Capone hit the deck, Galluccio jumped on his back like a cat. He slashed at the neck of his adversary three successive times with his sharp pocketknife, attempting to sever Capone's jugular vein while Capone tried without success to flip himself over and grab hold of his attacker.

The conflict lasted but a few seconds. Galluccio, thinking he had finished Capone off, stood up, took a fast look around at the patrons who had observed the chaos in horror, and made a dash for the nearby rear exit, disappearing into the crowded street. Sham Brown came too late to be of any help to Capone except to compress the wounds with bar towels and see to it that Capone was driven to nearby Coney Island Hospital to attend to the three slashes, the worst of which had been administered to his face.

Galluccio grew worried in the days that followed because some of his closest friends were avoiding him and the word going around was that his days were numbered. Johnny Rassi was the first to bring him the troubling news.

"Some heavy hitters from Yale's gang, three of them as a matter of fact, stopped by the pool hall on Baltic Street," Rassi said with a serious look on his thin face. "They were asking for you and they wanted to know if anybody in the pool room knew where you lived. Naturally, everybody clammed up. No bullcrap, Gallooch, those guys were mean-looking."

Galluccio's face turned pale at the unsettling, whispered words emanating from the corner of his friend's mouth. "My brother Louis was there, too," Rassi continued, "and he claims he recognized one of them as Sham Brown. Everyone in the pool hall had the same impression, Frank. The big bastard looked to be packing a rod."

Galluccio shook his head in disbelief as Rassi asked him, "Whaddya do, Gallooch, knock up the don's daughter?"

Galluccio's first thoughts were to pack up and leave Brooklyn for a relative's house in faraway Los Angeles, but he thought he should first confide in his chum, Albert Altieri, before undertaking such a drastic move. He had told Altieri about his plans to take his sister, Lena, and a date to Coney Island that day, and it was Altieri who suggested they pay a visit to the Harvard Inn while they were there, and to mention his name at the door.

After Galluccio informed him of his plight and how it came about, Altieri felt somewhat responsible for telling Galluccio to go to Yale's place that fateful night and for that reason, he thought he should help him.

"It's best if you keep your ass at home," Altieri advised Galluccio. "And pray I can get Joe the Boss in on this. He's the only one that I know of who can possibly get you out of this mess, providing you explain what happened exactly as you did to me."

Within a few days, the first meeting with Joe "The Boss" Masseria took place in a secluded section in the rear of a restaurant on Broome Street in Manhattan. Masseria was munching on some spareribs while the remnants of some type of shellfish filled a large bowl beside him. Dropping a morsel back into his dish, he stood up from his chair, wiped his grease-covered fingers on a napkin, and extended an arm across the table to shake hands with them, requesting that they be seated.

Altieri started the session off, speaking as was the habit when in a public place, in soft tones and in the mother tongue.

"Don Giuseppe," he said, "this is a good and loyal soldier whose name happens to be on Frankie Yale's shit list because of something he could not avoid. It was an insult of a personal nature that started the incident." Masseria smiled and patted his lips with a napkin. Gently, he said, "Please don't tell me the story about somebody messing around with somebody's sister, because I've already heard that one." He folded his hands in his lap and leaned back in his chair. "Tell me, Frankie G," he continued, "did this big bully Capone break her cherry or what?"

Galluccio remained stone-faced, feeling intimidated and belittled, until Altieri spoke for him.

"Don Giuseppe," he said, "you see this man before you. He's not a very big man, nor has he been known to get into fights, especially with strangers or in unfamiliar surroundings." Altieri placed an arm around Galluccio's shoulder as he continued. "But let me tell you one thing, Don Giuseppe: If I were placed in the same situation, I think there's a good chance I might have reacted the same way." Galluccio saw a glimmer of hope now, because the grin had vanished from the don's face and Masseria was questioning him directly.

"Have you ever met this Alphonso Capone before that evening?" Masseria asked. With a wave of his hand, Galluccio emphatically responded, "No!"

"And I assume you never had any dealings with him before the fight?"

"No, Don Masseria, I never saw him before that evening. Because he was a friend of Albert's, I figured he should have shown a little more respect for myself and for my young sister."

Galluccio was sweating as Masseria scratched his chin, then turned to Altieri and remarked, "Yale is a reasonable man. Maybe I can get somebody to act as your *consigliore* at a table. Let me see. Who can I get to handle this for us?"

Galluccio's downcast appearance changed when he realized Masseria was willing to try getting him off the hook. "I want you to stay off the streets and out of sight until you hear from me. Is that clear?" Don Giuseppe said, "I think maybe Charlie Luciano can handle our side of it. Don't forget, provided Capone's people agree to the meet, whatever is decided at that table is binding for both of you and must be obeyed to the letter. Understood?" Both men nodded their heads in full agreement. "Now, let's have something to eat and a little bit of wine," Masseria roared as he raised an arm and shouted to get the waiter's attention.

• • •

GALLUCCIO ARRIVED AT the meeting first, along with Charles Luciano as his spokesman. They were led by Sham Brown into Yale's office at the Harvard Inn, where they awaited the arrival of Galluccio's adversary. About five minutes later, the door opened and for the first time since that dreadful evening, little Frank Galluccio witnessed the damage he had inflicted on the face of the big brute called Al Capone.

The ground rules for the interrogation were known by both sides, but Yale, who was acting as the consigliore for Capone, thought it wise to repeat them for his charge when, after being seated, Yale noticed Capone's hands were trembling and his eyes cocked in a maniacal death stare as if saying to Galluccio, this is the beginning, not the end of it.

"Neither one of you are to leave your seat or show any disrespect or anger in any way," Yale began. "Speak only when you're asked a question by my good friend, Lucky Luciano, or me, and answer truthfully and to the point. Do you understand me?" Frankie Yale then stood up, walked behind Capone and held the big man's face by the lower jaw. Gently turning Capone's head to the left, Yale displayed the terrible damage Galluccio had inflicted upon Capone's face.

Galluccio was visibly shaken and squirmed in his seat as Yale ran a finger along the length of the major scar.

"Look at what he did to this face, Charlie," Yale said. "This young man will be wearing this for the rest of his life. Do you think the insult suffered by Frank Galluccio called for going after somebody's jugular?" Luciano studied the three jagged lines carved into Capone's countenance and agreed that although his man was wrong for not thinking about the consequences of his actions, he still felt justified in protecting his sister from an over-eager stud. The skinny, dark-eyed Luciano looked into the face of Capone. "Alphonso," he said, "in your own heart do you feel you had it coming to you?"

"Not really," Capone responded. "If I deserved anything that night, it was to have a date with his sister." Galluccio stirred in his chair, willing to go all the way to put a stop to Capone's shit once and for all, but looking around he noticed at least three good reasons to control his temper. Those three reasons were the firepower that could erupt his way at any second from Capone, Yale, and even his ally, Luciano. Not to mention Sham Brown and whoever else was on the other side of the door.

"Wait a minute!" Luciano screeched. "Just what are you saying, Alphonso?" Capone sat close to the edge of his chair as he spoke directly to Luciano.

"First off, Charlie," Capone explained, "Galluccio's party demanded to sit all the way in the back of the place when there were no other customers in there, making it tough for the servers. Only later did I realize he had bad intentions from the start. That's why he wanted to sit close to the rear door." Galluccio nearly sprang from his chair at the inference, but Luciano, who practically threw himself on the man, urged him to keep calm and assured Galluccio he'd shortly get the chance to tell his side of the story. Capone continued, "During the course of the evening, the guy vomited on the pool table, which had to be shut down for a week so it could be washed out and allowed to dry. Being perfectly honest about it, I really liked his sister's looks a lot and what the hell, I'm around her age, so what was the big deal anyway? I figured a guy shown such courtesy by the Harvard Inn shouldn't be so touchy about somebody liking his sister."

"Did you go into my place looking for a fight?" Yale asked Galluccio.

"No!" Galluccio responded. "I would never seek trouble when my sister, Lena, is in my company. The reason we sat close to the exit was because my girlfriend's mother trained her to always sit near the door in case a fire, a shooting, or a fight breaks out. I may have drank too much that night, but I certainly would remember throwing up, which I did not do."

"Well, I can tell you right now," Yale interrupted, "somebody *did* toss up a belly-full of food that night, because like Capone said, the pool table had to be steamed clean and dried." Yale made a motion to Luciano, and the two mobsters stepped back from the table to huddle in private for a few minutes. When they separated, Luciano came away rubbing his chin while Yale returned to his chair.

"A fight is something that happens from time to time," Yale said, "and there's hardly a way to avoid these things, especially when it concerns family." Galluccio raised his head from the constant stare he had directed at the Persian rug Yale had installed in his office. "Alphonso," Yale continued, "you tried to take advantage of one of Don Masseria's people and we find much responsibility is with you. A sincere apology is necessary from you to Galluccio. As for the injury and disfigurement you have suffered, we both feel it was a little extreme of Galluccio to try killing a man, even a total stranger, in a place where people are drinking, eating, and trying to have a nice time."

Yale was interrupted by a knock at the door. It was Charlie the bartender, who handed Yale a receipt for a delivery of booze while Luciano sauntered over to Galluccio to relate the rest of their decision.

"Gallooch," Lucky reported, "we feel this man deserves to be compensated for the scars to his face to the tune of fifteen hundred dollars to be paid by you to Capone within ten days. Is that clear? That will settle this thing once and for all."

"But Charlie," Galluccio pleaded, "I can't pay that kind of money right now and I can't see how I'll be able to pay it that soon."

Yale opened a drawer in his desk, pulled out a cash box, and counted out fifteen hundred dollars. "I'm laying out the dough for you, Frankie G," he said. "And Charlie Luciano is gonna send the same amount over to reimburse me. You'll settle with Charlie, who's the guy going to bat for you." Yale placed the pile of C notes in front of Capone, whose eyes beamed at all that cash. Luciano patted Galluccio's arm and assured him, "You don't have to pay me back in one shot, Galooch. I'll spread it out so it won't be tough on you."

Galluccio nodded his head but was really disheartened by the decision in which Capone received a nice bundle and he just a promise of no retaliation on the big guy's part. But after thinking it through, he kind of liked the notion of being into guys like Lucky Luciano and Joe the Boss. This practically guaranteed they'd find a decent spot for him, somewhere, to make enough dough to pay them back . . . plus.

"I want to see both of you shake hands and consider this dispute over and finished with for now and forever," Yale said. He stood alongside Luciano, and both looked down on the two men still seated in their chairs. After ordering them to rise to shake hands, they all stood together in a show of unity.

"Both of you agree to abide by the decision made here today," Yale said, concluding the sitdown, "and both of you understand that if either one of you breaks this contract, both me and Charlie here promise you will go to the cemetery."

9

Ma, Dance with Pa!

THE SUDDEN WINDFALL of dough provided by the Galluccio incident helped fund the wardrobe of expensive suits and other fashionable attire Capone began acquiring in the early part of 1918.

In March of that year, he had the opportunity to deck himself out in lavish style in order to attend the wedding reception of Frankie Yale's niece. It was a must-attend affair because Yale was his boss and Alphonse considered it an honor to be invited.

Dressed in his finest, Capone could pass for a businessman, or, to be more specific, an important executive on his way to catch a taxicab to Wall Street or Madison Avenue. However, upon closer scrutiny, one might wonder about the brown spats that covered his patent leather shoes and also the wide-brim hat on his head. Of course, the .38 caliber revolver in his shoulder holster was always hidden from view.

As he departed his house, his thoughts were on the girl he had recently met, an Irish lass named Mary Coughlin who he sometimes called by the one syllable sound, "Mare." Her gentle voice and pleasant nature were unlike any other girl's he'd known before. The fact that Mary also drove her own car was a big plus, too. Because of this, Capone started bringing her along with him to various family functions, and this one was no exception. It was a nuptial celebration to be held at the Knights of Columbus Hall at the corner of Prospect Park West and Union Street, near Grand Army Plaza in Brooklyn.

The large ballroom was already packed when they arrived at the entrance, where they were told they were to be seated at table number two. Weaving their way through the crowd, Alphonse and Mary were scanning the crowded auditorium in search of their table when he heard somebody calling him.

"Alphonso," someone was saying, "over here." The voice belonged to "Little Augie," another of Yale's henchmen, who had as his date a young, blonde woman named Sophie Olson, who was recently widowed. Sophie was an attractive woman who decided to get on with her life and was now keeping steady company with the shortest member of Yale's crew. In the many months Augie had known her, she was adamant about refusing to enter into a sexual relationship with him. However, Augie never gave up trying to get the golden-haired beauty in the sack. Meantime, he constantly bragged to Capone about what a fantastic sex partner she was and offered that as the reason for buying her expensive gifts.

Capone knew better, though. As a matter of fact, he, more than anyone else in the place, was aware of Sophie's strong sex drive. But believing her to be a good person at heart, the youngster never informed Augie about her long-ago affair with officer Walter Sheaf or that he'd humped her a few times himself. Nor did he relate the tale of her tits. Sophie had accidentally fallen down onto a garden rake in her backyard as a child, sustaining an injury to her chest that required surgery. The lasting result of the injury was that Sophie's left breast never really developed enough to match the fullness of her right one. Capone figured that Augie hadn't even gotten that far yet, or else he would have mentioned this to him. But realizing that the bullshitter was treating her well, Capone did the gentlemanly thing by keeping his mouth shut. He felt genuinely sorry for her and the situation she found herself in. Sophie had lost her husband in a mugging incident, and was forced to work hard in a little tailor shop alone in order to provide for herself and her growing boy.

Mary Coughlin knew Sophie from a church group they both belonged to. They sat next to each other exchanging greetings while Yale's wife, Maria, chatted with them, remarking how nice they both looked. Young Al Capone stood in the aisle conversing with Little Augie, his brawny arms on the back of Mary's chair. "The boss hasn't arrived yet," Capone remarked, studying the crowd that had gathered for the wedding reception.

"I think he had some business at the Sunrise," Augie responded, "but I've already talked to the bandleader."

"How so?" Capone asked, wondering what the little guy was talking about.

"You'll see in a few minutes, Al, here comes the boss now," Augie said, moving a chair out of his way. He stepped into the aisle to stand beside his cohort.

The large wooden doors leading to the reception hall were flung open by a gray-haired man with spectacles, an usher, who smiled and said, "Good evening, Mr. Yale!" as the mobster boss handed the man his hat and overcoat. He was flanked by his loyal bodyguard, Sham Brown.

"Your hats and coats will be in my office when you are ready to leave," the usher said, pointing them in the direction of the first table, which was reserved for the immediate family.

With a cue from the bride and groom, the band's rendition of "Banks of the Wabash" came to an abrupt halt. The strange momentary silence baffled those on the dance floor, but immediately, the orchestra started up again with another tune.

"For he's a jolly good fellow," they sang in Yale's honor. He was well respected by his community, known for his generous and warm-hearted nature. Yale gracefully accepted the elaborate welcome with a smile. Waving his hands, he motioned everyone to sit down and continue on with the party.

Relatives and friends waddled up to the Brooklyn Godfather, planting the traditional kiss on his cheek. Some offered Yale their best wishes on his newly remodeled dance hall in Coney Island. Capone stood in awe of his charisma and the way others fawned over the veteran gangster. His eyes followed Yale as he worked his way around the table to where his mother, Isabella, and father, Dominico, sat close to the wall.

"Mama, you look beautiful tonight," Yale said, holding her hands as he kissed her forehead. He then turned to his father and kissed him on the cheek saying, "Where did you get the suit, Papa? It looks great on you."

"I went to your own tailor, Frankie," Yale's father said, "Mr. Yarloff, down on Columbia Street. Do you really like it?"

"I think you two are the best-dressed young couple here," Yale said. He smiled and seated himself at the table next to his wife, Maria. Sham Brown squeezed his large frame into a chair near Little Augie at the next table and immediatly poured himself some wine from a bottle.

"Gee, this place is nice," Sham said. But before he could put the glass to his mouth, he heard Capone say, "Sham, have you ever heard the expression, 'He who drinks alone, dies alone'?" Sham's hand froze. He put his glass back down on the table and displayed his characteristic faraway look.

"Whaddaya talking about, Al?" Sham asked. "There's other people drinking here too, ain't there?"

"What he means, Sham," Augie piped up, "is that you should always offer some of what you're drinking to other people first. Do you understand?"

"Oh, I'm sorry!" Sham said, apologizing to everyone at the table as he waved his glass around. They thought he was about to offer a toast. Instead, with his usual blank expression on his face, he stared at the bottle on the table, put his glass of wine back up to his lips and muttered, "Hey everybody, have some wine." Then he emptied the contents of the glass down his throat.

Sham Brown had balls. Yale trusted him after the confidence he'd earned from many years of loyal service to the godfather and the innumerable tight spots he helped Yale see his way through. Sham was never regarded as being much of a genius or a conversationalist, though. For that reason, Yale sometimes found him dull company. But in his heart, he knew when it came to covering his ass, Sham Brown was the best around.

Capone was having some laughs with Little Augie, who was bragging that he could out-drink everyone at the table, whispering in the youngster's ear, "That's with the possible exception of the Swedish widow." Being very careful that Sophie didn't hear what he was saying, Augie leaned a shoulder toward Al and confided, "When I go out drinking with her, I'm stiff as a board when the night's over and she's as sober as my own mother in church. I don't understand it, Al."

"Maybe she's got a wooden leg or something," Capone chided.

"Oh, no!" Augie bragged, "I happen to know for a fact that her two legs wrapped around my head are real. Beautiful flesh and bones."

"Maybe, by that time, you're too drunk to know the difference," Al said, smiling at Little Augie's inclination to lie about his conquests.

The fifteen-piece orchestra was playing some of the old Italian tunes, music with a Neopolitan flavor such as "O Sole Mio" and the like, when suddenly they broke out with a song that reminded Yale of his younger days. He remembered how his mother enjoyed listening to it time and again. Its name was "Santa Lucia." He imagined her in the kitchen, preparing supper and humming along with the music coming off the Gramophone.

Now, he could see his mother's face brighten when she heard the first few notes. He saw her lips moving as she began murmuring the words to her favorite song softly under her breath. What a wonderful time, Yale thought, for everyone at the wedding party to see what true, enduring love was really like.

Capone was busy attending to his second course, an antipasto dish that had all the things in it that the big kid loved, such as Genoa salami, provolone cheese, and black olives. Lifting his head up for a second, Al heard his boss, Yale, urging his mother, "Ma, why don't you get up and dance with Papa?"

"Oh no, Frankie, not tonight," she replied, placing a hand gently on his. "I'm really very tired from all the walking around I've done today." Capone heard his boss's plea once again,

"Come on, Ma, dance with Pa." Capone recognized the look on Yale's face. It was something he'd become familiar with when the boss was on the verge of exploding. Capone watched him get out of his chair and step a few feet back, then pull out a .38 caliber nickel-plated revolver and blast three shots into the floor, just inches away from his own mother's feet.

The band stopped playing immediately and retreated to a safe place behind the stage, while the terror-stricken crowd jumped from their chairs and hysterical women screamed out the names of their small children in a mad scramble to flee. Most people had no idea what the hell was going on as they began a thunderous stampede toward the hall's main exit. Capone had seen it coming but was still shocked at Yale's actions. Nevertheless, he quickly got up and yelled to Sham, who was seated on the end of the table, "Sham, get the doors. Hurry, don't let anybody out." Capone hustled himself to the center of the deserted dance floor to address the cowering crowd.

"Please everybody, calm down," Capone begged. "Someone dropped a pistol on the floor. Nobody got hurt. It's all over." Capone turned to the orchestra leader, who peeped out from behind the curtains, and ordered the man to start playing music again. The man's refusal to bring his musicians onstage was met by Capone's apologetic assurance that there was no longer any danger present. Slipping him a twenty-dollar bill, Capone finally persuaded the hesitant leader to resume playing.

"Number twelve," the conductor's wavering voice told his band, which had left their instruments onstage when fleeing the madman with the gun. Reluctantly, they returned to their former positions and started to render a popular tune, "By the Light of the Silvery Moon." Barely into the first few notes, the band heard a voice screaming, "No, no, no! Santa Lucia, Santa Lucia." Yale stood on his feet looking down on his parents as the band quickly complied with the request.

"Ma, dance with Pa," he said again, softly. The horrified woman tugged her husband up from his chair. They strolled with shaking legs to the dance floor and began a fox trot to the melodious strains of "Santa Lucia." Frankie Yale walked to the side where his brothers, John and Angelo, were sitting and nudged the younger one. With his hands waist high and his palms turned upward, he said, "Ah, don't they look nice dancing? Look at Ma, look at Pa! I love it! I love it! It does my heart good to see them this way." With his brawny fingers clasped together in a prayerful attitude, he asked, "Right, John? Right, Angelo?" Quaking like little schoolboys, their immediate response was, "Oh yeah, Frank. It's wonderful. It's really great."

Capone settled back in his chair to finish his salad and thought to himself, if Yale was nuts enough to toss shots at the feet of his own mother in a place like this, something was wrong with anyone who doubted he'd have nerve enough to kill anybody, anywhere, on the spot.

In reality, a study of Frankie Yale's life revealed the fact that he fit the classic illustration of a person possessed with a Jekyll and Hyde personality, a schizophrenic who at times displayed the behavior of a cold-blooded murderer and at other times was warm and affectionate.

Because he adored children, Yale established a tradition every Sunday after the eleven o'clock Mass. He would stand on the sidewalk outside the doors of St. Rosalie's Church alongside Monsignor Cioffi, who took great pleasure watching the generous parishioner flip silver dollars from a bag loaded with the shiny coins to the children of poor families in the neighborhood.

The locals who read of his gangland reputation as reported in the New York newspapers refused to believe, or couldn't care less about the negative depiction of their hero in the press. Their only interest was in the results obtained by his charitable works in the community.

Alphonse Capone became Yale's prize student in crime, learning a lesson from him that he never forgot: "The Lord does love a cheerful giver."

10

Chicago, Here I Come!

THE MOB BOSS of Brooklyn waited impatiently for one of his underlings, Al Capone, to arrive for a scheduled appointment at his Sunrise Café. Yale was dressed in a double-breasted, charcoal-gray suit and a light-gray necktie with a diamond-studded stickpin that held the tie firmly in place. He was downing his third demitasse of coffee laced with anisette, and holding a notepad in one hand.

"Sonnafabitch!" he said aloud. "That guy will be late for anything except women, whiskey, and gambling—in that order." Yale's eyes glanced once again at the wall clock just as Capone's hulking figure trudged through the door, still counting the change he'd gotten from the cab driver.

Capone's first words to his boss would have to be carefully chosen, because past experience had taught him that Frank was tough on his hired help. The words he always objected to, and detested hearing from any of them were, "I'm sorry, boss." He especially disliked hearing them when they came from Capone or Sham, two of the people he most relied on for his personal protection.

Capone slid into the chair while Yale's fingers drummed the table top.

"Do you realize I've been sitting here for thirty minutes waiting for you?" Yale inquired. "I have so many things to do today and you come in here like nothing's wrong." He shoved the small notebook across the table at the younger man.

"Well, what the fuck happened to you, or do I have to guess?" Yale snarled.

"I made a stop on the way over, Frank," Capone said. "One of those late collections from old man Hornsby. Being I was in the neighborhood, I thought I'd pay him a visit. Good idea, no? And guess what, Frank? He paid me all the money he owes you, including the interest." Capone counted out two hundred dollars, all in twenties, and slid the cash over to Yale, whose anger was softened by the sight.

"That notebook contains all the people with outstanding balances due on their loans," Yale said. "I want you to go after them this afternoon and be sure to bring home something from each and every one, *capisci?*"

Capone eyed the names on the pages, which numbered five. Three of them were located in the general area, businessmen on Fourth Avenue, and the other two were longshoremen in the vicinity of the Fulton ferry slip situated at the foot of Fulton Street in downtown Brooklyn. "You should be waiting for these two guys down near the docks when they knock off from work," Yale remarked, then added, "That'd be around five o'clock, so try being there about ten minutes before."

"Yeah, boss," Capone assured him. "I know what them guys look like enough to spot them in a crowd." Capone rubbed his chin while conjuring up images of the two customers, Eddie Giffara and his cousin, Tommy "Zipper Nose" Marrinelli. "Those two guys are easy to spot because Giffara is a fat bastard they call 'Squeaks' and the other guy has a long, jagged scar running down the middle of his nose that looks like a fuckin' zipper. Don't worry, Frankie, if they went to work today, I'll find them."

"You got them pegged right, Alphonso," replied Yale. "And don't let them give you a sob story because they get paid today. Those two skells borrowed the dough from me last month and to date they owe four weeks vig."

Capone asked Yale if he had time to have a bite to eat. Yale summoned his cook, Umberto Cassano, from the kitchen and Al asked him to bring a steak, potatoes, a few vegetables, and some bread.

"I thought all you wanted was some coffee and toast," Yale complained, "not a full course meal. What the hell time you gonna get on with it?"

"I got time," Capone said. "Don't worry, boss. Umberto, do me a favor, please. Cook it up fast." Yale shrugged his shoulders as he reached for his coat in preparation for departing the café, but before leaving he imparted a bit of advice to his underling.

"When you go near the waterfront, be careful not to stumble into that fuckin' maniac, Bill Lovett," Yale warned. "That's White Hand turf down there and you know he's a fuckin' pyscho." Capone didn't seem the least bit worried by the warning, and as he unbuttoned his jacket, he told Yale, "I hear you, but have no fear, Frankie. I won't advertise to let the Irish know why I'm in the neighborhood. I like to blend in with the surroundings." Capone stood up from his chair and remarked, "Hey boss, dressed up as I am, can't I pass for a hard-working man?" Yale smiled at the navy coat and the cap with ear flaps that Capone was carrying.

"When you finish, bring the cash to my Coney Island place. I'll be there from six on, got that?" Capone sat with his arms folded while he waited for the food and nodded his head affirmatively.

Yale opened the door and stepped outside in his shirt sleeves because he had spotted a nun waiting for the streetcar on the corner of 14th Avenue and 65th Street. Fishing a twenty-dollar bill out of his wallet, he handed it to the grateful sister, telling her to use it toward helping the poor. When he returned to his place of business, his coat and hat were waiting for him by the door. He threw the dark-blue coat over his shoulder and waved to Capone when he saw his car pulling up with Sham Brown behind the wheel.

After he finished eating, Capone walked to the curb where his chauffeur for the day's work, Lefty "Crater" Piccone, was lounging in the front seat of a black 1917 Buick sedan. Piccone's eyes were focused, as usual, on the *Daily Racing Form*. Capone entered the back seat and chided the wheel man.

"Lefty, could you leave those fuckin' nags alone long enough to take care of some business?" The man slid behind the steering wheel of the car, started the motor, and drew away from the sidewalk. The Buick roared off in the direction of New Utrecht Avenue and made a left turn with its exhaust fumes billowing as it rolled due north toward downtown Brooklyn.

"Hey Al," Piccone piped, "Who do you like in the big race today?"

"Put a cork in it willya, Lefty? I lost my drawers on those friggin' nags last week and I don't want to hear anything about them for a while. Okay?"

Lefty Piccone watched Capone's face turn sour in the rearview mirror and decided he'd better clam up.

Their first stop was a butcher shop in the vicinity of Prospect and Fourth Avenues. When Capone exited the automobile, he buttoned his coat and turned up the collar in order to repel the buffeting winds, which seemed to be gaining in force. Holding his cap down on his head, he approached the market. When he entered, Capone gave the place the once-over. Capone walked to the counter, his shoes kicking up some sawdust that was sprinkled on the floor. He noticed two customers in the place and three men with white aprons behind the counter cutting steaks and cutlets for their patrons. One was a gray-haired, stocky man with a pudgy face and a big, round nose who looked like W.C. Fields, except this man wore a thick, long handlebar mustache.

Capone's eyes were drawn to the unusual whiskers on the overweight man. He thought it must have required about a pound of wax in order to curl up both edges of his comical mustache in that manner. It made him smile to think the man could probably support the weight of a suit of clothes on his face. But Capone did not smile for long.

"Can I help you, sir?" the man asked.

"Is your name Nunzio Assidia?" Capone replied, unbuttoning his coat. The meat handler's eyes widened as he answered.

"Yes, that's me," he said, jabbing a stubby thumb against his breast several times. "What can I do for you? How do you know my name?"

"Your name was given to me by a mutual friend of ours," Capone responded.

"Who might that be?" the man inquired. Staring into the butcher's eyes, Capone placed both hands on the meat counter and leaned toward Assidia, who stood on the opposite side of the display case. Capone's voice was just a whisper.

"Frankie Yale." The name seemed to freeze Nunzio in his spot as Capone's gray eyes fixed him in a harrowing gaze. "Didn't you borrow five hundred bucks from my boss a month ago, promising to pay the interest until you were able to repay him the full amount?"

"Yes, I did, sir," the butcher stammered, nervously twirling the tips of his mustache, "but I don't have it on me right now. Could you please wait a minute and I'll see what I can do?" Capone reached inside of his coat and the act suggested to Assidia that this rough-looking man was about to pull out a gun. He could feel a warm, wet feeling run down his leg as he reached down to pull the front of his pants away from his skin, tugging at them for a second.

"You must give me at least forty dollars in interest right now," Capone said. "Do you *capisci*?" Assidia walked over to where another butcher was busy trimming some meat for a customer toward the front of the shop and in a little while he returned with the cash. Capone counted it and put it in his pocket, warning the butcher that he would personally come to collect the juice every week if the man did not go out of his way to make payment himself.

"I'll stop by the café every Saturday, I promise," Assidia said, wondering how he was going to walk in and out of the icy meat storage room all day with his pants soaked.

Capone returned to the Buick, which was parked in front of the store, and Lefty Crater drove away from their first stop. The Crater, whose proper name was Tulio Piccone, received both monikers early in life. First, he was called Lefty because of the fact that he was left-handed. The nickname Crater was bestowed upon him for his unfortunate bout with chicken pox as a child. The disease left his face spotted with countless pock marks and the heartless kids in his neighborhood declared it reminded them of the craters on the moon. Crater was driving along Fourth Avenue and turned left onto Pacific Street, coming to a halt just off the corner. Capone stepped out of the car and placed a cigar between his lips, cupped his hands and lit it as he swaggered into a fine jewelry shop close to the corner of Atlantic Avenue, across the street from the Long Island Rail Road's underground depot.

Hyman Cohen, the owner of the store, was next on Capone's list. The jeweler was one grand in debt and the vigorish due was one hundred smackers. All Capone had to do was mention Yale's name and Hyman succumbed to the messenger's demand, coming up with the money immediately. Alphonse found no need to display the intimidating, maniacal stare that he had featured at the butcher shop. This collection was a snap.

Hopping back into the auto, the next stop on his collection rounds happened to be a doctor by the name of "Doctor Joe" Vitarina, who considered himself an expert in proctology. Vitarina shared Crater Piccone's obsession with the ponies, but the good doctor was losing much more money at the racetrack than he could ever earn in his practice. Capone found Vitarina to be good-natured and very businesslike. The doctor forked over his required interest, apologizing for his tardiness by saying that he missed payment because he was out of town for a while. Capone left the office as soon as the doctor asked him if he was interested in undergoing a medical check-up as long as he was there.

"I'll charge you my special rate of only three dollars," Vitarina said. "What do you say, sir?" Capone turned around and walked out of the doctor's office without uttering another word.

Passing through the empty waiting room Al brushed past a sickly looking man who was holding his jaw, seemingly in a lot of pain.

"Is this the dentist's office?" the man asked. Capone was about to tell him that he had the wrong office, when from behind him he heard the doctor's voice urging the man, "Come in, come in, sir! There are many things that I can do to relieve your pain immediately."

When Capone returned to the car, he remarked to Crater, "Never go to this man for medical treatment, no matter if you're dying. Believe me Crater, you'll live a lot longer if you stay away from him."

"Maybe he got his license from Saratoga or the University of Churchill Downs," Crater spoke as though he was an expert on such things.

"I wonder if he meant to help the man with the toothache by exploring his asshole," quipped Capone. Both men were laughing and seemed to enjoy their small departure from things of a serious nature.

The strong winds that had been so prevalent during the afternoon had changed into a bone-chilling swirl that filled the streets with litter and dust as Crater turned the car toward the river.

"Do you know where the ferry slip is?" Capone asked.

"I certainly do," Crater said. "I've known the area all my life. When I was a small kid, my brother Claudio would bring me swimming there. Sometimes we'd sneak into the firehouse near the edge of the water and ring the bell while the fire wagons were out. That never failed to bring all kinds of people outside to see what the hell was going on."

Capone sat back in the car, listening to his wheelman reminisce about the good old days and his mind drifted back to the time in his life that he personally referred to as the "poor old days." He was taking the opportunity to relax for a while, until he noticed the heavy traffic that was going in the same direction as they were. Lifting his large frame, Capone leaned forward and rested his arms against the back of the driver's seat. "Step on it a little, Crater. It's getting late!"

Crater responded by turning on two wheels only to find the road blocked by a brewery wagon when he turned onto Furman Street. Capone suggested that they take another route, to which Crater responded, "If we go the way you're talking about, we're bound to see even more traffic because a lot of these fucking horses are so scared shitless about being driven over the Brooklyn Bridge that they're always creating traffic tie-ups around the entrance. This way we avoid all of that by coming up Fulton Street close to the water. Don't worry, Al," he added, "I'll get you there before they come outta work."

He did get Capone there in time. As a matter of fact, Al had a few minutes to spare and remained seated in the car, which Crater had parked right on the cross corner of Fulton and Furman Streets. This gave them a splendid view of the gatehouse. Capone waited until he saw the first group of workers—four longshoremen—exit the gate, then left the car to stand next to the security guard's shack. He watched the passing parade of heavy-booted men. Most of them were carrying large, pointed baling hooks on their shoulders. Then he spotted the two guys he was laying in wait for. He turned his back to the crowd, allowing them to pass. Then Capone followed close behind the rotund Giffara and the other one, Zipper Nose Marrinelli, as they crossed the street, headed in the direction of the Eagle warehouse while making their way to Court Street. Capone swooped down from behind and pushed the pair into a dark part of a large building that turned out to be the Teamsters' loading zone. There, the two men found themselves cut off from the view of people on the street, not knowing what was happening to them and who the hell this crazy man was.

"Hey, what the hell is going on here?" Marrinelli asked with a yelp in his voice. The other one, Fat Eddie Squeaks, made the mistake of grabbing for the handle of his longshoreman's hook tucked under his belt. Capone pushed him against the loading platform while the other cringed in mortal terror at the sight of Capone's .38 caliber Smith and Wesson revolver. Capone shoved it against the thick neck of Fatso Squeaks as Zipper Nose groaned in agony from the impact of his back striking the truck platform. Capone wrapped his free hand around the neck of the cowering Marrinelli and pulled him toward Squeaks, slamming their heads together with such force that a gash opened above Zipper Nose's left eye.

"Do you guys think you can borrow money without paying it back?" Capone asked. He increased the pressure that he was applying to both men. One arm now held the pistol to Squeaks's face, while the other arm held the head of Zipper Nose in a vice-like grip.

"Please, fellow, turn me loose. I'll do whatever you ask," Marrinelli cried. "I got the money to pay Frankie right now." Capone stepped back a few paces, releasing the hold on Squeaks.

"How much are we talking about? Be quick about it!" growled Capone. "The ledger shows you owe a hundred apiece."

"I can give you all of it right now if you take the gun out of my face, mister," Giffara begged. Capone pushed the heavyset man back to the ground and repeated, "C'mon, c'mon, be quick about it. Get the dough up." The two men shuffled deep into their work pants and together they came up just a little short of having enough money to pay off both loans.

"You won't have to look for us to pay off the rest, we both promise that to you," said Squeaks, whose head dripped a mixture of blood and sweat while he was trying his best to appease Capone. "Please mister, you can relax and get that thing away from my face. It's liable to go off. "

"If you don't make the effort to resolve this, you can be sure we'll meet again," Capone said. "Next time," he warned Tommy Marrinelli, "I'll add another zipper to your schnozzola. And you, Fatso Squeaks, I'll make sure that your shoes never squeak again because you'll be carried off in a burlap bag. Get the picture?"

"Sure, sure, fellow," they chorused, "we're gonna do the right thing from now on." Capone wriggled the revolver back into his holster under his left armpit.

"Now get the fuck out of here, both of you," Capone yelled, his statement bringing a quick response from the would-be welchers as they limped out of the warehouse clutching various parts of their aching bodies. Capone followed them into the waning daylight of the street, turning in the opposite direction.

"You guys know where to bring the money," he shouted after them. "Fourth Avenue and Union Street. So be sure that you start keeping good habits."

When Capone reached the locked car, he found Crater fast asleep behind the steering wheel with his head still in the race sheet. Capone's rap at the window brought him to a rude awakening. Sitting up straight in his seat, Crater tried to show he'd been awake all the while by pretending that he was still reading the paper. He slipped an arm up to release the door while Capone remained standing on the sidewalk.

"Hey, Crater," Capone said, "my throat's as dry as Kelsey's nuts. What do you say we go for a nice brew?"

"None for me, Al, I got heartburn now," Crater responded. "But get in the car and I'll drive you around the corner. The Ferry Slip Inn is right there. You don't mind if I wait for you in the car, do you Alphonse? I wanna read my paper some more."

"You can go back to sleep, Crater," Capone said. "I'll see you in a few minutes."

• • •

FULTON STREET WAS not only very wide, but also a naturally elevated artery that provided a splendid view of the harbor. Capone saw the setting sun, which made the river seem afire with bright red and silvered hues, a sharp contrast to the path he was walking, where the somber shadows created by the limestone towers of the Brooklyn Bridge followed his every step. As was his custom when on enemy turf, he constantly looked over his shoulder.

Gold lettering on the window read FULTON SLIP INN and it was sparsely occupied when Capone ordered a glass of tap beer. Tipsy Murphy was behind the bar and responded to the request with an amiable smile and the small talk usually associated with his friendly service.

"Getting a bit cold out there, isn't it?" he offered, while filling the glass with the foamy brew. "My name is Danny, but everybody calls me by Tipsy. Don't get that wrong though, I don't drink enough to get tipsy. It's just a name hung on me by my friends because, they say, in my younger days as a waiter, I was always knocking over glasses and dropping dinner plates. Are you from around here?"

"Not anymore," Capone answered, "but I was born not far from here, at 95 Navy Street." Lifting the beer to his lips, Capone noticed that the two men standing near him were getting ready to leave and that there was only one other patron in the place, at the extreme end of the bar.

"Hey, do you know what?" the bartender responded while wiping the countertop in front of Capone, "I was born just a few blocks away from there, at 195 Front Street. Say, everybody in that neighborhood had a nickname. You know mine, so tell me, what did the other guys call you out on the street?" It was at this moment that the bartender first noticed the terrible scars on the side of the stranger's face. Worried that his new customer might be sensitive to whatever attention his disfigurement attracted, Tipsy wanted to kick himself for asking the question. But Capone's friendly response relieved his anxiety.

"All my friends call me Skippy!" said Capone, mindful not to give his right name to a stranger. No matter how nice the stranger might be or how insignificant the inquiry might seem at the time, he knew you had to play it safe when you were in White Hand territory.

Tipsy wiped his hands on the apron he wore and extended a hand over the bar. Capone responded by shaking the smallish hand with a pleasant, contented smile on his face.

"What do you want now, Criss-Cross? I'll be right there." The gregarious bartender was interrupted by the call of the only other customer in the place. He excused himself. When he returned, he slid another full glass of brew for "Skippy" across the surface of the bar. Presenting it to his new friend, he said, "Please Skip, have a beer on me." Capone thanked the man and finished off the rest of his first beer, ready to enjoy another.

"Where's the toilet?" asked Capone, feeling the need to relieve his bladder.

"First door on your right, in the back there," said Tipsy.

Capone paid scant attention to the slumped-over figure that occupied a small table off to one side of the bar as he passed by, but he noticed that the man had a terrible smell about him—something like a combination of mildew, sweat, and alcohol—which fouled the air in that end of the bar. Later on, Capone would learn this man's name was Artie Finnegan, alias "Criss-Cross." He was tagged with that name because of the superior skills he acquired playing tic-tac-toe, which he always referred to as criss-cross. He was also a minor associate of "Wild" Bill Lovett's White Hand gang.

Capone never thought he'd welcome the change of air provided by a less-than-classy men's room, but within seconds, he heard the door opening and the same stink fill his nostrils once again. Capone tried to hurry his bodily functions so that he could get the hell out of there as quickly as possible. He raised one hand to cover his nose and mouth. Just as he was about finished, he saw the man pull up to the same urinal and let out a stream of urine that missed the target completely, splashed against the side of the cabinet, and wet the cuff of Capone's trouser leg.

"What the fuck are you doing, you fucking skell?" Capone howled. "You got piss on my clothes!"

"It was an accident, wop," Criss-Cross said. "Just an accident, that's all." If that wasn't enough to set Capone off, the man's next sentence did. "Nothing to complain about, scarface!"

Capone saw blood. He pounced on Finnegan's beefy frame, grabbing him by the neck and pulling his head down toward Al's rising knee, which he struck with overwhelming force. Over and over again, he smashed his kneecap into Finnegan's nose, jaw, and head while the man screamed, "My head! My head!" Then Capone held his slumping antagonist, bleeding from his mouth and ears, against the wall. Grabbing hold of the wise guy's hair, Capone proceeded to pound the victim's head with all the force he could muster against the wooden partition. Smashing the unlucky Irishman's head at least six times and then spinning him around, Capone continued to hold him by the hair, slamming his face against the wall several more times.

The mirror on the opposite wall reflected the terrible beating Capone was handing to Finnigan and throughout the whole turbulent assault the mirror clearly showed Capone's eyes. The psychotic gaze was there, all right. Only this time, it was not there to instill fear. It was the real McCoy.

When Capone thought the man was finished, he let his adversary's body drop to the floor, turned, and raced out of the place. Crossing the street, he entered the car. This time, Crater was awake and responded immediately to Al's hurrying pace, which he knew spelled trouble. He slammed the car into gear and roared off toward Court Street with a piercing squeal of tires that skidded wildly around the corner and turned once again down a side street.

Tipsy Murphy was a dedicated bartender, but the reason he refused to leave the tavern was not from any "don't give up the ship" attitude—he just figured it was safer there. When he heard the pandemonium in the men's room, he feared for his life. Tipsy tucked himself under the bar in the spot reserved for towels and things, worried that shots could be fired at any time. Whoever came out of that toilet and saw him standing there might shoot him dead right on the spot, because, as the saying goes, dead men tell no tales. After hearing the footsteps stomping past the bar, he remained in that spot for at least ten minutes. In fact, Tipsy didn't even know who it was that ran out of the place and eventually worked up the courage to investigate the washroom. After seeing Finnegan's bloodied body laying on the floor, he quickly called for an ambulance.

Turning the car onto Clinton Street and moving along with the normal flow of traffic, Crater was happy to realize they weren't being followed. He started to feel more relaxed when the booming voice of his passenger shook him again. "Take me to my apartment right now," Capone screamed. "That stinking son of a bitch got his sticky blood between my fingers."

Crater Picconi thought he'd keep his eyes straight ahead. The remote possibility of diverting the young hood's anger in his direction had occurred to him. He'd heard other members of the gang remark on Capone's volatile nature, and whatever mayhem Capone caused in that tavern was none of Piccone's business. He stole a nervous glance in the rearview mirror and noticed that Capone was pulling a handkerchief from a hip pocket and pouring globs of saliva into it.

• • •

CAPONE HAD EXPERIENCED difficulty at the hands of the Irish throughout his young life, from neighborhood tough guys to his teachers in school to the cops on the corner. His most recent misadventure was against Criss-Cross Finnegan, that stinking son of the Emerald Isle he nearly iced at the Fulton Slip Inn.

Looking to the future, Capone was sure that he could expect more of the same coming from the Irish waterfront rats called the White Hand. But to say he hated the Irish, or didn't care for their culture, would be a misstatement. Being raised in neighborhoods that included so many Irish families, he'd always thought of them as good-hearted people. When Capone met one of their fairest daughters, a girl named Mary Coughlin, he fell in love. Her gentle and affectionate manner caused the tough Capone to rethink his desire to remain single until at least age twenty-five. Besides, the U.S. military was not including married men with children in its draft, so he planned on fitting that deferment category as soon as possible. After a short courtship and having already sired a baby boy, Albert Francis Capone, nineteen-year-old Alphonse and Mary exchanged vows at Saint Mary's Star of the Sea Roman Catholic Church on Court Street in Brooklyn, on December 30, 1918, in a fairly large ceremony.

"I now pronounce you man and wife," declared Father James J. Delaney, servant of God. "You may kiss the bride." Capone embraced and kissed his beloved Mary at the altar while flanked by his best man, James "Jimmy Boy" DiVico, and the bride's sister, Anna, who stood just a step below. The families were thrilled with the marriage and both Bridget Coughlin, the bride's mother, and Capone's mama, Teresina Capone, had tears of joy streaming down their happy faces all through the ceremony. When it was over, Capone's brothers rushed to the rear of the church to greet the newlyweds and to offer their congratulations as Capone raised his six-year-old sister, Mafalda, the little flower girl, in his arms and smothered her with kisses.

The newlyweds got into a black Cadillac limousine parked in front of the church and Mary's eyes shone like two hazel stars as the limo pulled away from the curb. She smiled and waved to the crowd while smoothing her gown to fit the car's interior.

"Al, darling, I'm so relieved and glad you didn't do to me what Frank did to Maria when they left the church." She was referring to the unusual event that occurred a little more than one year earlier when Capone's boss, Frankie Yale, departed his own wedding service. It seems that after placing his bride, the former Maria Delapia, in the rear of a chauffeured limo, Yale jumped into a maroon Chevrolet roadster driven by James "Sham Brown" Caponi. His new bride traveled to their reception sitting alone in the backseat of the bridal limo with two of Yale's bodyguards for consolation. Sham and Frankie led the way while a third car trailed close behind.

Alphonse kept the real story from his new wife, not telling her of the tip Yale received on the morning of April 29, 1917, which prompted the boss to play it safe by putting Maria in a separate limo. The tipster, evidently a nut, reported that an enemy was out to spoil Frank and Maria's wedding plans that day. Although nothing ever came of the threat, reason demanded that Yale take unusual precautions, including the "invitation" that most of his goon squad attend not only the Church ceremony at St. Rosalie's on Fourteenth Avenue but also the banquet. As a matter of fact, it was a small army that accompanied the couple up until the time they boarded a Florida-bound train in the wee hours of the morning.

Capone looked at his Mary, seated next to him in the car, as he held her soft hand in his. "You know, you really do make a beautiful bride," he remarked. Indeed, she did. She wore a white, flowered bonnet, a satin, white gown with lace trimmings, and she still held a basket of red- white- and peach-colored roses in her lap, which filled the automobile with their sweet fragrance. Mary smiled and kissed the marred cheek of her husband. "Al, I want you to know that I'll always try my best to be a good wife for you, my darling," she said. "Everything has been perfect so far. Don't you think so?" Capone nodded his head approvingly and smiled all the while during their short trip to the Park Slope section of Brooklyn. The reception was to be held at the Prospect Hall, an elegant ballroom that had recently been remodeled. Built in 1892, the structure was originally designed for use as a German opera house and remains in use to this day, catering to all kinds of social functions.

Yes, Capone would be the first to agree, everything was perfect on his wedding day. But that was only because he still hadn't heard the rather disturbing news that would change his life forever. It took almost a month to reach his ears. Another of Yale's henchmen, Salvatore "Sammy" Pollaccio, first reported the tidings to his boss in January, inside Yale's Sunrise Café.

"Listen, Frank," he said. "I heard that Wild Bill Lovett is prowling around, looking for some guy with a scarred face! The left side of his face, that is, boss!" It took a few seconds to sink in but the last part confirmed it. The man Pollaccio was referring to was Capone, but unaware of the incident at Fulton Slip Inn, all Yale could do was scratch his head and wonder why the White Hand leader would single out his young protégé.

"What the hell did he do to get himself on the shit list of that crazy fuck?" Yale asked. His facial muscles stiffened as he glared at Pollaccio, who really didn't enjoy being the bearer of this kind of news. "Tell me whatever you know," Yale said. Pulling a chair out for Sammy, he encouraged him to relax by pouring him a glass of wine. After all, he thought to himself, Pollaccio was certainly doing the right thing by warning his boss first about a serious threat to another man he considered a friend, as well as a fellow employee of Yale's.

Pollaccio knew where Capone lived and maybe things would have turned out differently if he had gone directly to him first, but knowing something about Capone's quick temper, Sammy thought the big fellow might decide to go off half-cocked, trying to get the drop on Wild Bill first.

"The word is the bartender in a joint near the ferry slip, around Pier Four, described a stocky Italian guy with a badly scarred face as the one who knocked around one of Lovett's pals named Artie Criss-Cross." Yale was starting to grow more furious by the minute. Getting out of his chair, he began to pace the floor. "Did he finish the guy off?" he inquired.

"Well, this Irishman didn't die, boss," Pollaccio said, "but I heard his head was fractured and he has serious brain damage. Fractures of his nose and cheek bones, too," he added. "Just left for dead by the guy who done it."

"That fucking Capone didn't say a word to me," Yale roared. "That's what gets me burned up." He turned to Cassano, his waiter at the Sunrise, and said, "Umberto, put your coat on and drive over to Capone's house." After tossing his car keys to the obliging man, Yale sat down next to Sammy Pollaccio and yelled, over his shoulder, "Make sure you bring him back with you. Do you hear me?" Cassano turned to acknowledge the order and left in a hurry.

When Capone arrived, Pollaccio was already gone. Yale ordered Umberto to close the café and then locked the door behind the waiter, leaving the two of them alone in the empty, dimly lit restaurant. They were seated across from each other at a table in the back, when Yale spoke his piece.

"I want to ask you something and please, Al, give it to me straight," Yale said. Capone wiped his nose on a handkerchief he pulled from his pocket.

"Sure boss," Capone said. "Why would I bullshit you in the first place?" He had been at home asleep when Umberto rang his doorbell, and still didn't know what his boss wanted. All he knew was that judging by Frank's tousled demeanor, a serious situation was at hand. Yale looked deeply into Capone's eyes and questioned him.

"Remember when I sent you to collect on my loan book way back in November?" Yale asked. Al thought for a minute. Then the scene flashed in his mind. "Alphonse, did you have any problems down by Pier Four, near the bridge?"

Capone's response was quick and honest. "Yeah, after I finished the rounds, I stopped in a place called the Fulton Slip Inn for a beer. When I went to the shit house, this guy came in there, stood next to me in front of the piss pot, and got his piss all over my shoe and the cuff of my trousers, too!"

"Go ahead!" Yale urged, "Don't leave anything out. I want the straight story." Capone clasped his hands together in front of him on the table and watched his boss as he squirmed in his chair, evidently upset about this thing that happened so long ago, which Capone considered so insignificant he'd dismissed it from his mind.

Raising himself from his chair, Capone pointed down to his leg as he related the incident. "Well anyway, I tell this scurvy prick, 'Hey, mister, you pissed on me, do you know that?' He says to me, 'An accident, wop. That's all, scarface, an accident.' Dammit, Frank, I held back when he called me a wop, but that scarface shit I couldn't take from that stinking asshole, so I went to work on him. That's all."

Yale jumped from his chair and began pacing the floor again. This time, he started mumbling something to himself. Then, turning to the young hood, Yale roared at him. "'That's all,' you say? Do you have any idea what you've done, you big fuck? I distinctly remember telling you not to *lose* your head, but to *use* your head while you're in that fucking White Hand territory. Don't you remember me telling you that? You almost made a stiff out of the guy. His name is Artie Criss-Cross, and now it seems Bill Lovett is hunting for the guy who did it."

Yale walked to where Capone was sitting and grabbed his right cheek with his thumb and index finger. Tugging it gently, Yale said, "What do you wanna do, start a fucking war or something? You fuck up a good friend of Wild Bill and you pooh-pooh it? Don't you know that crazy fucker don't fear anything or anybody?"

Capone's half-closed eyes were wide and alert now. The drowsy feeling he felt when he first came into the Sunrise was replaced by a nervous, intuitive reaction. He checked to see if the revolver in his pocket was fully loaded. "You hit the jackpot this time, Alphonse," Yale said. "Now you have Lovett and his right-hand man, Peg Leg Lonergan, looking for you." He watched the youngster spin the cylinder. "That pistol won't do you any good, Alphonse," Yale remarked. "It's a wonder that you didn't give them your right name too. But sooner or later, they're gonna find you anyway. The description they have of you, those scars on your kisser, they'll find you."

What else could Capone do but sit there, quiet as a mouse, and listen to his boss pronounce his death sentence. Frankie, the man he looked up to and admired most, the one he served faithfully, was informing him of the consensus of opinion among the dons. "In a year or so," Yale said, "when the Irish get fucking tired of sleeping with one eye open, Alphonso, that's when we make our big move and if it's done right, the whole fuckin' waterfront will be in our hands." Yale's persuasive argument included the discouraging report of the don's unwillingness to risk an all-out war at this point. "That's the reason I can't have all this other shit going on around me. Do you understand what I'm saying?"

Sweat streamed down Capone's forehead and reached his eyes, turning them into two burning slits. Yale, noticing that Capone was using his damp handkerchief to help relieve the stinging perspiration, reached for a nearby towel and tossed it his way. Yale felt sorry for Capone, figuring, who wouldn't be nervous knowing that Wild Bill Lovett—winner of the Distinguished Service Cross in the First World War, ace machine-gunner of the Eleventh Infantry Division, and now one of the most feared triggermen in Brooklyn—was after his ass?

When Capone got his chance to speak, his loud response was quickly tempered by the boss's two hands pushing him hard against the wall. "Do you mean to tell me that I lost the right to defend myself?" Al asked, in a belligerent tone. Yale released the hold on Capone's chest only when he realized that the younger man was ready to talk rationally. He managed to lead his peppery underling to a chair.

"My advice, Al, is for you to take a powder for a while," Yale said. "How about I call Johnny in Chicago? I'm sure that he could find a spot for you there with no trouble at all."

"Chicago?" he blurted. "Frank, what about my wife and baby?"

Capone's hands nervously patted the gun in his pocket, a sign that he had not given up on the idea of the boss okaying a hit on the White Hand leader. "I like it here," he pleaded. "Besides, my whole life is Mary and the baby. You should know that by now."

"Who's saying they can't go with you?" Yale responded. "You can take them with you to Chicago and come back in a year or so. Maybe by that time we'll be calling on you anyway for the big push against the Irish."

"Why the fuck should I have to run away and leave?" Capone asked. "I'll be okay right here." Standing on his feet, Capone suggested they speed things up by bringing the White Hand leadership down in a series of well-organized attacks. "We can do every don a favor by getting rid of that Irish bastard once and for all," Capone said.

Growing weary of listening to Capone's pitch, Yale strolled over to where the angry youngster stood. With a big smile on his face and his arms extended, Yale's sudden display of affection took Capone by complete surprise. Only moments ago the boss had acted like he wanted to kill him and now he was offering his fond embrace. Yale gently placed a kiss on the right side of Capone's face. Cupping the young man's wide jaw in his hand, he looked Capone straight in the eyes while his lips trembled, as if he was having trouble getting the words out. "Go to Chicago, you prick, or else you don't work for me tomorrow!" he said. "Do you hear me good?"

Capone's task of breaking the news to Mary was made easy because of her concern for her man, especially when he warned her that if they wanted to remain in Brooklyn, they'd have to get used to a life of locked doors and shuttered windows. Explaining the move to the rest of the family was a bit more difficult. "Chicago?" brothers Ralph and Frank chorused when Al informed them of his plans. Caught by surprise, both of them refused to believe his statement at first, but the glum expression on his face told them he was serious.

Charlie Fischetti remained calm while heaving a deep sigh. He had already heard about his cousin Al's tussle with Criss-Cross Finnegan from none other than Frankie Yale, who at the time assured Fischetti that Wild Bill Lovett's manhunt for "a big Italian with a scarred face" would soon be settled in Alphonse's best interest.

Fischetti had it figured. This sudden revelation of Al's confirmed the rumor that was going around saying Frankie Yale was looking to get rid of the big guy anyway. Cousin Charlie heard it from more than one person regarding Yale's disappointment in Capone, beginning with the unauthorized icing of the immigrant, Perrata, after the craps game. He complained that Capone was becoming a real liability in turning the heat of "Wild" Bill Lovett right inside his own inner circle.

Frank Capone was still flabbergasted at the prospect and hoped to change his brother's mind. "Who'd want to live in that chilly burg except some cold fish like Johnny Torrio?" he said, before grasping the reality of the situation at hand. In a short while, he and the others in the room realized that Alphonse wasn't exactly thrilled with the idea of pulling up roots either, but that he had no choice. "How soon are you talking about?" Ralph asked his youngest, sullen-faced brother. "The baby has a little cold right now," Al responded, "but as soon as he's all right to travel, we're off!"

Charlie walked to where Capone stood and placed a hand on his shoulder. "Al," he said, "if there's anything I can do to help, let me know, heh?" He offered Capone his own simple solution to the problem: Eradicate the impending menace. "I found out that Wild Bill likes the racetrack," Fischetti remarked. "Maybe we can catch him there and make sure he departs a loser." Ralph jumped at the idea. "Yeah, a stone-cold loser," he said.

The threesome declared their intentions to act as his personal body-guards and not to rest until they got rid of the Irish crime boss, but Alphonse nixed the idea. "They claim there's nothing to be done without starting an all-out war with the White Hand," Capone retorted. "Charlie, how can I go against orders from my boss? He's telling me to go to Chicago, to work for Torrio for a while. Being a good soldier, I'll go. But you can be sure of one thing," he said, raising a ham-like fist over his head, "when I do come back home, it'll be in style." A few days later, Al, Mary, and little "Sonny" Capone left for Chicago by train.

The address Capone sought out was 2222 South Wabash Avenue, hence the name of the place, the Four Deuces. Torrio's boss, "Big Jim" Colosimo, had his own high-class eatery just down the street from where Capone was promised steady work in Torrio's employ. Colosimo's well-heeled clientele, comprised of mostly—but not exclusively—men, would cap off their meals by strolling over to Torrio's Four Deuces to satisfy a different appetite.

"Welcome to the Four Deuces, Alphonso," Torrio said as Capone walked through the door that his new boss, looking as suave as ever, held open for him. Capone couldn't help thinking about the first time he'd been to Torrio's place in Coney Island. That's when that little thief, Shorty Annie, was the one who welcomed him.

"What do you think of my place?" the older man asked, a broad smile on his face. Capone remained speechless while pumping Torrio's hand. He was too engrossed in studying the lush surroundings to know that his abrupt move past Torrio was noted with some alarm by the early hour housekeeping crew and others who were busy at work. Torrio laughed while assuring his workers that this threatening-looking man was his good friend, Al Capone. Still wearing his coat and cap, Capone walked past the bar. Following closely behind him was Torrio.

Capone's curiosity was finally satisfied when he was able to get a good look at the glass-enclosed patio attached to the rear of the building. He realized that the bright objects lining the sides of the cobblestone courtyard were indeed slot machines. "I'm really impressed, John," he declared, while throwing his head back in an effort to see where the wide staircase ended.

"The floor above is actually the gaming room," Torrio informed him. "I just keep those slot machines out there so that the customers are constantly reminded of what's available to them upstairs. I'll take you on a tour of the place in a few minutes. First off, Alphonse, I want you to stand still long enough for me to take a look at you!" Capone walked to where the older gangster stood and allowed his boss to inspect the package he was buying. Torrio considered it to be more like an investment, to be able to stake the young hood in getting his family settled in town. He knew full well that having this bulky, bulldog-looking youngster with the cold, penetrating eyes working for him would serve to keep the occasional, troublesome customers on the third floor in check.

"You're looking just great, Alphonso," the puny Torrio declared. "Come this way now, and take that coat off. I'll introduce you to Tony Spinella, my bartender." A middle-aged man wearing a red-and-white-checkered vest and black suspenders emerged from behind the bar to shake hands with Capone, and in doing so cringed at the icy grip the young New Yorker offered. "I want you to meet Al Capone, my new supervisor of the third floor," Torrio said.

"Would you like some brandy?" Spinella asked, while offering to take Capone's hat and coat.

"Good idea, Tony," Torrio said. "It's cold outside. Bring a bottle and three glasses to the table. My friend Big Al needs something to warm him up. He's too spoiled by the balmy climate of the South, where he comes from."

"What South?" piped Spinella. "I thought he came from Brooklyn."

"Yeah, South Brooklyn!" his boss cracked. Capone laughed. Poor Tony didn't quite understand what was so funny. "Don't worry, Alphonse," Torrio continued. "You'll soon learn to adapt to the weather here. It's not so bad as long as you keep in mind that you can't go outside on even the nicest of days without a coat."

"And a tight hatband," Spinella added.

"Is that why you guys from Chicago have no brains?" Torrio kidded his bartender, a local man. "Do you mean to tell me that people in Chicago go around all day long with added pressure on their smart part?" Torrio laughed while raising his glass to offer a toast of good health to all. "How does Mary like the place that I got for you?" he inquired. "Not bad, huh? I got you that nice apartment because I knew it'd be easy for your wife to get around to all the nice shops and for you to come to work."

"We both like the place a lot," Capone assured Torrio. "Mary feels pretty good about it and I guess that's what's most important. Only problem is that she's got to learn to do things for herself now, because she doesn't have her mother to rely on for help anymore. But I know that eventually she'll be okay." Torrio refilled their glasses while gently nodding his head in complete agreement.

"Nobody can say what's in store for any of us," Torrio said. "Who knows? Maybe in a little while, you might find yourself in a position to lure your mother-in-law as well as others from your family to join you here in Chicago."

"Yeah, Johnny," Capone responded with a smile, "I was thinking the same thing." The slick-haired gangster reached across the table and placed a thin hand on Capone's arm. Looking straight into the younger man's eyes, Torrio suddenly changed the subject from the introductory small talk to some pre-employment advice.

"Alphonse, here at the Four Deuces we're very careful to avoid any kind of customer dissatisfaction and when I heard that you needed a job, I said to myself, 'That Capone, he knows how to handle people.' That's the reason I couldn't believe it when Frankie told me about the fight you got into with that White Hand guy in the heart of their territory. What came over you? I heard that you put one of them in the hospital. Is that right, Al?"

"Yeah, I guess that's what happened, Johnny," Capone said. "I beat the shit out of him because the fucking guy had the nerve to call me scarface!" Tony Spinella made a mental note of that remark, reminding himself never to mention that he even noticed the young man's scarred face. Torrio frowned. "You almost killed a stranger in a toilet because he called you a name?" he asked. Torrio set his glass down on the table and clasped his hands together, while studying the deep gashes on Capone's face.

"Well, that was really just part of it," Capone said. "That was the final straw. The fuckin' bastard first splattered his piss on my leg."

"Look, Al. Do me a big favor, will ya?" Torrio implored. "Put some cotton in your ears if you're gonna work here. I don't want any violence in this place and if someone pisses on your leg here, it'll be Nina's little pooch. Anyone else pisses on your leg, you have my prior permission to tear them apart. Okay, Al? However, I want you to keep that temper of yours in check at all times. Do you understand?" Capone nodded while raising his drink to his lips. After draining the contents of the shot glass, he patted his lips with the back of his hand.

"John," he said, "just like I told you when you gave me my first steady job, I'll always do my best for you."

"I know you will," Torrio replied, exhibiting a pained expression on his face as he rose from his chair. "I must be getting too old to satisfy some of my young girls anymore," he said, clutching his back. "Nina, the woman who takes care of my flock, tells me that I should stick to the lazy boy style from now on."

"Lazy boy style?" Spinella retorted. "What the hell his that?"

"See what I mean, Al?" Torrio replied. "I told you the guys in this burg wear the hats on their noggins too tight." Capone himself was mystified at the term, but smiled and nodded his head.

"You're familiar with doggie-style sex, aren't you?" Torrio asked the bartender. "There's also Greek style, English style, and French style. Am I right?" After Tony had acknowledged that he was aware of the outlandish requests that came from many of their customers, Torrio continued. "Then, there's the missionary position," he said with a chuckle, "which I'm sure you've tried a few times yourself, Tony. Finally, there's the 'lazy boy.' You just sit in a chair, drop your trousers and let the bitch *gamahuche* you with her mouth. Saves time and energy." Capone roared with laughter while Tony remained speechless. "Come with me, Alphonse," Torrio advised. "I want you to see where you'll be working."

They climbed the thickly carpeted steps to the next floor while Capone carefully examined the framed autographed pictures and playbills of famous opera stars that lined the wall of the staircase. "Gosh, Johnny, it's like a fuckin' museum in here," Capone remarked while coming to a halt midway up the stairs. He was inspecting one of the photographs, which included a smiling Johnny Torrio posing with a whole troupe of singers. "Where's Caruso?" he asked.

"I haven't been able to make it to Big Jim's place when that guy stops by, but I'll get him to pose with me for a picture yet," he said. "Have no doubt about it."

"Johnny, maybe I could ride gun for you when that happens," Capone suggested, "because I'd love to see the great Caruso in person. Grand opera is the berries, as far as I'm concerned."

"Alphonse, you're gonna see plenty of big names around Colosimo's place and, once in a while, in this place, too. But we don't make a big fuss over them here, or do anything that would sacrifice their anonymity while they're spending their money with us. Who knows, Alphonso?" he snickered. "Maybe Caruso will pay you a visit on the third floor someday."

Capone noticed that the second floor had small white and gold lanterns hanging down in neat rows through the whole length of the balcony, where a worker was busy sweeping the carpet. The walls were lavishly decorated with murals of Roman battle scenes, hand-painted in delicate shades of tawny orange and gray.

Capone came to a stop behind his boss at the foot of the stairs, while the worker winked and began to slide one of the big twin doors on its track, just wide enough to allow them to enter. Stepping inside, Capone's eyes were drawn to the magnificent crystal chandelier in the center of the room, which sparkled brilliantly in spite of the sparse light that seeped through the curtains. A roulette wheel stood idly by, awaiting the evening's action while six card and dice tables were placed around the perimeter of the room, sharing the wall space with a couple of money wheels.

"Looks like I should be getting rich from this floor alone, doesn't it?" Torrio asked, brushing a hand across his forehead.

"I think this setup brings in a few dollars," Capone grinned.

"If you want to know something, there's more profit in our business on the third floor," he answered. "This casino does okay, but occasionally we do get a big winner who takes a good chunk of the house's money outta here. Besides that, the investment and overhead is too great to ensure a high profit, but upstairs is different. The whores each got their own room, which they rent from me, plus I get a percentage of every humper that enters. Of course," he went on, "all that is besides the drinks the johns consume while they're in the club."

Leading Capone out of the gaming room, Torrio's attention was drawn to the sound of a female voice coming from downstairs. "Who is that, Tony?" Torrio yelled.

"It's a girl that's looking for Nina," he answered. "She claims she's supposed to start hustling here tonight and being in the neighborhood, she thought she'd drop by early to check the place out. She's real nice, boss."

"Walk her over here, will you, Tony?" Torrio said. "I wanna take a look at her." The redheaded girl sauntered over to the bottom of the balcony, being led along by the horny bartender who couldn't wait to sample her talents himself. They stopped at the foot of the stairs.

"Yes, dolly, I'm the boss here," Torrio said. "Who were you looking for?"

"Nina told me to stop by to say hello to John Torrio," she said. "Is that you, sir?" The two men studied her curves as they leaned over the balcony.

"Hey, John," Capone remarked, "she's got good manners."

"That's not all she's got," Torrio quipped. "She's got my attention, too."

"What's your name?" Torrio asked the beauty.

"My name is Rhoda Fuller, Mr. Torrio. If it's a bad time for you now, I'll come back when Nina comes in. Okay?"

"No, no," he replied. "If you don't mind waiting around a little bit, I'll be finished with this business and we can have a little talk."

"Johnny," Capone kidded, "a little while ago you were complaining about your sore back." Torrio's eyes were riveted on the beauty below as she began an exaggerated wiggle, making her way back to the bar area. His dark eyes now flashed a reply to Capone. "Lazy boy," Torrio whispered, exhibiting a lusty smile and rubbing his hands together. With Torrio, business was always the prime consideration, although he was never reluctant about testing the merchandise himself. As a matter of fact, the procedure was that Johnny Torrio reserved the right to "interview" any one of the girls before they started to work in his club.

Trudging up the carpeted steps with Capone following behind, Torrio stooped over to lift a medicine ball that lay against the railing near the top step. Tucking the ball under an arm, he stopped alongside a desk that stood in front of the entrance to what appeared to be an unoccupied room. He retrieved a notebook from one of the drawers of the desk and thumbed through the pages, briefly describing its contents.

"This is the health club's appointment book," Torrio explained while shaking his head wistfully. "It seems as though every single night has become party night for a good portion of the fellows in Chicago these days. I can't really complain about that, but shit, it seems like the club is in for another real busy one tonight, Al. By the way, when can you start work?" Capone ventured a few steps closer to his new boss and waved his two hands in circles. "I came here ready for work this morning," he said, "and I'll start right now if you want me to." Torrio's face beamed with satisfaction. Same old Alphonso, he said to himself while reaching for the youngster's face. He gently pinched the scarred cheek between his fingers. "I really need you to straighten this floor out for me, Al," Torrio said. "Do you know what I mean? Give it a little order so that it runs as smooth as a factory, heh?"

"I'll do what I can to bring it up to snuff, Johnny," Capone said. "Can you fill me in on the layout?" Capone walked behind Torrio as his new boss rolled the medicine ball along the floor with his foot. Then Torrio pushed it past an open door of what turned out to be a large, beautifully decorated living room.

"In a few hours, after the housekeeping is done, you'll see all the benches in here crammed with whores," Torrio said. "This is where the 'rubberholes' hang out between tricks. It's the room where a customer without an appointment comes to select a girl from my available stock." Torrio held a finger in the air for emphasis and said, "We don't allow any johns to hang out in here! If they wanna wait for a certain girl that's busy at the time, they can sign the date sheet at the desk, but they have to do their waiting downstairs near the bar. Don't worry about a thing. Nina, the broad who's in charge of the desk chores, basically runs the business operation up here and you'll catch on fast with her help."

Standing just outside the doorway, Capone could see that the whole upper floor had been divided into separate, tiny cubicles, each one with its own entrance facing the balcony.

"Shit, Johnny, how many girls you got working here?" Capone asked, suddenly struck with the immensity of this flesh market. Torrio sat down on one of the padded benches with a hand extended and urged the towering Capone to do likewise.

"We should have between ten or twelve girls working tonight," Torrio said. "Five or six additional girls come around on weekends. But don't worry about that now. What I really want to know is, do you really think you can start work tonight? I mean you must be awfully tired from the trip."

"I'm okay, Johnny," Capone answered. "As a matter of fact, I was ready for anything when I arrived this morning. You just say the word, boss."

"Good man," Torrio shouted. "What I want you to do is, go back home now, get some rest, and play with the baby a little. Come back around six tonight. That's when I'll go over your job with you in more detail. Okay, Alphonse? Now, if you don't mind, I promised that I would interview this Rhoda with the long, red hair. So, if you want to leave, I'll show you the way many of our customers come and go here."

Torrio ordered a worker to go downstairs to retrieve their coats, then opened a door that led to a steep staircase. They took the stairs down to the street where Torrio expressed his desire to expand the club by purchasing an adjoining building. They strolled down to the corner and turned back to the front of the club, where they stood chatting for a bit. Capone took notice of a black Pierce-Arrow sedan loaded down with some tough-looking mugs inside. The car was rolling straight toward them in a sudden maneuver that made him think it was going to jump the curb where the two of them were standing. Capone reacted in a flash, grabbing Torrio's arm in a halted attempt at pulling the surprised club owner into the doorway of his club.

"What the fuck is wrong with you?" Torrio shouted while prying himself loose from Capone's grip. "Relax," he urged, as the wheels of the car straightened out. "That Irishman in there happens to be a friend of mine."

"Hello John, how's tricks?" the front-seat passenger inquired with a wave of his diamond-studded hand. Someone in the back seat let out a loud laugh, reading the quip as an intentional reference to Torrio's bawdy reputation. The driver slowed the vehicle down long enough to hear Johnny's response. "I can't complain, Deany. How are things with you?"

"Just great, John. Nice seeing you," he said, ducking his head back inside the window. Capone and Torrio remained standing close to the curb and watched the vehicle continue its steady roll up Wabash Avenue.

"Did you get a gander at that guy?" Torrio asked Capone. "That fucking Irishman is the one you probably know by name only. His name is Dion O'Banion, the brains and power behind the North Side mob and most of the rackets in this town. We do plenty of business with him."

"I'm sorry, John," Capone said. "I guess this'll take some getting used to. It seems like my Brooklyn days always seem to get the better of me. It's like all I could see was this car bearing down on us. Then, I realized it was loaded with rosy-cheeked muscle guys, and . . . "

"That's okay, Alphonse," Torrio interrupted, reaching up to place an arm around Capone's muscular shoulders. "Here in Chicago it isn't much different than back home. Only here we have an opportunity to co-exist with the Irish. You know I've always been a firm believer in the idea that there's plenty of dough to go 'round." Torrio faked a blow to Capone's bulging midsection. "You big fucker," he said, "you don't realize how happy I am to have you around. You are one observant guy. I'll bet that President McKinley would still be around if he had you for protection."

• • •

AFTER WORKING AT the Four Deuces for about a year, Capone had risen in Torrio's organization in rapid fashion. He went from being an energetic sidewalk hustler who would steer male passersby on the street into the club with the spiel, "Hey, fellow, come inside, we got some nice young girls upstairs," to someone who was considered by everyone, including his boss, to be a junior partner. However, Capone's propensity for getting into personal disputes due to his volatile temper was unmistakably unchanged.

A newcomer to the club, Sam Genna, was there one night on account of some business deal he had with Johnny. He was putting on his coat and hat, about ready to leave, when the casual conversation escalated into a spirited discussion of grand opera. "How about you join our little poker game?" the affable Sam Genna said to Capone. "The card game is not the main attraction, you see. One of my brothers happens to be a collector of opera music and we listen to the music on the gramophone and enjoy some tasty food while we play cards."

"That sounds great to me," Capone responded. "See you on Tuesday."

The music was good, all right, and the food was fine, too, but the card game turned out to be something more than Capone imagined.

He had been drinking, but not as much two of the other players in the game, Angelo and Mike Genna. Their boisterous attitude had begun to grate on Capone's nerves, mainly because it served to drown out the music he'd come to hear. The fact that he was losing money at a rapid clip didn't help, either. "He didn't see the bank! So how can he be in the game?" Capone complained to Sam Genna, who puffed on a cigar.

"Aww, come on, Al," Genna said. "I saw him throw in his money."

"Sure I was in the pot. What's the matter with you? Do you think I'm a cheater?" Angelo snapped.

"How about we count up the pot to find out?" Capone suggested. Angelo Genna rebuked the inspection. Instead, he slid the money from the pot toward his own bank. Al felt helpless. Here he was losing all of his money to a trio of brothers plus one of their cohorts in the weirdest game of cards he'd ever had the misfortune to be a part of. "Look, you mugs," he said. "Do you think I'm fuckin' stupid or something? I know what's going on and I'm quitting right now." Capone rose from the table, a move not taken lightly by Genna brother Mike, a.k.a. "The Devil," who thrust a hand in his pocket.

"So, you think you're getting cheated, do you?" Mike Genna yelled. "Well, what the fuck are you gonna do about it, heh?" There was, in fact, very little Capone could do. Outnumbered four to one and unarmed, he had little recourse except to leave. "I really don't care to press the issue right now so I'll just go," he said meekly. "But who knows? Maybe the next time we meet, I'll have one of my pals with me. That'll help make it a little more fair."

"Who's this pal of yours?" Mike Genna sneered. "One of Johnny Torrio's whores?" The room rocked with laughter while Capone's blood boiled, but he nevertheless left the premises quietly after confessing that he was drunk and profoundly apologizing for his rude accusation.

"That's okay, Al, think nothing of it," piped Sam. Taking the cigar out of his mouth and spitting a wad on the floor, he added, "You know you're always welcome at our game." Slipping out the door,

Capone could hear the snickers and the muffled laughter of the four men at the table who, because of their riotous state, neglected to follow him in order to throw the bolt back on the door.

Capone had figured that carrying a gun on the street was unwise because when he had pulled his car in front of the Genna house, he noticed a bluecoat stationed on the corner. For that reason, he decided to leave his rod, a .45 caliber Colt automatic pistol, where it lay in the Buick's glove compartment. Snatching it from its cradle now, Capone inspected the clip to assure himself that it was fully loaded. Using both hands, he cocked the weapon in order to load a round into the chamber, tucked the gun into his waistband and headed back to the Genna brothers' card game. He burst into the room with a furious roar.

"Okay, you fuckin' rats," he shouted. "My 'whore pal' here wants to see all eight hands on the table, right now! Now, you two, grab each other's hands," he commanded, pointing to Sam and Angelo. "Yeah, that's right, Sam, you better hold Angelo's hands real tight because I'll blow your ugly head off. You guys, do the same thing," he said, motioning to the others. "Hold each other's hands on top of the table. The first one that moves gets it. Do you hear?"

Capone's round face, scarred and crimson in color, resembled an ugly caricature of the moon, while his sharp, penetrating eyes darted around the table. "My whore pal here is forty-five years old today and if you want, she'll blow out all of your candles! What do you say, Angelo? Do I get my money refunded?" Capone stepped around the table to where Tony Genna's pile of dough was.

"Fifty-six dollars, and put it in front of you, now!" Capone screamed directly into Tony's right ear. Sam relaxed the hold on his brother's hands while Capone growled, "Hurry up, you shit." Sticking the barrel of the gun closer to the oldest brother's cheek, Capone watched the sweat roll down the man's face while he inquired of him, "Which pocket is the rod in?"

"Right-hand trousers," Sam replied.

"Stand up, but don't you move a knuckle off the table," Capone ordered. He removed the gun from the arched man's pocket and put it into his own. Working his way around the table, he forced them to their feet one at a time, asking the same question. "Which pocket is it in?" When he was finished, he had in his possession two handguns plus a derringer pistol. Stuffing the guns and the cash into his coat pockets, he backed slowly out of the room.

"Thanks for the eats and the music, boys," he said as he exited the door. "Sorry I can't stay any longer. Oh, by the way, if anybody follows me, he's gonna be surprised. And dead! Do you hear me?"

· · ·

A FEW MONTHS after this incident occurred, on January 16, 1920, prohibition became law. The National Prohibition Act, also known as the Volstead Act, was introduced to the legislature by Congressman Andrew J. Volstead of Minnesota. This bill made it a federal offense to manufacture or possess alcoholic beverages, and the enforcement of this unpopular attempt to legislate morality was placed in the hands of federal agents under the authority of the Treasury Department. By shutting the taps on alcohol consumption in America, the new law opened the floodgates for illegally bootlegged products, creating a real bonanza for the shady, privately owned clubs. The neighborhood "speakeasy" was fast becoming the main outlet for the throngs of displaced boozers in the land. Almost overnight, Torrio's Four Deuces evolved into a more discreet establishment, one that screened its drinking customers on the rear steps through a small crack in the door. The front of the place was left unchanged in order to retain its demure "dining room" appearance, but the interior of the rather large, four-story building had been completely renovated to accommodate the hundreds of new customers who plunked down their cash each week just for the privilege of indulging in drink. The joint's red, white, and green painted sign that advertised FOUR DEUCES was pulled from its place on the roadway, broken up and eventually used for firewood because Torrio needed no other draw (nor unwanted attention). Word of mouth alone ensured a full house almost every evening, and the dough kept rolling in.

11

Crazy Benny's Watery Grave

THE STEADY INROADS on the Brooklyn dock rackets made by Frankie Yale's gang in 1920 were having a dire effect on White Hand co-leaders Dinny Meehan and Bill Lovett. When informed by a sympathetic employee of a large shipping company that his boss was slated to deliver an envelope containing protection money to two "Italian-looking" guys, the White Hand bosses decided to put a stop to it immediately. Keeping their time-honored, lucrative waterfront rackets intact sometimes called for special measures. This time, it included the use of a death squad with the participation, and under the direct supervision, of both Meehan and Lovett. The explosive, deadly natures of these two men had been demonstrated time and again in past feuds with other gangs seeking to get a hunk of the waterfront pie and they figured these upstart Italians, who were their latest and most challenging competition, needed a good lesson in controlling their grandiose schemes.

The minor skirmishes and harsh words exchanged between the two sides had reached the boiling point with the violent demise of one Benedetto "Crazy Benny" Pazzo. The first shots were fired by the incumbents, on their own turf.

It seemed the Italians had managed to slide in right under the noses of Meehan and the rest of his mob on the highly prized waterfront, offering their services to some of the White Hand's premier customers. The damage and pilfering of the cargoes that were stored on the Brooklyn docks had ceased to occur under Black Hand protection, as one shipping company after another began relying on the Italians who were definitely more effective in their ability to control the damage. Frankie Yale, it seemed, could also be called upon to play the role of mediator when particular problems arose concerning their labor force.

Don Paolo Vaccarelli, coming out of retirement and using the influence of his position as an official of the Longshoreman's Labor Union, was the eventual recipient of some of the bribes that his "general," Frankie Yale, collected with the help of his soldiers.

• • •

BENEDETTO "CRAZY BENNY" Pazzo had an enviable reputation and was fast becoming one of the most effective collectors in Yale's stable. Known for his smooth manners and gentle tone of voice, Crazy Benny was definitely the man the Brooklyn crime boss considered the most capable and gutsy of his pack able to fill the spot in his organization vacated by Capone.

The slick gangster was assigned the job of going down to Pier Four in Brooklyn to get the promised grease (i.e., extortion money) from the pier management office. The amount due, probably between five hundred and a thousand dollars, was the weekly charge levied against this particular stevedore company and Pazzo had become accustomed to completing the task quickly and without incident, or so he thought. This day was different.

The city was undergoing a tough, icy winter and the usually frantic pace of pier activity had drawn to a halt as the relentless Crazy Benny Pazzo trudged his way through the new-fallen snow. His cohort and driver, Tony Scraps, had parked their vehicle beside a snowbank in front of the pier and remained behind the wheel while Crazy Benny elected to retrieve the envelope himself.

A group of men in front of the pier were hard at work shoveling the white stuff, and they paid little attention to the stranger whose fedora and upturned coat collar kept his face from view as he walked carefully measured steps over the slippery upgrade that led to the main office. Finally reaching the shed and finding refuge from the bitter wind, Pazzo lifted the brim of his hat and noticed a large wooden crate, which had been unloaded recently from a Japanese freighter. It stood right in front of him, blocking his path. Because he assumed the large case was stationary, he decided to follow a worker who was walking around it. Crazy Benny didn't realize that the heavy crate was on wheels until he had circled it and reached the far side.

Without warning, he heard a loud rumble as the heavy case began to move toward him. Trying to get out of the way, Pazzo wondered what became of the man he was following. The man had disappeared, and there was no other route for Pazzo to run except straight ahead.

In order to avoid being knocked down, Pazzo began screaming at the top of his lungs to the driver who was pushing the case, riding atop a forklift.

"Stop! There's people in front of you!" Pazzo yelled, over and over again as his nervous eyes searched for an escape from the menacing crate, which seemed to have a mind of its own. Then, just as suddenly as it had started to move, its forward motion subsided.

Because he found himself near one of the open cargo doors, he was secure in the knowledge that if the case started moving again, he would have an exit that he could reach quickly. But as he composed himself to confront the careless worker, Pazzo was surprised to see three well-dressed men coming toward him. He recognized them immediately, especially the one with the black coat and gray fedora: He was Dinny Meehan. The shortest member of the trio was Wild Bill Lovett, while the other bull was Richard "Peg Leg" Lonergan. Working as a team, the three had gained a nasty reputation around town as the White Hand "death squad."

Benny's eyes widened at the realization of what was to transpire as he tried desperately to reach a hand inside his long coat to get at his pistol. Unfortunately, he found his arms being forcibly locked behind his body by another two men who jumped out of the darkness like phantoms.

"Don't you know when you're beaten?" snarled Meehan as he retrieved the revolver from inside Pazzo's coat. The nervous Italian could do nothing but shake his head back and forth in disbelief as Meehan checked the fully loaded weapon and held the barrel to his forehead. "Drag him outside, boys," Meehan barked to the oversized hoods after personally patting down the luckless man himself. "This fucking bigshot's got all of twenty-four dollars on him, boys," he said. "What do you say we get some beer with the dough, heh?"

"Yeah, Dinny, let's blow it on a nice party for this spaghetti-snapper," chimed Lonergan while plowing his wooden leg through the snow. The handicap of having only one leg did not prevent Peg Leg from becoming one of the most dangerous killers among the White Hand notables, and few antagonists in his life viewed this infirmity as a reason to challenge him in a fight. It was well-known that when it came to performing deadly acts of violence, Lonergan had few peers.

The captive Benny Pazzo pleaded for relief from the pain being inflicted to his arms, which were still being held fast by the two brutes. "Please," he begged, "tell them to lighten their grip, Mr. Meehan. They're breaking my bones."

"How do you know my name?" Dinny asked. "I don't know yours." The Irish gang boss kept the pistol trained on Crazy Benny's face while ordering his men to release their hold.

"I happen to be a good friend of Joe Mack, who lived around the corner from your house," Pazzo answered. "Once, I paid him a visit there and he pointed you out to me on the street."

"Well, a small friendship is better than none, I would say," Meehan said. "Don't you agree? What are you called anyway?"

Pazzo snorted white puffs of smoke in the cold air. His bulging eyes inspected his right wrist, which was still limp and painful. "My name is Benedetto Pazzo," he said, "and I swear if you give me a break, Dinny, you'll never see or hear from me again. I promise you."

"You wanna know something, you greasy piece of shit?" Meehan snapped. "I've got an easy way of making sure of that. Let's go for a little walk around the back of the shed."

When the entourage turned the corner of the building, Pazzo spotted a lone seagull feasting on the remnants of a fish he'd caught. The large bird had obviously taken his lunch from the frigid waters below and upon being disturbed, the seagull grabbed the fish in his beak, flapped his wings, and took off for parts unknown. At that time, Crazy Benny wished he could be just like that bird, soaring away from his fate with a chance to exist beyond the moment. "Dinny," he pleaded, while stumbling and falling down in the snow, "what do you want to do this for? You know I was only following my boss's orders."

The Irishmen picked Pazzo off the ground and dragged his shaking body past the apron area at the end of the pier where the possibility of anybody witnessing the scene would be extremely remote. At this point, Meehan ordered his men to release the prisoner, which they accomplished by flinging him head first into a knee-high snowdrift. Pazzo's left shoulder took the brunt of the fall as he tried desperately to fight the numbness and the loss of mobility in his left wrist. Nevertheless, he succeeded in rolling his body over to face the killing crew that was converging toward him.

Sitting upright in the pile of snow, Pazzo commenced sliding his body along the ground with his back close to the shed while cringing in horror at the sight of the two approaching figures. The actual gunmen were Bill Lovett (using Pazzo's revolver) and "Peg Leg" Lonergan, who heard Pazzo's final plea for his life to be spared. "Please don't shoot me!" Pazzo screamed, as his dilating eyes desperately searched for mercy.

Two slugs fired by Lovett ripped through Pazzo's head while another four bullets from Lonergan's cannon slammed into his chest, tearing through his thick, woolen overcoat as his body slumped down into the freezing snow. "Grand day for a rub out, ain't it, Dinny?" the lanky

Peg Leg remarked as he looked out at the big chunks of ice that floated in the water.

"Help me get him over the side," said Meehan, who was bending over to lift Pazzo by his ankles. The three mobsters proceeded to toss Pazzo's corpse into the murky waters of the East River.

With the fingers of his right hand, Wild Bill Lovett tipped the brim of his hat and said, "Benedetto, you're about to be christened."

After the body of the murdered Pazzo splashed into the frigid water below, the White Hand death squad waited until they were sure the body drifted clear of the wooden pilings as it went under. Within seconds, the remains of Crazy Benny Pazzo were claimed by the swift and treacherous currents of the lower East River, headed for the open sea.

A tugboat pulling a coal barge skimmed its way along with the tide, passing rather close to the wharf. By that time, the White Hands were finished with the deed and promptly left the scene.

None of the crew aboard the tug paused long enough to take notice of the single laborer who was busy shoveling red-stained snow from the tip of Pier Four in Brooklyn Heights, where the first deadly rounds in the bloody battle for total control of the docks had been fired.

• • •

TONY SCRAPISETTI WAITED over two hours for his partner in crime to return before admitting to himself that Crazy Benny wasn't coming out. He pondered the idea of leaving the vehicle to conduct a search but froze in his seat when he spotted a suspicious-looking gray sedan pulling up to the gatehouse in front of the pier. The automobile was being driven by a White Hand torpedo whom he recognized immediately. It was Gary Barry.

Tony Scraps ducked his head below the dashboard and waited until the vehicle entered the pier. He then started his engine and proceeded to move the car across the street, where he would stand a better chance of going undetected while still maintaining a watch for his partner.

After a short while, Scrapisetti's worst fears were realized while peeking out the street-side window of his auto. He spotted three notorious White Hand biggies—Meehan, Wild Bill, and Peg Leg—laughing inside the same gray sedan. They left the pier in a casual manner as Scrappy Tony suddenly came down with a severe case of the jitters. He felt like he was ready to shit in his pants.

The occupants of the Sunrise Café, including its proprietor, Frankie Yale, were engaged in a game of cards in the rear of the joint when Scrapisetti parted the curtains. Shaken, he headed straight for the toilet while shouting in a loud voice, "Crazy Benny never showed up."

Yale threw down his cards and followed Scraps toward the bathroom. He stood outside the open door while Scraps sat on the toilet bowl muttering, "Can you hear me Frank? They done old Benny in for sure."

Exasperated at the bad tidings, Yale yelled into the bathroom, "Scraps, hurry the fuck up in there and come out and explain exactly what happened today. Just when things were moving our way," he said to his men, "these fucking Irish have to let the shit fly."

The others present in the room were Sammy "Crater" Piccone, Sham Brown, and Angelo "Mushy" Guardino. They remained speechless while Yale paced the floor mumbling an oath under his breath: "If those rat-bastards want to start this kind of shit, it's going to be all right by me."

Tony Scraps emerged from the toilet with his head dripping wet. Yale tossed him a towel and encouraged him to be seated. "First thing we gotta do," said Yale, "is to get somebody down there. You know, to make sure he ain't lying around somewhere busted-up and needing our help."

"The way they were giggling amongst themselves on the way out of the pier tells me they took Benny to his grave," Scrapisetti responded. "I'm sure of it, Frank."

"Mush, I want to see what you can do about getting a guy to make a good search of that fuckin' pier. Do you hear me? Get started on that right now," he bellowed to a red-faced Guardino, who reluctantly threw his cards on the table. "What the fuck is wrong with you, Mushy?" Yale said. "I tell you to do something for me and you make a face?"

"I had a full house, Frankie, and the pot should be mine," Guardino said in a meek tone of voice, reaching down to display his hand.

"Take your fucking dough, Mush," Yale said. "Just get the fuck going and do what I said . . . fast!"

"Sure, Frank," the hood replied while scooping up his winnings. "I'll get my friend, Jerry the Weasel. He works down there and I'll have him snoop around at first light. Okay, boss?"

"First light, my ass," Yale roared back. "I said right now! Did you hear me, you four-eyed fuck?"

. . .

DINNY MEEHAN AND Bill Lovett were cocky enough to assume that rubbing-out a single Black Hand collector would put an end to the challenge coming from the upstart Italians. The White Hand leaders figured all they had to do was to keep a sharp eye and a keen ear in the direction of the stoolies they had placed (using their influence) in strategic jobs around the docks and that would give them the needed advantage to stamp out any further intrusion in their waterfront rackets. They continued their customary business with the shipping and stevedore companies that operated the sixty-odd piers in Brooklyn, and work disputes were quickly settled (i.e., squashed) as long as the company came up with the right amount of cash.

A few of the other criminal ventures included in the White Hand repertoire were hijacking, labor kickbacks, shylocking, alien smuggling, and the increasingly profitable drug trade. The Brooklyn brotherhood known as the White Hand gang was truly an entrenched "super power," but so self-assured that they were, they completely underestimated the greedy determination of the Italians.

. . .

UNITED FRUIT COMPANY, operating on Pier Sixteen in Manhattan, was engaged in a prolonged labor problem with members of the dock union known as the International Longshoremen's Association. Meehan, aspiring to spread his wings of power to the Manhattan side of the river, crossed the bridge with around ten members of his tough crew in tow. His goal was to get the nod from United Fruit Co. officials to represent them in negotiating an end to the work stoppage. Instead, Meehan wound up in a heated exchange of words with an ILA business agent named Frank Madden. An ex-pug-turned-union-delegate, Madden dismissed the argument immediately after learning that the fruit biggies had already decided to hire a local group to negotiate the dispute on their behalf. The union official figured he'd won his point. Control of these New York piers would remain intact as they related to Madden and his cronies. He brushed off the attempted invasion of the Brooklyn-based Meehan–Lovett gang into Manhattan as simply "one of the things that goes with the territory." Nonetheless, the shouting match he had with Meehan would come to haunt him in the near future.

The White Hand leaders considered their excursion across the river for the recruitment of new business an exercise in free enterprise, while Frankie Yale, the "interloper," was busy recruiting the services of a Cleveland torpedo named Giovanni Sciacca in mid-February 1920.

Keeping the medium-built import busy and paying his way until the opportune moment arrived was not a simple task for the Brooklyn boss, who considered the olive-skinned Sciacca too nervous a man to practice in this most delicate profession. "I better send somebody with him when the time comes. Somebody that's reliable," Yale told himself.

As luck would have it, March 31, the day after Meehan and Madden's verbal run-in on the New York dock, Yale became privy to information on the whereabouts of Meehan's residence: 452 Warren Street in the Gowanus section of Brooklyn. Yale also learned that the White Hand boss had a tendency to sleep quite late in the day whenever he'd been out drinking the night before.

Yale's spies reported that Meehan had been spotted in the rear of his car being driven home in an absolute, alcoholic fog. The Italians decided they had to act fast. Around three-fifteen in the afternoon, a black sedan slid to a stop and parked about fifty feet from Meehan's apartment. Three men exited the auto, walked to an apartment house near the corner, and climbed the steps leading up to the hallway. Little Augie Pisano, Giovanni Sciacca, and Sammy Pollaccio located the door to the room where Yale's snitch had reported they would find Dinny Meehan.

Little Augie stood to one side of the door with a hand inside his coat, gripping the handle of the automatic weapon he carried in a shoulder holster. Sciacca's nervous left hand slowly tried the doorknob while Pollaccio, the huskiest of the three men, stepped back a few feet to get himself in position to kick the door in.

Suddenly, Sciacca's face brightened. "It's unlocked," he whispered. Stepping into the room, the three Italians found two partially covered figures, one male, one female, in peaceful slumber. They stepped in for what appeared to be an easy kill.

Little Augie poked Sciacca in the ribs with an elbow, urging him in a low voice, "Shoot the Irish fuck right now, you slowpoke. His wife is starting to get my cock hard." Sciacca tiptoed up to the bed, putting the muzzle of his .38 caliber pistol scant inches from Meehan's skull, and blasted a dum-dum bullet into Meehan's brain. The second shot, fired in rapid succession, went clear through the man's neck and entered the forearm of his panic-stricken spouse, who promptly fainted away without retaining a clue of the attack.

Sprinting away from the building, the assassins scrambled into their waiting vehicle and roared away from the scene. Within minutes, they were headed for parts unknown.

Brooklyn homicide detectives in the Eighty-Second Precinct tried to pin the killing on Madden. Someone had tipped the law concerning the argument that occurred over labor problems down by Pier Sixteen (the United Fruit pier) just the day before. They questioned him and dogged his life for awhile, but gave up on the idea after learning that fourteen witnesses were ready to testify that Madden was attending an executive board meeting at his union headquarters in Manhattan at the exact hour of the White Hand gang chief's demise.

When news of the slayings reached the street, residents in the area began engaging in all sorts of gossip. Some actually thought the body taken to the morgue that afternoon was caught up in some kind of lover's triangle. Others claimed that the woman shot her husband dead, accidentally catching one of the slugs in her own arm, while those who knew the couple personally kept their speculations concerning the ghastly killing to themselves. They would also get used to the incident being referred to as "the pajama murder."

12

The Interrupted Honeymoon

C OLOSIMO'S CAFE WAS a very popular night spot for anyone willing to spend top dollar for the best in Italian cuisine. On a given night, one might observe in the large dining room such notables as Broadway producer Florenz Ziegfeld, George M. Cohan, former heavyweight champion "Gentleman" Jim Corbett, and even the world famous tenor Enrico Caruso, all of whom were accustomed to being fussed over by its owner.

The classy regulars were the first to notice the change in Colosimo, and began whispering behind his back, "What the hell is wrong with Big Jim?" Even the Great Caruso was appalled at the indifference shown when Colosimo tendered him only a mild greeting.

Caruso had called to him in Italian: "Jim, come over here, will you? I want you to meet some friends." Colosimo responded by dragging Dale Winter over to Caruso's table, quickly introducing her as his soon-to-be wife and immediately leaving the scene with his head still in the clouds and Dale on his arm.

Caruso, the pudgy, round-faced singer whose voice could shatter a row of champagne glasses with little effort, was left speechless. He remained sitting there with his valuable mouth open while his dark eyes searched the room for an explanation to Jim's sudden lack of interest.

In mid-April, Jim and Dale eloped to French Lick, Indiana, for a quickie wedding and a short honeymoon. They returned to the windy city on May 2, 1920, and set up housekeeping in Big Jim's mansion at 3156 South Vernon Avenue, only about a mile from his famous eatery.

On May 11, 1920—the last day of his life—Colosimo climbed into his chauffeured limo while promising his new wife that he would send Woolfson, the driver, back to the house to pick up Dale and her mother to take them shopping.

He had promised Torrio, who complained about a diarrhea attack that kept him up all night, that he would go to the restaurant to oversee the reception of two rather large loads of alcoholic beverages.

"Jim, I know you'd want one of us to be present for such an expensive shipment," Torrio declared, certain that Colosimo would agree to personally go to the restaurant to accept the delivery. Torrio had already dispatched Capone's former Brooklyn honcho, Frankie Yale, to offer the man a surprise greeting. But not without first sounding a warning to his hired gun. "Frankie," he pleaded, "make sure you get him from behind and don't give him a chance, because the big prick always carries a fully licensed .38 caliber revolver."

The first truck to arrive that afternoon was the load of moonshine whiskey, which was delivered by an unpretentious step-in van emblazoned with a sign on its doors that read MAHONEY FLORISTS. Colosimo's strict business sense required that he count each and every case of booze as it was placed in the cellar himself. When he finished that chore, he talked a little business with his bookkeeper, Frank Camilla, in the small office he maintained, and after that, Big Jim chatted with some kitchen help, including his chef, Antonio Ceasarino, about his latest dinner menu.

Colosimo's attitude about life was upbeat, especially after settling into a nice groove as restaurateur extraordinaire while his underboss, Johnny Torrio, had the "privilege" of attending to the daily routine. This also allowed more time for the forty-three-year-old man to spend at home with his new, young wife Dale, who deserved his full attention.

Jim was not averse to brag to his close associates, "This is the sweetest period in my whole life, thanks to her."

The shadows gathering in the empty aisles reminded Colosimo that time had slipped by. Within an hour or so, the restaurant would be open for business, and he considered sending the beer back to the warehouse.

Colosimo figured that early customers shouldn't be present while an illegal shipment of beer was being unloaded. So he decided to check the street for the delivery truck. The swinging glass partitions parted as Colosimo strolled out of the dining room across the porcelain floor of the lobby on his way out to Wabash Avenue.

On one side of the lobby was a cloakroom facing a cashier's booth and a coin box telephone, which happened to be ringing off the wall. Colosimo stopped over to answer it, unaware of the threat that loomed behind his back. The sinister figure hiding in the cloakroom raised his right hand, which clutched a revolver, and zeroed its sights in on Colosimo's upper body. "Hello, say . . . who is this?" Big Jim inquired in response to the indiscernible sounds coming from the receiver.

Just then, two shots roared from the muzzle of Yale's pistol, twin salvos that splashed across the glossy interior of the vestibule and caused powder burns to remain on the victim's scalp and neck. The subsequent investigation would reveal that the blasts also scorched the sheer curtains that hung beside the cloakroom.

Only the first of the two bullets, discharged at close range, actually plowed through Colosimo's skull. The second shot missed the target completely, burying itself in a wall.

Big Jim weakened at the knees and dropped head-first onto the tiled floor as blood gushed from the wound behind his ear, matting his dark brown hair.

Frank Camilla peeked out the door of Colosimo's office in the rear of the dining room and found Ceasarino and another worker looking puzzled as someone turned on all the house lights. Camilla realized that the others were also disturbed by the ominous blasts. "Where's the boss?" he inquired of them.

"Only a few minutes ago he was swearing he'd send the truck away if it didn't show up soon," answered Ceasarino. "Maybe he left already?"

Before dismissing the loud blasts as backfire coming from a motorcar, the three men decided to check it out. They exited the restaurant from a side door because Ceasarino claimed, "That's where the sounds came from." The early evening street scene they found included only a horse-drawn ice wagon with an elderly driver slapping the reins while cursing at the nag's refusal to go faster.

"I'm gonna take a look around the front," said the heavyset bookkeeper to the others. Extending the search to the corner, he turned onto Wabash Avenue and glanced into an alley on the other side of the building. Camilla decided the reports they heard would simply have to remain a mystery and was about to shrug the whole thing off when he attempted to re-enter the establishment through the main door.

His push on the engraved glass panel met such firm resistance, however, that he assumed it was locked, so Camilla started fishing in his pocket for the key. Then, casually glancing through the glass door he spotted Colosimo's brown shoes on the tiled floor and his body lying in a crimson pool.

Screaming for help, he forced the door open wide enough to squeeze through and proceeded to climb over the lifeless hulk that lay crumpled against the door. Camilla tried desperately to stop his nervous fingers from shaking, at least long enough to ring the operator in a call for an ambulance. The brutal scene in front of him, compounded by the sudden awareness that the killer might still be in the vicinity, had him worried stiff. It took the rumbling footsteps of Ceasarino and one of his crew arriving in response to Camilla's loud yelling that enabled him to regain his composure. "Antonio, you call up the ambulance . . . I hate the sight of blood," Camilla said, clutching his stomach.

"Do you think we should call the police, too?" the cook's helper asked in a shaky voice.

A call placed for an ambulance always resulted in a police inquiry and a simple investigation by a bluecoat. This case was different, though. When the desk sergeant heard that the victim was Colosimo, he notified Chief of Police John J. Garrity, who arrived on the scene accompanied by Thomas Mooney, chief of detectives, and several other sleuths on loan from the state attorney's office.

Detective Lieutenant Thomas Nolan of Chicago's homicide squad spoke to the press:

"We believe the killer did the nasty deed while the deceased was using the phone because the receiver was found off the hook," he said, "and judging by the trajectory of bullets, we have a strong suspicion he was gunned down by someone hiding in the cloakroom. That's all we can say right now. The fingerprint guys are still in the process of doing their work so we'll see what happens next."

Alfred "Jake" Lingle, a reporter for the *Chicago Tribune* who had some rather devious ties to the mob himself, raised a question: "Where on his body did Mr. Colosimo sustain the mortal wound?"

Lieutenant Nolan silently responded by raising his right index finger to a point just behind his right ear.

"Does the department have any leads or clues at this time about who the responsible party is?" asked another reporter.

"I can't reveal our suspicions right now," said Nolan.

The small crowd of newsmen then asked a barrage of the usual questions, including inquiries regarding the victim's age, marital status, and so forth, while one scribe inquired whether or not the rumor of possible extortion being levied against Mr. Colosimo by local gangsters had any validity.

"Gentlemen, that's about it for now," Nolan insisted. "All your other questions in regards to this will be answered soon. I can assure you that every avenue and alley will be explored until we nail the killer. Please leave your business cards with Officer Stevens and he'll get in touch with your office when something new develops."

The following day, most of the employees of the bistro were questioned at the local station house by a four-man team headed by Lieutenant Nolan and Sergeant Michael Walsh, a six-foot, athletic-looking man with light skin and gray peepers that always seemed to be squinting. The potential witnesses remembered that curious feature; even back in the gloomy confines of the shuttered restaurant, his eyes appeared as miniscule gashes in constant battle with a blazing sun. The questioning started with Ceasarino offering only a cool response to the series of barbs being fired at him by Sergeant Walsh and company.

When asked directly if he had seen or heard anything unusual, his remarks were identical to his prior quote. "All I heard, officer, was two loud bangs," he said.

The stocky bookkeeper, Camilla, wearing a pair of tan trousers and a white shirt topped off with a straw boater, held the summer head-piece in his hand while fanning it in front of his face. "Lord God, it's hot in this place," he said. "Can't you fellows do without the spotlight shining down on me and broiling my ass?" He sat in the chair tugging at his collar, answering the same questions over and over again, adding nothing new to his story.

Several others, including Ceasarino's apprentice and a dishwasher who was on duty that day, were also quizzed at length, but to no avail. Interest suddenly grew with the account given by a porter, Giuseppe Gabreala, who was dumping garbage late in the afternoon on the day in question. He reported seeing a stranger walking through the alley beside the building.

"I thought very little of it," he said, "because it was still daylight and the man didn't seem to be up to anything fishy."

"Can you describe this man and the way he was dressed?"

"Let me think for a moment," a jittery Gabreala responded, brushing a hand across his temple, where beads of perspiration made tiny trails down to his cheek. "I saw a guy about average height. Five foot seven, maybe. He was built like a bulldog, you know what I mean. You know, solid. That's the best way I can describe him."

"Can you remember how he was dressed?" Walsh asked.

"I told you already, I only spotted the guy for a second," Gabreala answered with a cynical smile. "How the hell was I supposed to know if a normal-looking person like this one was up to some dirty work? In answer to your question, sir, I don't recall how the man was dressed."

"You said, normal-looking, Mr. Gabreala," Walsh said. "What was it about the man that put you at ease with his presence that day?"

"Because lots of people pass that way, that's why," Gabreala answered.

"Do you mean to say, four o'clock in the afternoon and lots of traffic comes through an alley?" Walsh asked. Gabreala looked around at the other cops in the room who seemed to be hanging onto every word spoken.

"I didn't say that," Gabreala said. "I just said I paid little attention to him."

Gabreala's answer to Nolan's next question caused a stir in the room. "If you ever saw this character again," Nolan asked, "do you think you'd remember him?" Gabreala squirmed in his seat and pulled a handkerchief from his trouser pocket. He proceeded to mop his sweaty brow.

"Yes sir, officer," Gabreala announced. "I think I could."

"Finally, we're making some headway," Nolan said.

· · ·

THE NEXT STEP on the Chicago police's agenda was to assure Gabreala of the city's intention to reimburse him for time lost from his job in going through the mug files. He did so in a fruitless yet sincere attempt to identify the man thought to be involved in the murder of his boss.

A break in the case came with the revelation that a Brooklyn torpedo named Frank Ioele had been detained at a railroad station immediately following the crime. After being questioned by police that day, they found little reason to hold him and allowed him to continue on his way to New York. This new information caused Chicago police to request a mug shot of Yale from the New York authorities and promptly brought in Giuseppe Gabreala to check out the suspect's photo.

One look at the face plastered above the numbers on the upper-left-hand corner of Frankie Yale's yellow sheet caused Gabreala to jump from his chair. With a stubby finger, he pointed to the photo and exclaimed, "That's him! That's the guy I saw that day."

Chicago detectives assigned to the case immediately called the Bath Beach precinct in Brooklyn, requesting they pick up Yale on suspicion of homicide. He was apprehended and transferred to the Raymond Street jail to await the arrival of the star witness. Gabreala was quickly hustled to New York by Chicago cops, who, along with their New York City counterparts, salivated at the thought of finally nailing the elusive Yale.

Chief of Police Garrity considered it wise to send Gabreala out of town to identify the suspect in New York instead of waiting for Yale to be brought to Chicago, because he didn't want to allow additional time and opportunity for Chicago thugs to get to their witness. While they waited for Gabreala to arrive in New York, the investigation continued at home as statements were taken from anyone who had business or social interactions with Colosimo. The story made front-page headlines in Chicago, while an outraged public demanded results. Capone and his boss, Torrio, were invited downtown for an interview with homicide investigators. Torrio, playing up his grief, held a handkerchief to his tearful face while exclaiming, "Jesus, officer, how can you suggest I had anything to do with this? Jim was like a brother to me. I loved the big guy very much."

Capone repeated the same story. "Johnny and me were shooting pool down on North State Street. You can check that out with about ten others guys including the beat cop, Eddie Murphy, who happened to come in for a drink of water." Capone smirked and turned his head toward the wall. When his face came back into view, his voice was booming. "Goddammit," he said, "I wish to hell you guys were out looking for whoever killed Big Jim, because if I could just get my two hands on him first, I'll crack his fuckin' skull wide open. Then you fellas would have good reason to bring me in here."

"Okay, you guys can leave now," said Nolan. "But you know, we're gonna check out your story." Motioning to a subordinate, Nolan said, "Let's have the other two."

Victoria Moresco, Colosimo's former wife, and a brother were brought in, questioned, and released after an extensive period of time, with no new clues or leads provided by either.

· · ·

SONNY COSMANO, A Black Hand figure who was rumored to have put the squeeze on Big Jim in an attempt at extortion, was ruled out as a suspect because the tall, heavyset Cosmano had spent May 11, 1920, in a Cicero jail cell for one of his many criminal capers.

Under the pretense of offering assistance in planning the funeral extravaganza, Torrio and Capone paid a "sympathy call" to Colosimo's wife, Dale. With flowers in hand they proceeded to abuse the woman with a tirade of insults, holding her personally responsible for Colosimo's death. She remained seated on the couch, bawling her eyes out while Capone busied himself by rummaging through her late husband's personal effects, confiscating large amounts of cash and jewelry and leaving behind only those valuables that wouldn't fit in his pockets. They left the vivacious beauty with the warning, "You better not tell anyone what went on here today," Capone told the widow, "do you hear? Unless you want to join your husband in the hole that's waiting in the cemetery."

Word had trickled down to Torrio about the police department's plan to ship Giuseppe Gabreala off to New York for the Yale lineup. On the evening prior to his departure, the porter was relayed a message from Capone advising him not to cooperate with the police if he valued his life. "If you do as they say, they're prepared to offer you a fine job spinning the roulette wheel in one of their new, classy spots opening in the loop next month. And when you get back from New York, two hundred dollars cash will be waiting for you, but only if you don't rat. Otherwise, you'll wind up in a box like your boss," Capone promised.

Yale sweated in the Raymond Street Prison in Brooklyn while three Windy City detectives guided Gabreala onto a train headed for New

York. The jail resembled a classic medieval dungeon. It was a solemn place to visit, let alone spend a period of time as a "guest" inside its walls. The most unfortunate languished there because they were too poor to afford a good legal defense. But Yale was neither poor nor unfortunate, having as his legal counsel the well-connected and brilliant defense lawyer, Samuel Liebowitz, who promised Yale that his stay there would be very short indeed.

Yale looked past the steel bars to the sky outside his vermin-infested cell and watched the sun going down. He hoped the new day would bring word that they'd gotten to Giuseppe Gabreala. But soon Gabreala and the three Chicago lawmen arrived at the jail. They walked into the sterile, tunnel-like foyer until they were constrained by a wall of steel rods that jutted down from the high ceiling.

"Captain Cummings, please," officer Walsh said to the uniformed guard who was checking his book for confirmation of the scheduled conference. They saw him press a button and the curtain of steel bars that separated them from the main building began to slide along a track and disappear into the wall.

Lieutenant Nolan handed his official credentials to another guard who scrutinized the documents and handed them back to him.

"This way, please," the guard said, directing the four men inside of a cage-like section, where the surrounding steel bars seemed to engulf Gabreala. "How the fuck did I get into this?" he asked himself as he nervously followed the three cops into the interrogation room. When they entered, a trustee was hard at work arranging a number of chairs that had been strewn about the twenty-foot by thirty-foot cubicle, which was used specifically for questioning prisoners.

Captain Cummings introduced himself to his three counterparts from Chicago, then offered a smile to Gabreala and the warmest handshake the maintenance worker could remember as the Brooklyn cop encouraged the witness to be seated. Gabreala felt isolated from reality for a moment, thinking he was doing his civic duty. It was something the boss's real friends should admire him for. "But where are they?" he pondered. Where was Torrio, Colosimo's manager, to advise him on the situation? If he lied to the police, he knew he'd probably wind up in this place or another just like it for a long time.

Gabreala was loosening the collar of his shirt as the door swung open and a handcuffed prisoner was led to a spot around six feet away from where he sat while the porter's eyes studied the contours of the stocky body. The guard removed the cuffs and turned the prison-garbed Yale around by his shoulders to face his finger man.

Yale's glaring eyes were cemented on Gabreala's in an ominous exhibition that almost forced the quaking man to vomit the bacon and eggs he had eaten for breakfast. It was the same demented demonstration of eye contortion Yale had persuaded Capone to practice. The terrifying visual message came across loud and clear. Gabreala held his hands in the area of his esophagus and turned away from the man's face while a voice drifted in.

"Is this the man you saw around Colosimo's restaurant when your boss was killed?" Nolan's voice was loud and clear, but Gabreala hesitated with his answer until the lieutenant repeated the question. "I'm asking you, Mr. Gabreala, is this the man?"

This time, Gabreala collected his words in his mind and shook his head saying, "No, I'm sorry. That's not him!"

"What did you say?" Nolan shouted as the other officers muttered curses and threats at the eyewitness. Detective Walsh slammed a fist down on the table and kicked the wall in a rage.

"This is the same guy you picked out of our mug files," he blared. "Shit, man, does he look so different in person?"

Gabreala remained motionless, a blank expression on his face. Yale's attorney, seizing the opportunity, reprimanded the Chicago police for accusing his client of murder simply because he was on vacation in Chicago at the time somebody got killed. On the way out of the prison, the captain informed all concerned that there was no case against Yale and tore the arrest warrant into shreds in the presence of both Yale and his attorney.

Lieutenant Nolan tossed the return train ticket at the feet of Gabreala with disdain written across his ordinarily mild-looking face.

"Fuck up one time when you get back home, you fuckin' lying bastard," he sneered. "Fuck up just once and I swear I'll nail your ass to a lamppost."

Frankie Yale went immediately to his home for a bath and a change of clothes. Within hours, he was being driven to Grand Central Terminal for the first train back to Chicago. It took an unholy trinity, Torrio, Capone, and Yale, to topple Big Jim Colosimo from his throne. But it was Yale who provided the corpse for the first of Chicago's many big gangland funerals.

13

New Underworld Order

I **T WAS A** rather cool and breezy day in Brooklyn on Thursday, November 14, 1920, with temperatures barely reaching forty degrees, as Gabriele Capone prepared to leave his Garfield Place residence to meet a friend for their usual game of "eight ball" down at the local pool hall.

"Why don't you tell Gaetano that you're not feeling so good today?" his wife suggested as she stood by the kitchen sink washing the breakfast dishes. "You're looking pale and you kept me up half the night with that cough of yours," she said in Italian as she looked at his face and studied his stubby chin. "Really, Gabriele, I think you should go to see the doctor instead of your friend Gaetano in the pool room. If you want, I'll go with you. Okay?"

Teresina Capone realized her concern was falling on deaf ears as she watched her fifty-two-year-old husband grab a hairbrush from a drawer and disappear into the bathroom.

Gabriele cursed under his breath at the stranger-than-usual sight that confronted him in the mirror. His cheeks seemed sunken, and his eyes were puffy and watery. With a trembling hand, Gabriele stroked the side of his head while letting out a quiet sigh. He wasn't at all happy with his appearance on that portentous morning, but he attempted to dismiss it from his mind by finding a cause. He attributed the way he looked and the nagging pains in his chest to the spicy food he had eaten at a family get-together the evening before, a feast he had really enjoyed.

Proceeding to groom his hair, Gabriele stuck his head out of the bathroom door and asked his wife to pour him a small glass of milk. "I think maybe that'll make me feel better," he said. Teresina strolled over to the icebox in response to his request, while her husband reached into a closet for his brown, three-quarter-length coat.

The sluggish man threw the fur-trimmed coat over one arm and walked into the kitchen. "You better put the coat on and button it up to keep your chest covered," Teresina chided him as he drank his milk, his eyes glued to the kitchen wall clock.

"Where do you think I'm going, on a trip?" he responded. "I'm only going a few steps down to the corner to meet Guy, then into the pool room. That's all." Slipping the bolt of the door, he waved a hand in the air in disgust and stepped outside. No sooner had the door closed behind him than Teresina heard his voice sounding through the door. His words offered something they both considered an apology.

"I'm buttoning up my coat, Teresina," he said. "See you later."

The two-family brownstone the Capones lived in had wide steps, which Gabriele descended slowly, sliding a hand along the handrail as he greeted the bakery deliveryman who was carrying a box containing an apple pie to the house next door. The green and cream Duggan Bakery van was a regular early morning visitor to Garfield Place and the surrounding area, buzzing through the streets in a methodical pattern while offering freshly baked goods to customers at home.

"I can smell it from here," Capone remarked in his broken English while holding his nose in the air. The deliveryman responded to Gabriele's appreciative comment with a sales pitch. "What can I sell you today, Pop?" he said.

"Nothing for us today," Gabriele replied. "I'm afraid that my wife wants me to cut down on my sweets. You know, on account of my heart condition."

"Duggan's bread is the greatest thing in the world for the ticker," the deliveryman exclaimed.

"Maybe the cakes or the pies," Capone said, "but not the bread. That's for sure."

The deliveryman stopped in his tracks halfway up the steps in order to respond to the old-timer. "You don't like my company's bread?" he said. "That's funny, I thought your family always bought some."

"We sometimes buy it for the kid," Gabriele said. "She likes it. I only eat regular Italian bread from Valducci's," he boasted.

"That bread is for the birds," the Duggan man kidded.

"Chirp-chirp," Gabriele intoned with a lilting voice, attempting to force his heavy legs to respond to the urging of his friend, Gaetano, who was standing on the corner waving to him. "You can't wait to lose, eh, Gaetano?" he shouted.

"What the hell is wrong with you today, Gabriele?" Gaetano said. "What's the 'chirp-chirp' for?" The former barber, unaware that his lips were still moving in response to the deliveryman, walked behind his friend through the wooden archway of the pool room. "Don't mind me," Gabriele replied. "I was just thinking of something funny the bakery driver said."

"Are you all right today, Gabriele?" his friend inquired.

"Sure, Gaetano, c'mon, we flip for who breaks," he said.

After they removed their coats and selected their favorite cues from a rack, the oldest member of the Capone family suddenly stiffened as he complained to Gaetano about the terrible pains he was experiencing.

"Gaetano, my chest," he said. "It feels like an elephant is sitting on it. I feel sweaty." Gabriele's eyes suddenly dilated, and he started to choke violently. Gaetano raced around the table, grabbing Gabriele's body as it went limp, and struggled to get his good friend seated in a nearby chair. "Help him, somebody help!" Gaetano screamed, trying to unbutton Gabriele's shirt collar.

The proprietor of the pool room alerted Barney Colson, a veteran of the First World War who had seen enough wounded and dying soldiers to render first aid. Colson, who was outside the building working on his car, rushed inside and made a frantic attempt to resuscitate the stricken man, but it was for naught. He finally realized there was no sound coming from Gabriele's chest and decided it was over when he saw the color of the man's lips go livid.

"He's gone!" Colson announced to the small crowd that had gathered. "Somebody better tell his family. Maybe they'll want us to carry him home."

Alphonse's older brother, Ralph, telephoned Chicago to relay the bad news. "A heart attack, Alphonso," Ralph sobbed. "We kept telling him, 'Papa, you gotta lay off the vino and stuff. Do you understand? Papa . . . The doctor says your blood pressure is awfully high . . . .' Oh, Al, I'm really gonna miss having him around, especially for Mama's sake."

"How's Mama taking it?" Capone asked.

"Pretty rough," Ralph said, "because she blames herself. Mafalda's taking it bad too, Al. The kid hasn't stopped bawling her eyes out since he died."

"Where are you planning to wake Papa?" Capone asked.

"Well, he's in his bedroom now and Mama says she wants to wake him right here in the house," Ralph said. "What do you think, Alphonse? I know you'll want to come in to see Papa. But you got that fuckin' Irishman who's still looking for the man with the scars on his face."

"Ralphie, do me a favor," Capone said. "Stay close to the phone for awhile. I'll get back to you right away."

• • •

"NEW YORK?" MAMA Capone cried when she learned the news. The suggestion compounded her grief as she begged to know why Gabriele's friends and relatives were being subjected to the inconvenience of traveling all the way to lower Manhattan to pay their final respects.

"Mama, Alphonso says he'll have a car right in front of the house for anyone from the neighborhood who wants to go," Ralph said in a soft and reassuring voice. "We'll shuffle them there and back, even if it takes ten cars to do it."

In Chicago, Mary Capone got busy packing the family's luggage and preparing their two-year-old son Albert, nicknamed Sonny, who would be traveling to the wake along with an increasing number of friends who expressed a desire to attend the funeral when word of Gabriele Capone's death spread around the Windy City.

Johnny Torrio appeared genuinely grieved about a man who he referred to as "one of the nicest men I've ever known."

Deany O'Banion, decked out in a double-breasted black suit adorned with a white carnation pinned to his left lapel, had dropped into Colosimo's restaurant, which was now being managed on Torrio's behalf by Big Jim's father, Luigi. Flanked by "Schemer" Drucci and Hymie Weiss, O'Banion also expressed a desire to make the trip. But when Capone was informed that Samoots Ammatuna, a fugitive of the New York justice system, wanted to tag along, he reminded the Sicilian triggerman of the dangers involved in such a trip. "Listen, Samoots," Capone cautioned, "you got the cops after your ass back home and I gotta advise you against taking such a chance."

"Don't worry, Alphonso," Samoots insisted in Italian. "I promise to keep out of Brooklyn while I'm there. Besides, I don't really think I'm on anybody's shit list."

"Would you do me one favor, Samoots?" Capone asked. "Could you leave your tool at home? What if, by chance, you happen to get frisked by the law and they find a pistol on you? Your Sicilian ass would be dragged in front of a judge in no time," Capone said, answering his own question. "I know what I'm talking about, my friend. If that happens, you know . . . there's that outstanding warrant against you."

Reluctantly, Samoots agreed to leave his sidearm in Chicago. "I'd like to attend the funeral of your Papa at my own expense," he said.

"Of course, Samoots," Al replied.

A small fleet of automobiles arrived intermittently throughout the day at Vanella's Funeral Home on Madison Street in lower Manhattan. Some brought flowers, while others offered only their prayers and expressions of sympathy to the family. In the crowded chapel sat such underworld figures as Giuseppe Masseria, Arnold Rothstein, Batista Balsamo, Vincenzo Mangano, and retired godfather, Don Paolo Vaccarelli, former leader of the Five Points brotherhood. From Chicago, Torrio traveled with his new accountant, Jake Cuzik, a talented individual charged with the extremely sensitive chore of keeping the company books in proper order. Also in attendance from Chicago was Schemer Drucci, who saw personal advantage in making the trip because he'd never been to New York before and thought of it as a chance to see some of the sights. He also figured it would be a good opportunity for him to meet and perhaps even break bread with some important people who were going places in the world.

Earl "Hymie" Weiss, Tony Lombardo, and Miguel Merlo (the Frankie Yale-appointed president of the Chicago chapter of the Unione Siciliana), along with other notorious figures from Chicago's underworld, also made the trip in to pay their respects.

After three days of lying in state, Gabriele's bronze coffin was shouldered by eight family members. Dressed in black suits, they had all remained unshaven since the death of their beloved relative, an old-world custom. They carried the casket into Our Lady of Peace Roman Catholic church, where Father Rinaldo Fiumano performed a Requiem High Mass set with a choir and an organist in which the somber crowd was assured of Gabriele's entrance into a place of "light and refreshment."

Johnny Torrio was struck by those in attendance. "A regular League of Nations," he told himself. While Italians made up the majority of the crowd, Cuzik was of Polish extraction, Arnold Rothstein was a Jew, and Deany O'Banion, naturally, was Irish Catholic.

"If only people would forget their cultural differences and come together more often, there'd be peace and harmony in the world," Torrio thought to himself. Taking that noble thought one step further, Torrio was suddenly struck by the idea of setting up such an underworld order where everyone would be allowed the freedom to operate in their own territories without fear of competition or intrusion by one mob into another's turf.

A few months prior to this brainstorm, Torrio had invested large amounts of money in the manufacturing of illegal alcohol, buying half interests in several breweries. That's when he began his association with Joseph Stenson, the youngest and most savvy of four brothers who were the long-time owners of the Stenson Brewing Company of Chicago. Torrio, with Stenson's production techniques and financial backing, also gained major interest in four other beer-producing plants in Chicago: The Manhattan Beer Company, the Best Beer Company, the West Hammond Brewery, and the giant Sieben Beer producing plant, located at North Larrabee Street.

Deany O'Banion had already been doing business with the Sieben family when Torrio became a third affiliate. Now, Torrio was more than just another outlet for O'Banion's illegal liquor; he was a business partner of the North Side gang leader. O'Banion had also bought a controlling interest in the William Schofield florist shop at 733 North State Street, directly across from the Holy Name Cathedral. When asked by the police or reporters about his mob ties, Deany would remark, "Who me? You got it all wrong! I run a respectable florist business." Despite his legitimate front, however, O'Banion could not hide the fact that he was considered a suspect in no less than twenty-five murders in the previous fifteen years.

The blue-eyed, sandy-haired North Side gang chieftain stood about five feet, seven inches tall, with broad shoulders and powerful arms. A strange quirk of his was to pack three pistols on his person at all times in special pockets in suits that were tailored to his particular specifications. A hidden compartment was sewn into his garments under his left armpit, another pocket was hidden inside his trousers, and a third pocket, near his groin, concealed the smallest pistol in his cluster, a tiny, German firearm, a Walther 25 caliber automatic.

As a youngster, Deany was accidentally hit by a mail truck, and the subsequent surgery caused his right leg to remain four inches shorter than the left. For this reason, O'Banion was forced to wear special shoes with a thick sole on the one leg in order to compensate for the handicap.

Well on his way to becoming a millionaire, the "Beer Baron" had come a long way from his safecracking and stickup days. While only sixteen years of age, Dion "Deany" O'Banion obtained a job as a singing waiter at a Northside saloon called McGovern's, where his glee club would occasionally assist him in removing someone from the premises who they considered to be drunk and disorderly. After singling out the mark, they would run him into the alley and pick his pockets. Sometimes, they would beat the hell out of a victim who resisted, but most times, they were content with just clipping the drunk's dough.

• • •

TORRIO PLANNED ON calling a forum of the interested parties to consider his grand scheme of dividing Chicago's criminal enterprises into individual, private territories. When informed of Johnny's serious intentions, Capone wondered how he'd pull it off, but knowing his boss, he knew he would find a way.

"This effort requires the involvement of someone with the prestige of Deany O'Banion in order to succeed," Capone advised Torrio.

"Alphonse," Torrio responded, "we gotta hook the big fish first. We have to encourage the Irishman to throw his weight behind the plan."

Without uttering a word about the future meeting to O'Banion, they started the ball rolling by speaking to an associate of Joe Saltis, who went by the name of John "Dingbat" O'Berta. Torrio contracted him and his boys to hijack a few truckloads of O'Banion's booze while promising them an immediate, "top dollar" reward for their services. But he didn't stop there. Torrio also victimized another competitor, the Genna brothers. Their operations were set into a tizzy when two loads of their illegal moonshine were also lifted within a matter of weeks.

Setting the stage by creating turmoil and baffling the various gangs, who didn't know who was responsible for the hijackings, was all part of Torrio's campaign, which paid dividends in the late spring of 1922. His blueprint for bringing Chicago's organized crime despots together in one place was finally realized when a meeting was called to order in Colosimo's restaurant.

Each leader came into the meeting with the understanding there would be no preconditions, only that they leave old grievances at the door and listen to the offer with an open mind. Every leader present was allowed one or two advisors. For most, it was the underboss who served in that capacity. Besides Dion O'Banion and Earl "Hymie" Weiss from the North Side, there was Mike "the Devil" Genna and his brother, Angelo, from Chicago's "Little Italy" district. Ralph Sheldon from the South Side and William "Klondike" O'Donnell, who represented his brother's West Side interests, were also invited guests.

A sign reading CLOSED FOR RENOVATIONS! was posted on each door of the restaurant to ensure that no outsiders would interrupt the proceedings that were soon to transpire at Colosimo's.

Torrio sat at the head of a long banquet table while Capone reclined in a chair beside him. On the other side was Capone's older brother, Ralph, who was being introduced to the Chicago scene after yielding to his brother's passionate appeal. "Ralphie, I know that as soon as you come out here, Mama will follow right behind," he said. "All I want is my whole family close to me so they can share in my good luck."

Ralph was the first of the Capone brothers to join Al in Chicago, where he found a well-paying job awaiting him. The rest of the family relocated soon after Capone furnished the nice but not overly lavish home he purchased on South Prairie Avenue. The older Capone was seated alongside Frankie Lake, who was representing the Valley area just south of Klondike, O'Donnell's Westerly turf.

Torrio started the meeting by introducing himself to the many unrecognizable faces peering up from the jammed banquet table. "I'm Johnny Torrio," he said, "and I sincerely hope I haven't excluded anybody from this conference that's gonna make a difference in any decisions that come out of this room tonight."

"C'mon Johnny," urged Deany O'Banion impatiently. "Stop the horseshit and tell us why we're all here."

Smiling all the while, Torrio reacted to O'Banion's outburst by raising his hands in front of his chest and spinning them in a circular motion as he continued to talk. "Seated at this table and looking around at the uneasy faces on you mugs, I say, is a little like my first day in school. The only difference is there are no teachers here, because all of us have already learned our Ps and Qs the hard way. And there's no principal here either. Because, my motto is: Never tell another guy how to operate his own business. But I think we'll all learn something very important here today, as well as very profitable."

Watching the raised eyebrows and puckered lips of the North Side mobster, O'Banion, who continually puffed on a cigar, Torrio pleaded his case. "All of us at this table represent business interests that are struggling to expand their operations and bring in cash with the least amount of interference from the law. Right? What we don't need is one of us stepping on another's toes in order to form protective alliances that split profits.

"By God," Torrio continued, raising a finger in the air, "what we have here in Chicago is a money machine. A gold mine. Do you fellows hear me? There's plenty of dough to go around. Probably millions for all of us, including Pollack Joe Saltis, who is the only one that couldn't make it here today. But I can assure you, he's made known his intention to go along with any plan that promises more opportunity for his boys."

Capone observed the interested faces seated around the long table as Torrio continued his rehearsed speech.

"All of our individual enterprises must be protected," Torrio said, "or it'll come back to haunt us the next time Mayor Thompson comes up for reelection. If the public clamor over gang activity increases, we're liable to see a reform candidate get into the mayor's seat."

It was at this point that O'Banion interrupted Torrio in order to offer his advice. With his thick, Irish accent, O'Banion confirmed the truth of Torrio's statement with a raised fist.

"Bill 'The Builder' Thompson is a personal friend of mine," O'Banion said, "and you're right, Johnny. Something has to be done to stop the shit that's happening all around us, or we're liable to lose a mayor who looks the other way when it comes to the wet stuff."

Mike "The Devil" Genna sprang from his chair to express his agreement with the opinions offered. "I gotta say, the mayor is'a berry nice'a guy. It's'a true, no?" he said in his broken English.

Torrio's eyes widened and his chest expanded proudly at the way things were going. "Do you see boys?" he piped. "I'm not alone with this idea of keeping this mayor in office. From now until the election and afterward too, I think we'll find real peace and harmony in the idea of drawing lines across certain areas of the city where a certain gang can operate."

"What area do you consider mine?" inquired Klondike O'Donnell. Torrio reached across the table to unfold a large piece of paper, a map, which had territorial designations outlined in various colors.

"The West Side, as it is now, is yours, Bill," Torrio said. "We're not taking anything away from anybody with this plan. Get it?" O'Donnell seemed satisfied with Torrio's response, and the others rose from their chairs to gather around the map.

Chicago's underworld thrived with Torrio's apportion arrangement and for a period of time, it looked as if their man, Thompson, would be a shoo-in for reelection. Until trouble erupted in the streets, the hijacking of booze delivery trucks belonging to Torrio and O'Banion was the result of long-simmering anger on the part of Spike O'Donnell, who was not to be confused with the Westside O'Donnells.

Spike, whose gang occupied an area in the far Southern tip of Chicago, had just been released from prison after serving time for bank robbery. He was insulted and became furious when informed that not a single member of his gang was invited to the big meet.

"We can't have every wise mug who's got a brother or two in on this," Torrio explained to an intermediary. "Why doesn't Spike and his boys try joining up with one of the gangs that's in the order?"

After a while, Torrio and O'Banion learned the guilty party was, in fact, Spike O'Donnell, and with 1923, an election year, approaching, they realized that an impetuous gang leader such as Spike could very well upset the applecart.

The Chicago peace, initiated by Torrio, was under siege as O'Donnell, aside from his hijacking ventures, ordered his members to shoot up the employees of the Torrio-O'Banion-Capone combine. "I can whip that bird Capone, any day of the week," O'Donnell roared. "Fuck Torrio, fuck Capone and that other monkey gimp from the North Side."

Now the combine was forced to defend not only their business interests, but their very lives as several gunfights erupted upon the streets. The one thing Torrio dreaded came to pass. "Actions like these will only serve to arouse public outrage and the voters will cast their ballots in favor of William E. Dever," Johnny warned.

Dever was a reform candidate whose campaign promise was to get tough on organized crime and that's exactly what came about. Thompson withdrew as a candidate in January 1923, not only because of all the bullets that were flying around the windy city, but on account of the stunning indictment of Fred Lundin in a much-publicized school board scandal. Lundin was a key figure in the Thompson administration.

Capone and Hymie Weiss were designated the field generals, leading the troops into battle against the pesky South Side O'Donnells.

• • •

DURING THIS PERIOD of time, some rather good news did reach Capone's ears, but it was not in regard to the current situation. Instead, it was from back home in Brooklyn, concerning a Sicilian-born ex-Brooklynite named Vincenzo Gibaldi. In a case of mistaken identity, in 1913 Gibaldi's father had been blown away while having his shoes shined in one of the bootblack shops in downtown Brooklyn. Nevertheless, Gibaldi learned that the assassins were two White Hand soldiers who became known to him through a private inquest he had started many years earlier. After being certain in his mind about who committed the slaughter of his father, Gibaldi spent the next few months finding out where they lived and what their habits were. He stalked the responsible hoods and eventually shot them both dead. After the bloody deed was done, Gibaldi placed a nickel in the right-hand palm of each of his victims.

Before fleeing Brooklyn, Gibaldi decided that in order to be completely satisfied, he would also have to take out the leader of the Irish gang, Capone's dogged antagonist, Wild Bill Lovett. Paying the sum of two hundred dollars to an informant for a layout of Lovett's flat on Front Street, Gibaldi waited until he thought the time was right. He even went as far as to court a less-than-ordinary-looking spinster six years his senior, simply because she was Lovett's next-door neighbor.

When the opportune moment arrived, Gibaldi went to the rear of the building and climbed a ladder to reach his prey, who was relaxing in his home with no inkling of the impending attack. Firing his pistol through an open window, Gibaldi thought he finished Lovett off when he saw the .38 caliber slugs rip through the Irish gang leader's chest. What Vincenzo didn't realize was that two of the missiles struck Lovett just above the heart and the third inches below. Lovett would miraculously survive the attack.

Gibaldi sprinted down the fire escape after tossing a shiny nickel into the open window, grinning a sardonic smile as he watched the coin roll close to the fallen gang leader's hand. The three nickels Gibaldi dispensed among the fallen bodies represented the money his father held in his fist on the day he was murdered. Having just finished getting his shine, Thomas Gibaldi was gunned down while holding two nickels in his right hand as payment for the shine. The third nickel was a tip intended for the bootblack. This was his son's way of paying them back.

Although the effort to completely eliminate Lovett was a failure, Capone admired the man's boldness and tenacity for the attempt. Gibaldi immediately fled to Chicago where he was warmly welcomed by Capone and offered a spot in his organization. Later, Gibaldi would gain notoriety as "Machine Gun Jack McGurn," believed to have been the mastermind behind the "Saint Valentine's Day Massacre" and the main triggerman on behalf of his boss, Capone.

The attempt on Lovett's life and his subsequent absence from the Brooklyn scene while convalescing only served to heighten the desire of his rivals. The so-called Black Hand network of Yale affiliates in Brooklyn jumped at each new opportunity offered.

With the violent death of Dinny Meehan, the White Hand Gang had lost a feared and effective leader. Now, with Bill Lovett still nursing his wounds, the daily responsibility of running things on the docks was left to Peg Leg Lonergan, who was primarily known for his deadly nature and not for any special ability to delegate authority. So, true to the adage, "while the cat's away the mice will play," Yale's people pushed their way through the door that opportunity created, until word came down in the fall of 1923 that Lovett was back in action and almost as good as new.

"He moves around a little slower, but he's the same old Bill," stated Joe Flynn, trying his best to negate the hushed conversation at the corner of the bar in the Loader's Club, a local longshoreman's dive, by putting a positive spin on the incident. At the other end of the room, Lovett was just beginning to return to his old form by bending an elbow and lapping up the sauce with renewed vigor. He remained in the place drinking, long after his meeting with a labor union treasurer regarding kickbacks collected in their "under-the-table" employment agency. They would supply new faces (and backs) to the dock-loading and warehouse services in return for a small fee (dues) collected in advance from the job-seeking men. Lovett was at the Loader's Club to pick up his share of the proceeds.

Outside the club, a short, muscular junk dealer named Angelo Petti pushed his cart down the cobblestone street while a cowbell hanging from a wire clanked his impending arrival. He was nicknamed "Penny's Worth" by the residents in his neighborhood because of his miserly habit of offering mere pennies to the youngsters for the copper, lead, and other recyclable articles they obtained, which Angelo promptly sold for much greater profit at a local junkyard.

He rounded the corner of Water Street, turned his cart onto Bridge Street, and slid it alongside the curb in front of the door of the Loader's Club, where he rested for a moment.

His parched throat and the sight of a youngster toting a beer pail filled with the sudsy brew caused him to wonder what this place had to offer and decided to try it out. Entering the club, he stole a backward glance through the window at his junk cart, which was filled with stacks of newspapers, empty bottles, and other discarded treasures that he had collected over the course of the day. Petti noticed the room contained a good-sized bar, where a number of people sat drinking alcoholic beverages while engaging in light conversation. Smiling at the bartender, Michael Tucker, Penny's Worth inquired, "Say, how much is it for a glass of beer?"

"This here's a private club and we don't serve strangers," Tucker replied as he wiped down the area of the bar next to where Angelo Petti's arms were rested.

"Aww, go ahead Mike, sell the man a glass of beer," a sympathetic voice from the sidelines urged.

"Beer is five cents a glass," the annoyed bartender said, manifesting his disapproval of the request by snapping at the junkman. "Do you want some or not?"

"Is it too much to ask for three pennies' worth?" Petti inquired.

This statement caused an uproar to rise from the other customers, whose laughter subsided only with the intervention of a man who had been drinking heavily all day. "Sell the poor ginzo a beer," the drunk said. "I'll lend the fucker the other two cents."

"Thank you very much, sir," Petti replied to the kind offer, tipping the brim of his tattered fedora in the direction of the brown-eyed man who was busy lifting his glass to his lips.

From a vest pocket, Penny's Worth pulled out an old leather snap purse and dug out three pennies, which he placed on the counter before him to the tune of the bartender mumbling aloud, "Guess I shouldn't even think of getting a tip from this cheap prick!"

After finishing his beer, Penny's Worth was able to get a look at the face of the man who made it possible for him to drink at a cut-rate price and realized he'd seen it before. Undoubtedly Irish, he thought. Then, it struck him like a bolt of lightning. "Why that drunken fuck is the one that's called 'Wild Bill,'" he said to himself, as he watched the man place his head on the bar in peaceful repose.

Penny's Worth soon had his revelation confirmed by Tucker, who asked, "Are you all right, Mr. Lovett?"

"Yeah, I'm okay," Lovett slurred. "What happened to my drink?"

"It's right in front of your left hand, Bill," Tucker replied in a meek tone, offering a shrug of his shoulders to another onlooker seated at the extreme end of the bar.

Petti's curiosity was aroused by the quiet conversation now taking place in the rear of the bar between the bartender and a few of his customers, as his dark eyes spotted the shoulder holster inside the sleeping man's disheveled trench coat. Penny's Worth decided it was time to leave. Besides, the generosity offered by Lovett was taken in a casual manner. Now that he was aware of who this drunk was, Petti remembered the remarks he'd heard about his violent nature, especially when he had a little too much booze in him. His reputation as a hotheaded killer told Petti that he had no business remaining on the scene he'd stumbled upon in the Loader's Club that Halloween evening.

The gang leader was really plastered and therefore out of the picture, but it was hard for the junkman to avoid the icy stares of some of the other patrons as they very gently encouraged Wild Bill to lay his body down on a long bench that sat in a corner.

He watched as the man who was later identified as Joe Flynn took off his plaid lumber jacket and, with the bartender's assistance, placed the rolled-up garment under the sleeping gangster's head as a makeshift pillow. Flynn folded his jacket in such a way that when Lovett finally came around, he would be certain to spot the name tag of such a thoughtful person and perhaps think more kindly of his friend, Joe Flynn.

Penny's Worth was able to hear every word the bartender uttered. "Yeah, Joe, I'll leave him sleep it off for a few hours, then I'll wake him up when I get ready to close for the night," Tucker said.

"He should be able to leave under his own power by that time," chimed Flynn.

Petti sucked up the last few drops of his brew and quietly slipped out the door, immediately beginning to push his cart along the street with the bell clanging and the spoked wheels clanking. He felt he was armed with important information that certain parties would be very interested in obtaining and, perhaps, even pay for. Bringing his junk wagon to a stop in front of Jimmy Kelly's gin mill opposite the Long Island Rail Road's Flatbush Avenue depot, Petti waddled in the front door.

"Awww . . . what the fuck do you want in here?" shouted a bartender.

"Hey, we threw you outta here for good, you penny's worth of shit," yelled another. "You'll be in an awful jam if me boss sees you in here. Now be gone!"

"That's just the man I'm looking for," Petti replied with a smug expression on his face. "Your boss, Jimmy Kelly, or his son-in-law, Little Augie Pisano."

"Get outta here right now or I'll give you a swift kick in the seat of your trousers," one of the bartenders threatened.

"Hear me out first," Petti pleaded as the angry bartender made a move to come from behind the bar.

"Just a minute, Duffy," said a booming voice. "I'm friends with Little Augie. What do you want that guy for?" Sham Brown slid down from a bar stool and swaggered toward Petti with a mug of beer still clenched in his brawny fist.

"I have some information he might find valuable," Petti said. "It just so happens that the one they call Wild Bill Lovett is passed out drunk in a nearby bar."

"What's the name of the joint?" Sham inquired of the junkman, who seated himself in a booth reserved for special customers. "It's all right, Mack. You just tell me where to find that Irishman and I'll buy you a drink. Okay?"

"I'll take Scotch whisky," Petti said. "You can call me Angelo."

"Gimme a glass of Scotch for my friend, Angelo," Sham said to Duffy. Then, turning to Petti he said, "Now, c'mon, out with it, or I just might break your fuckin' head right now."

"But you see, it's like this," Petti said. "I need dough fast. My poor wife is sick with consumption and I don't have the money to take her to a doctor."

"Okay, okay," Sham said. "I'll stake you to a ten-dollar bill. Now, are you gonna talk?" Neither Sham nor the people who regularly came in contact with Petti were aware of the small fortune Petti had amassed and secreted under his mattress at home, which was a single room atop a garage.

The junkman paid very little rent for the dwelling because he also served in the capacity of night watchman for the fleet of coal trucks the landlord allowed to park there. If people had known of his true fortune, they might have chosen to nickname him "Pretty Penny" instead of Penny's Worth. Petti was a bachelor who sailed to America from Trapani, Sicily, in 1913 and looked forward to the day when he would return to the town of his birth as a rich man.

Petti was surprised at Sham's excited response to the information he dispensed, and watched Sham make a dash for the telephone. The Yale associate was busy gathering the troops in an effort to catch the Irishman off guard and, according to the snitch, vulnerable to a surprise visit.

The junkman's eyes lit up at the sight of the twenty-dollar bill he'd been presented with. While the amount of money offered exceeded his expectations, he pointed down to his empty glass.

"Give my friend the whole bottle," Sham said aloud. Then, in a whisper, he said, "Duffy, I want you to keep this fucker here until I get back. Get it?"

"Why sure, Shammy," Duffy said. "Judging by the way he's sucking on that bottle, I don't think I'll have a bit of trouble holding him here even after closing. If that's what you want."

"That's just what I want," Sham replied. "And I don't think it'll be that late."

Sham had called Yale to verify his boss's approval of the long-anticipated opportunity to terminate Lovett. Naturally, Yale happily agreed to the operation, but reminded his hireling of the importance of taking tactical precautions.

"Anybody who knows about this piece of work has to be dealt with, too," Yale told Sham. "Do you understand?" After hearing Sham's affirmative response, Yale dispatched two more of his charges, Johnny "Silk Stockings" Giustra and Vincenzo Mangano, who were having dinner at Cafiero's restaurant on nearby President Street. Mangano promptly called his brother, Philip, who in turn notified a neighborhood hatchet-man, Willie Alterie, a.k.a. "*Dui Cuttedi*" (Two Knives), who was known to do odd jobs at a price.

• • •

THE TWO AUTOMOBILES parked near the base of the Brooklyn Bridge on the darkest corner of Water Street had been quickly emptied of their sinister passengers, who piled into a third car, which had Sham Brown behind the wheel. They listened intently to Sham's description of the Loader's Club's layout as it was revealed to him by the junkman, Angelo Petti.

After discussing their scheme in a matter of minutes, they paired off once again, re-entered their respective vehicles, and started a three-car procession by rolling slowly around the dimly lit block. The first car came to a stop a little bit short of the door to the Loader's Club, while the others lined up behind it. Young-looking Philip Mangano hopped out of the lead automobile onto the street, walked to the door, and began peering through one of the windows. At first, the place seemed empty of life, until he noticed a man wearing a white apron, sweeping the floor behind the bar.

"Excuse me, sir, does your name happen to be Tucker?" the younger of the Mangano brothers inquired, placing a dollar bill on the bar.

"You got that right, lad," said Tucker. "Now, how do you happen to know me name?"

"A friend of mine by the name of Joe told me this was a good stop on the way home," Mangano said.

"You talking about Joe Flynn? Why, he just left the place a little while ago," said the bartender. "Where do you know him from?"

Mangano's eyes darted about the the large room while he tried to discern whether or not the bench hidden in the shadows in the rear of the club actually held their target.

"I'm to start work in the morning with his crew," Mangano replied. "How long have you been working here, Mr. Tucker?"

"I've been tending bar here for around six months now, but as soon as me ship comes in, I'm gone," Tucker said, reaching down for a bottle of hooch. "You'll have to drink up fast, lad, because I'm gonna close the place soon."

"Tell me please, Mr. Tucker, where's the toilet?"

"Straight off to the right," Tucker said." Pointing a finger, he added, "Please, son, don't be disturbing me friend who's lying down in back. He's sleeping it off."

That statement assured Philip Mangano that the information was true, and he decided not to waste time. He poured the shot of whiskey down his throat, said a quick "so long, Mr. Tucker," and disappeared out the door.

A few moments later three of the six men strolled into the place. Two of them, Vincenzo Mangano and Johnny Giustra, headed straight to the back, while Alterie subdued the bartender by holding a knife to his ribs. He barked an order to the panic-stricken worker to remain quiet and docile if he didn't want to die.

Meanwhile, Philip Mangano, standing halfway out the door, was keeping an eye on the street. Philip broke the tension of the situation by remarking to Alterie, "Hey, Willy, bring that bottle on the bar along with you. That stuff's not too bad."

"Where are you bringing me?" the shaking bartender inquired of his assailants as tears welled in his eyes. He noticed that the two men headed to the rear of the club were drawing their pistols as Alterie pushed him out the door and into the front seat of a waiting car, where Sham Brown kept a pistol trained on his head.

Dui Cuttedi heard the sound of gunfire when he headed back inside, and when he reached the scene he saw Johnny Silk Stockings and Vincenzo Mangano still blasting away at Wild Bill's body. After firing about eight rounds (only three bullets finding their mark inside the chest of the sleeping gangleader), Lovett stirred from his drunken stupor and made a futile attempt to claw his own .45 automatic from under his left armpit.

The finishing touch was applied when Alterie raced past his cohorts waving a sharp meat cleaver that caught a glimmer of light from an overhead lamp. Alterie swung the butcher's chopper down full-force at the victim's head while screaming an eerie epithet: "Trick or treat, Bill!" That brutal act ended Lovett's protest as well as his life.

The men calmly walked out to the waiting cars and drove to Flatbush Avenue to gather the other loose thread, Angelo "Penny's Worth" Petti. He was briskly hustled into the car commandeered by Sham Brown, who ordered the whiskey-saturated snitch to return the twenty dollars he had so generously paid him and drove the car across town to a remote, swampy area near Jamaica Bay called Bergen Beach. There, both Petti and Tucker were shot in the back of the head and their bodies dumped into two hastily dug graves.

The Halloween-night murder of Wild Bill Lovett proved catastrophic for the Irish in the violent battle that raged for the docks. With Dinny Meehan gone and now his partner, the much-feared Bill Lovett, permanently out of the way too, the Black Hand organization soon gained control of most of the action on the moneymaking Brooklyn waterfront.

• • •

A VOTE FOR Dever is a vote for law and order! So it was trumpeted, and so it came to pass. William E. Dever, the reform mayor of Chicago, kept his campaign promise to rid the town of its criminal element and did so in an effective manner. The new mayor appointed a tough, honest-minded Chief of Police named Morgan A. Collins and set him to the task of ridding the city of its booming liquor industry. Reminding Chief Collins that there was a national dry law in effect, Dever demanded that all the laws of the land be scrupulously enforced.

"Any policeman who looks the other way while criminal activity is taking place on his beat is assumed to be a part of the problem," he said. "Those doing so will be stripped of their shields and fired immediately."

Hundreds of padlocked doors were plastered with official police notices that read: RAIDED PREMISES—CLOSED BY ORDER OF THE POLICE DEPARTMENT—CITY OF CHICAGO, ILLINOIS, as one police raid after another racked the illegal booze parlors, gambling dens, and bordellos around town with a devastating loss of property and income for those concerned. Dever did make good on his promise to kick the combine out of Chicago.

After a short relocation of Torrio's headquarters to the Four Deuces, they were obliged to pull up stakes and leave town. Torrio settled on the idea of moving the operations to nearby Cicero, where the chances of making inroads in the upcoming elections seemed excellent.

Torrio's speculative plunge into the suburban political scene included the assistance of the North Side biggie, Dion O'Banion, who offered some of his goons to aid in the intimidation of voters and the bribing of local officials in order to assure that a crime-friendly government would assume control of Cicero in 1924.

A family tragedy befell Capone on the day of the otherwise triumphant election, though. His older brother, Frank, was shot to death by the police. Frank, his cousin, Charlie Fischetti, and a third Capone hood were standing close to the polls on Cicero and Twenty-Second Street, when two plainclothes detectives spotted them browbeating a voter to endorse their candidate, Joseph Z. Klenha. Detectives Philip McGlynn and Lyle Grogan fired their service weapons at the trio and one slug from McGlynn's .38 caliber revolver tunneled its way into Frank Capone's heart, killing him instantly. During the subsequent inquest, the detective claimed that Frank Capone had fired several rounds from his confiscated weapon. "All I did was return fire in defense of my own life," he said.

It was a case of mistaken identity on the part of Frank Capone, who may have yanked his gun out thinking one of the approaching detectives was a sworn enemy of the Capone family named Rodger Touhy.

Capone bought his brother an expensive, silver-plated casket for a grand farewell replete with over twenty thousand dollars' worth of floral pieces arranged by the mob's favorite florist, Deany O'Banion.

After Frank was buried at Mount Carmel Cemetery, Capone ordered his father's remains unearthed from his grave in Calvary Cemetery in Queens and shipped to Chicago for reinterment next to his brother. Frank's death greatly grieved Capone, but he could take some solace in the results of the elections. The local political hacks, fueled with promises of financial gain without limit, worked hard to ensure the criminal element's victory. Some of them actually believed they were following the progressive tenets of the grand experiment that was taking firm hold in Russia at the time, only this experiment promised: "From each according to their ability, to each according to his greed."

And it was greed that forced the Genna brothers to break their contract—a contract that now appeared to heavily favor the Torrio, O'Banion, and Capone combine while their own Chicago interests were constantly being harassed by the forces of good. Perhaps their peculiar territorial rights helped to force the smaller but driven Genna gang to rethink their status. Their shrinking empire, which consisted of whorehouses and rot-gut whiskey, was something that demanded immediate attention. When the Gennas learned that Torrio had offered O'Banion an interest in several Cicero gambling enterprises including a plush establishment called "The Ship," their jealousy reached a peak. Mike "The Devil" allowed his whiskey sales-men to enter O'Banion territory in an effort to line up customers for their three-dollar-a-gallon booze, which, although much inferior, was priced at half of what O'Banion charged.

"Those Gennas don't give a damn about the rules," O'Banion com-plained to Capone.

"Maybe you should go and have a talk with them before I make sure they have a worse time than the one I gave that fuckin' Spike O'Donnell and his crew."

The following day, both Torrio and Capone lunched with Mike and Angelo Genna at Diamond Joe Esposito's South Side restau-rant, Bella Napoli. By this point, the run-in Capone had with the Genna brothers over the crooked card game he was sucked into a few years prior had been long forgotten, and looked upon as a bad joke that went a little too far. But now, the Devil vehemently denied introducing his moonshine past the boundary lines set up by the combine. He claimed that freelancing outsiders were the ones responsible for the Genna brand of liquor turning up in O'Banion territory.

Speaking in Italian, Mike Genna claimed the North Side Irishman held a grudge against them simply because they were Italians. "He calls us 'foreigners' and thinks he can force us out of business with phony accusations and setting one Italian family against another," Genna said. "If it wasn't for Miguel Merlo (Chicago president of the Unione Siciliana), who my brothers and I respect, and his misguided friendship with that Irish prick, we would have done him in a long time ago, Alphonso."

Capone concluded the conversation with a stern warning. "Mike," he said, "if what Deany is accusing you of has any truth to it, you'd better cut the shit out. Do you understand?"

After the meeting with the Gennas, the encroachment into O'Banion turf was somewhat restrained, but the six brothers con-tinued dealing their whiskey in limited amounts throughout greater Chicago by independent jobbers.

To make good on his lost revenue and to teach the intruders a lesson at the same time, O'Banion ordered his henchmen to rustle a $30,000 shipment of booze destined for delivery to a small Genna warehouse in Little Italy. The brothers promptly brought their beef to Torrio's attention at his headquarters in the Hawthorne hotel and walked away without satisfaction.

Sometime later, around May 1924, O'Banion expressed his frustration to Torrio. "John, me bucko," he confided, "I'm seriously considering retirement as a way to avoid all the pressures that keep me from enjoying life. Yes, John, I'm planning to give it up and live out my days on my good friend Louie Alterie's ranch, in Colorado.

"Sit yourself down, John," he continued as his tone grew serious. "I have a good deal for you to consider."

Torrio's initial reaction to O'Banion's retirement talk was one of surprise and shock. But soon, a pleasant thought occurred to him, the possibility of conducting business with Deany's underboss, Hymie Weiss, who was considered by many to be the strategic force behind the excitable and often dangerous O'Banion's success story.

"Would you be interested in buying my share of the Sieben plant?" O'Banion asked.

"What price are you asking?" a smiling Torrio inquired.

"I'll sell it to you lock, stock, and barrel—the whole thing—for five hundred thousand," O'Banion said. "What do you think?"

"This is a shock to me," Torrio said, "but if you're really serious, Deany, I'll have the money ready for you within a day or so."

On the morning of Monday, May 19, 1924, the deal was finalized and the new owner of the brewery toured his plant to oversee a large shipment that was being prepared to leave the premises. Then suddenly, the place got raided. It was a military-style operation that included machine-gun toting police who handcuffed the brewery's startled employees and placed them all under arrest. Torrio and O'Banion found themselves caught in the middle of the roundup. Chief of Police Collins turned the despondent owner of the Sieben plant, Torrio, over to the feds for violation of the Volstead Act. It was a charge that made him subject to jail time, while O'Banion got off with only paying a light fine.

Torrio fumed while fighting the legal battles the ensuing months provided while he mourned the loss not only of the half million dollars he had paid O'Banion for the brewery, but his initial investment as well. He couldn't shake the nagging thought that a high-level police official had tipped O'Banion off to the raid in advance and that the Irishman had cleverly duped him into buying a shuttered plant.

O'Banion's refusal to return any part of the money Torrio paid him for the brewery aggravated Torrio, but O'Banion insisted that he had no knowledge of an impending raid and that a deal was a deal. In Torrio's favor was that the government order to lock the place was for one year only.

"After the dust settles, Johnny, in a year's time, you'll be owning the whole plant outright and you can reopen with a permit to continue the manufacture of legal 'near beer,'" O'Banion claimed. His assurances weren't enough to soothe the ego of the suave Torrio, who would never allow his inner feelings about the situation to be known to an enemy and smilingly accepted the Irishman's apology with quiet grace. Meanwhile, the Torrio-Capone company was rapidly running out of patience. Its stockholders, no longer believing O'Banion's retirement announcement, looked to forge new alliances for the future. But it was the news of Chicago's Unione Siciliana President, Miguel Merlo's, terminal cancer that helped seal O'Banion's fate.

The Genna brothers' loyalty to Merlo's prohibitive edict in regard to warring against O'Banion was to be honored as long as Merlo lived. But after he was gone, they figured on making some changes in the North Side territory. Miguel Merlo, a trusted advisor in business dealings, was essential in settling disputes among friends. Working diligently within charitable and political circles in Chicago, his respect extended to the community he served so well. Soft-spoken and likable, Merlo had always been a perfect intermediary for the mob's front organization.

The fact that a Sicilian, Miguel Merlo, took orders from Calabrian-born Frankie Yale, national president of the influential fraternal and benevolent organization until his death in 1928, definitely disproved the often-repeated statement that one must be of Sicilian extraction in order to become a member of the Unione Siciliana. As a matter of fact, the Unione counted among its growing membership thousands of Italians who came here from all parts of southern Italy, Calabria, Naples, as well as Sicily.

Capone tried to mend fences with the Genna brothers by inviting Angelo to the Ship, where Genna was treated like royalty and served complimentary food and drinks. But wouldn't you know it, he lost a bundle of dough in the process and asked for a marker. Closing time found Angelo Genna almost flat broke and despondent, when Capone walked over and tore up the marker as a personal favor.

One of O'Banion's cronies who was a witness to the scene promptly notified O'Banion, who still maintained an interest in the joint. O'Banion became adamant about collecting his share of the money, even going so far as to call Angelo Genna on the telephone, telling him that Capone had no right to make good on gambling losses and demanding that Angelo pay up.

This insult to the Genna clan drew the criticism of O'Banion's underboss, Hymie Weiss, who reminded his leader, "Deany, you might fashion yourself as being a top-notch gunman like Johnny Ringo or Billy the Kid with that fast draw of yours, but take my advice and stop insulting people like the Gennas or someday they won't allow you the time to draw." O'Banion laughed off the prophetic statement with the remark, "Fuck those dirty Black Hand ginzos."

A few days before Merlo succumbed to his deadly disease, Johnny Torrio placed a call to Frankie Yale in Brooklyn, advising him that his Chicago representative of the Unione was not expected to live out the week. Since Yale ran a legitimate funeral home on Fourteenth Avenue in Brooklyn as a front and was considered an expert in making funeral arrangements, Torrio asked the surprised national president of the organization for another "special request." "We hope that when you come to Chicago to pay your last respects to Merlo, you would consider making arrangements for another very important funeral that we're planning," he said. "This one requires your personal handiwork as an undertaker par excellence." Torrio put the flattened palm of his hand against his own lips and threw a kiss into the air when Yale made it clear that he understood his Chicago associate's statement and was in complete agreement with the proposal to lend a helping hand.

Yale arrived in Chicago accompanied by two of his men, Salvatore Pollaccio and a recent recruit named Gandolfo Civito, who used the alias "Frankie Marlowe." They went straight to a meeting at Colosimo's restaurant where they were greeted by Torrio, Capone, the Genna brothers, and an old Brooklyn friend, Frank Nitto, now Nitti, was recently corralled into Capone's Chicago camp with the offer of becoming head treasurer, or collector of revenues for Capone's expanding empire.

The well-planned hit on O'Banion would take place in his Schofield's florist shop, where the Irishman would be busy taking orders for floral tributes to the late Miguel Merlo. Yale asked to be driven past the shop by somebody who was familiar with the area, and Mike Genna offered to help in that regard. Yale was mainly interested in traffic conditions in and around the area and in selecting the best escape route to ensure a clean getaway.

Late in the afternoon, Yale was on the phone with O'Banion inquiring about the price of a large, white-rose wreath he wished to be delivered to the Merlo funeral. "Would it be possible for me to see the floral display or one like it before I pay for it?" Yale asked. "I'm not skimping on the price mind you. I just want to be sure that I like it."

Identifying himself as "Frank Notaro," Yale claimed the deceased was a cherished friend.

"I won't be able to attend the wake because I have to leave town by midday on the morrow to be at my ailing mother's bedside," he said.

"As a matter of fact, Mr. Notaro, I'll start working on it right now if you promise to stop by in the morning to pay for it," replied the obliging florist.

"Of course, good sir," Yale said. "And perhaps while I'm there, I will personally write out my expression of sympathy to his family on a card."

"You can pass by the shop anytime tomorrow after ten AM in order to view the piece and I'll be here to ensure the wreath is to your liking," O'Banion said.

The next step in Yale's plan was to select the actual hit team that would accompany him into the shop, and he asked Capone to assemble at least twenty of his best men for a meeting somewhere that wouldn't draw too much attention. Both Torrio and Capone agreed to include the Genna mob in the conspiracy, figuring that sooner or later Mike the Devil, who hated the Irishman, was bound to try getting rid of the North Side leader himself. The idea was to set a precedent in their new relationship by placing themselves in charge of the hit and giving the brothers a sense of inclusion at the same time. They also decided that half the gunners requested by Yale should come from the Genna gang.

The get-together was held in the basement level of the "Ship." Frankie Yale held a deck of playing cards in his hands and asked the assembled group, excluding Torrio and Capone, to spread themselves around a pool table. Soon, the shuffling movements stopped and the twenty-odd men stood looking down at the head of the table, where Yale was bending over with his hands extended. When he was convinced they were all watching, he flipped a single card face up in the center of the table. It was the ace of spades.

"Now everybody here knows what this card represents, *morto'rio* (a funeral)," Yale said with a grin. Then he reached over to place another card under it. Before doing so, he displayed the ace of clubs to the puzzled spectators and placed it underneath the other black Ace. "This means flowers for O'Banion!" He howled uproariously at his ironic exhibition, while the others looked around for an explanation.

"We're gonna do a piece of work on that florist guy in the morning right in his own flower shop," Yale explained. "This deck of cards will decide which of you guys will have the pleasure of going with me into the shop to do the actual work. Most of you will be driving cars to act as interference during the getaway. This is better than drawing straws. The two mugs who get hit with the remaining aces go inside the place with me, understand?"

Yale started dealing the cards around the table, turning them over one by one and tossing them in front of each interested party.

"Anyone who's dealt a picture card is considered to be a driver and can withdraw from the table," he informed Tony "Batters" Accardo, who received a king. Albert Anselmi didn't flinch when the ace of diamonds came his way, but he remained standing in place long enough to find out who his other partner would be. Eventually, the final ace was tossed in front of John Scalise. Both men were from the Genna gang.

After everyone's roles in the hit were settled, Yale assured them all of his confidence in the combined effort that would accomplish the work with no trouble at all. When questioned as to the best method of getting the drop on the quick-triggered O'Banion, Yale answered, "I'm gonna offer the man a handshake!"

The morning of November 10, 1924, saw a small army converging in six separate automobiles onto North State Street with the lead car, occupied by Angelo and Mike Genna, pulling close to the curb only a car's length past the door to the shop. The second car, driven by Sammy Pollaccio, held the pistol-toting members of the death squad—Anselmi, Scalise, and Yale—while four other cars stationed themselves in various positions in order to block traffic even if it took faking an accident to assure the safety of the getaway car.

Looking through the window of the floral shop, Yale immediately informed his partners in crime when he spotted their well-dressed prey, who was known to always have a white carnation pinned to his lapel. The plan was for Albert Anselmi to enter first and remain stationed near the door until they were assured that no surprises would come from the street.

Anselmi quietly entered the establishment acting like a potential customer, showing interest in a plant that hung near the entrance, and drew little attention from the busy man behind the counter.

Within seconds, Scalise and Yale also entered the shop and, as it turned out, their timing couldn't have been better because the only other person in the shop was an employee who was busy sweeping floral debris toward the rear of the store. Walking toward their target, Yale's inquiry was soft-spoken and courteous. "Are you Mr. O'Banion, sir?" he asked.

"That's right," O'Banion said. "You boys must be from Mike Merlo, correct?"

"Yes, I'm Mr. Notaro," replied Yale, extending an arm to offer a friendly handshake. "I ordered the white-rose wreath."

Still holding a pair of shears in one hand, O'Banion reached over the counter with the other hand, a smile on his unsuspecting face. Suddenly, the florist realized the vice-like grip applied by the strong hand of Frankie Yale had an insidious purpose when he saw that the browsing customer was brandishing a pistol. Upon hearing the first shot fired, O'Banion's employee flew out a rear door while his boss was being riddled by three guns pumping bullets into his body.

Two slugs plowed through the right side of his chest while a third tore through his larynx and another through the side of his neck. The fifth shot hit the left side of O'Banion's face as Yale finally released the victim's hand and watched the body slump to the floor. Yale knelt down beside the dead Irish gangster, pressed the barrel of his gun to the man's head, and fired the final round.

Pollaccio quickly flung open the rear door of the blue Jewett sedan as the blasts coming from the shop told him it was almost time to get rolling. He watched the first car, which had one of the Gennas behind the wheel, gunning his motor in preparation for a hasty departure as the three men bolted from the store and dived into the getaway cars. Pollaccio screeched the car away from the curb and followed the lead car, which raced past the Holy Name Cathedral with four backup cars trailing behind it, ready to run interference that was never needed.

Inside the main car, Yale offered congratulations to his efficient team consisting of Pollaccio, the driver, and especially to the hitmen,

Anselmi and Scalise, two Sicilians, who as a team, would participate in no less than thirty-one slayings in the future.

. . .

O'BANION'S BODY LAY in state at the Sbarbaro Funeral Home, owned by Assistant State's Attorney John Sbarbaro. Visitors claimed that O'Banion looked like he was sleeping as he reposed in a ten-thousand-dollar bronze casket fashioned with an eight-by-ten-inch plate glass window on the casket's lid, directly over the dead man's face. Over twenty thousand mourners filed past the coffin to view the remains of the fallen mobster; among them were Torrio, Capone, Frank Nitti, and the Genna brothers.

The murder of O'Banion, contrary to Torrio's hopes, brought about the most tumultuous era of gang warfare ever to descend upon the likes of Chicago. O'Banion's reorganized crew, now led by Earl "Little Hymie" Weiss, remained loyal to their new boss in memory of their slain leader.

The next round of violence took place only a couple of months after O'Banion's death and it was directed at Johnny Torrio, who the North Side mob held responsible for the hit on their leader. Earl Wojciechowski's genuine sorrow at the loss of his friend was turning him inside out, and the obligation to retaliate against Torrio grew more intense with each daily reminder of the now deceased good and generous boss who treated his men very well. Wojciechowski, a Polish American better known as Hymie Weiss, assumed leadership control of the North Side gang with an undeniable obligation to avenge the loss.

"That fuckin' sissy Torrio ain't gonna know what hit him!" the short, thin-faced Weiss told a member of his crew who had inquired about the hit. "Just let me choose the time and place." Weiss's crew knew when their new leader was pumped up. He was extremely volatile and many people considered him to be one of the most feared criminals in Chicago in the 1920s. Eventually, even the undaunted

Capone would learn to respect the violent nature of the new leader of the North Side.

Meanwhile, Capone had his hands full contending with the Genna brothers, who seized control of the Unione Siciliana immediately following Miguel Merlo's burial. They marched into the offices on South Dearborn street and gave notice to the clerical help that changes in staff were imminent, announcing Angelo Genna as the new president of the organization.

Capone registered his complaint with the national head of the Unione, Frankie Yale. Capone hoped to replace Merlo with his own man, Tony Lombardo, explaining to Yale that Lombardo had both the personality and the temperament to affect a smooth continuance of the good will that had been established in community affairs by Mike Merlo. Angelo Genna, Capone reasoned, was a hothead who couldn't be trusted.

Yale kept out of the internal bickering of the two sides with the acceptance of Angelo Genna as president of the society, advising Capone to allow the Gennas the opportunity to prove themselves both capable to run the Unione while hopefully remaining loyal to the same profit-sharing system as practiced by the deceased Mike Merlo.

With North Side leader O'Banion out of the way, the Genna mob, swollen in size and stature, quickly began to encroach within the northern boundaries that had previously been off-limits to their gang. This further enfuriated Hymie Weiss, who assumed Torrio had a hand in a double-deal.

That's when Hymie decided to take his vengeance out on Torrio. After having a few of his boys stake out Torrio's residence, he learned that Torrio had left his home with his wife to attend an auction. Weiss figured that the time was right for a surprise afternoon visit. It was a little past four in the afternoon on that unusually mild day in January, with the temperature around forty degrees, when Torrio's Lincoln sedan came to a halt in front of 7011 South Clyde Avenue.

Parked in a gray Cadillac were two other men besides Hymie Weiss: the wheelman, Schemer Drucci, and a dimple-chinned subordinate named George Moran, who gained notoriety as "Bugs" Moran, the late-arriving, albeit main, target of the Saint Valentine's Massacre, which in 1929 claimed the lives of seven members of the North Side mob.

Moran was of medium height and built like a wrestler, with a moon-shaped face and nerves of steel. He, along with the other members of the hit team, waited patiently for Torrio's arrival. Making their final preparations, Moran slipped a loaded clip into place on his .45 caliber pistol while his boss, Weiss, sat beside him brandishing a twin-barreled shotgun.

Torrio opened the door and held a hand out to assist his wife, Anna, in stepping out of the car, when the attack began. Bugs Moran rushed the Lincoln while firing his .45 at Torrio, catching Torrio on the right arm. Weiss fired a blast from his shotgun that hit the ducking target in the jaw. Three more shots discharged by Moran's .45 hit Torrio in the chest and abdomen.

It was truly a miracle, Torrio thought, when he finally regained consciousness following the surgery, that he could hear his wife's voice through the fog repeating what the doctors had told her. "With a little help from providence, he'll make it," she said. Anna had escaped the attack unscathed, while their chauffeur received only a leg wound.

Puny and frail upon his release from the hospital, Torrio turned himself over to authorities for a small jail term related to the outstanding charges against him for the Sieben Brewery incident. One day when Capone was visiting him in jail, Torrio informed his partner, "It's all yours, Al. I'm leaving Chicago for good. I'm planning to retire and get away from this dangerous situation as soon as possible." Torrio promptly turned over all his business interests to Capone and did, in fact, leave town and the rackets forever. He lived out his days in a quiet, anonymous fashion in Brooklyn.

As for the Gennas gone bad, Capone had plans for them that included an attack on May 25, 1925, by four of his hired hands against the first and most impugning member of that family, Angelo. After a wild auto chase, Angelo crashed his car into a lamppost and met his doom via a shotgun blast delivered by his pursuers. Newspapers at the time reported the incident was probably initiated by the rival North Side gang, but it's now believed that the orders for Angelo Genna's murder originated with Capone.

Sammy Ammatuna, one of the Genna's more aggressive soldiers, took it upon himself (with the family's approval) to assume the presidency of the Unione Siciliana, while his onetime pal, Capone, was fast losing respect for the audacious Samoots Ammatuna.

Less than a month later, on June 13, Mike "The Devil" Genna was cruising the streets in search of revenge. He was convinced that the North Side gang were the ones that did the job on his brother, so he recruited Albert Anselmi and John Scalise to drive around town with him night after night in search of some of Weiss's crew. On one of those excursions, another wild shoot-out developed. This one involved the police who cut off one of the two warring parties while the others made their escape. The Genna hoods were forced into a gun battle with the law. When it was over, there were two dead and two wounded policemen and a mortally wounded Mike Genna, who died en route to the hospital from loss of blood while his two cohorts managed to escape unharmed. If this was not enough to convince the remaining four brothers to quit the rackets, Capone's next message to the family certainly was.

On July 8, 1925, around ten thirty in the morning, Anthony "The Gent" Genna, received a call from someone known to him to arrange a meeting regarding a money matter. Anthony spotted the friend waiting for him in front of a grocery store on the corner of Grand Street, and was surprised by two other men who jumped out from a nearby hallway with blazing pistols.

James, Sam, and Peter Genna decided that enough was too much and grabbed their families and whatever resources they could muster and pulled up stakes, moving out of town and the rackets, for the sake of survival.

The deadly duo of Scalise and Anselmi decided the wise thing for them was to accept the offer from Capone to join his clique.

Ammatuna's reign as president of the Unione was short-lived, as he succumbed to gunshot wounds suffered while ambushed inside a barber shop at Capone's order.

The next day, the Unione would have its third president within a four-month period as Tony Lombardo, Capone's longtime friend and choice for the top position, finally assumed control of the organization.

14

Fish in the Barrel

WHILE FRANKIE YALE and the Mafia were busy assuming piecemeal control of the Brooklyn piers, the years 1923–25 proved to be an extremely hazardous period of time for any young man considering joining the ranks of the underworld. Though rare opportunities existed for the naive who aspired to higher status within their respective cliques, most found the route to be an extremely unhealthy one. As a matter of fact, the struggle between the Italians at the gate and the entrenched White Hand mob would eventually claim the lives of more than forty Irish and a little over half as many of Yale's Italian forces.

Most of those killed were expendable youngsters. But when the corpse turned out to be a man of Dinny Meehan's ilk, or Wild Bill Lovett's, it created a serious void. The losses of the two White Hand commanders were particularly hard for the gang's new boss, the killing machine known as Richard "Peg Leg" Lonergan, to take in stride. After being informed of the brutal slaughter of his sister's husband, Wild Bill Lovett, the impulsive Lonergan went into a rage and swore an angry blood oath against the man who ordered the hit.

The opportunity to strike against his Black Hand adversary would come in mid-November 1925. Yale had stopped by one of the several "speaks" he owned in Brooklyn; this one was located on

Neptune Avenue off the corner of West Fifteenth Street in Coney Island, just a short hop from his dance palace, the Harvard Inn. His mind may have been diverted by the crowded intersection filled with pedestrians, or perhaps it was the secure feeling of being so close to his Coney Island citadel that caused the Brooklyn crime boss to neglect eyeballing the Pierce-Arrow pulling away from the opposite curb.

Inside the stalking sedan, the redheaded Richard Lonergan (called Peg Leg only by those outside his circle) was directing his driver, Kid Eddie Lynch, to follow behind at a safe distance. Three other hoods in Lonergan's employ that evening were "Cute Charlie" Donnelly, Patrick "Happy" Malone, and Neil "Needles" Ferry.

"That's the dago fuck I've been waiting to get off-guard for some time," shouted Lonergan as he watched the Brooklyn crime boss enter his club. "We'll wait right here to see how many guys he's gonna have with him when he comes out. Then, we'll strike fast and hard. Ah," he murmured, "tonight he belongs to the ages!"

They waited around for a half hour before seeing the singular figure of Yale, with his dark fedora, exit the club and re-enter his black Buick with its wheels pointed toward Coney Island Avenue.

"That fucker is as good as dead," Lonergan proclaimed in a glee-ful tone, adding, "Eddie, when I give you the command, you'll pull alongside of him. Do you understand?"

"Gottcha, Richie," the youngster responded with a smirk. "This should be as easy as shooting fish in a barrel."

Near the intersection of Coney Island Avenue and Avenue U, Yale slowed his car down in response to a traffic signal.

"Quick, Eddie, get alongside of him," Lonergan urged his driver.

Two members of the artillery crew crowded the rear window and planted their sights on the moving target while the wild-eyed Lonergan leaned forward in his seat to accommodate one of the hired guns whose .38 caliber pistol also shared the front window of the soon-to-be-spurting automobile.

"Get ready to burn in hell, you dago fuck." Lonergan swore as his car drew parallel to Yale's Buick. "Now, let him have it!"

An instant before the actual blasts occurred, the Black Hand crime boss had been startled by the thunderous roar of the dark Pierce-Arrow sedan, which seemed intent on passing him. His first reaction was to accelerate quickly, moving his car to the right side of the street in order to give the maniac who was pulling alongside plenty of leeway. Just as the crescendo began, Kid Eddie nervously reacted to the deafening blasts with a sudden swerve that allowed the left tire to make contact with the trolley rails in the middle of the road. The resulting bounce caused the marksmen to completely miss their target inside the Buick.

Yale probably thought his luck had ran out when a volley of bullets ripped into the roof and upper portion of his car, and cursed when a deflected slug struck him in the left forearm. Fortunately for him, a uniformed policeman, George Meegan, was just exiting a grocery store a little way up the street when he chanced upon the gun play. Drawing out his service revolver, the officer fired a few shots at the instigators of the mayhem, the occupants of the Pierce-Arrow, which made a screeching left turn on Avenue U and promptly disappeared down the fog-laden street.

Yale was able to drive himself to the Coney Island Hospital, where he explained to police that he had no idea who his attackers were. Meanwhile, Lonergan was chewing out Eddie Lynch in the company of the rest of the gang. Seated alongside the shaky youngster, Lonergan was screaming in his ear. "You stupid fuck! You blew it for us," he yelled. "Do you know that?"

Lynch tried to explain. "What the hell was I supposed to do, Richie? I thought there was enough room to pass and the tire hit the trolley track, it could have happened to anybody."

"Yeah, well I say it's your fucking fault, you prick," Lonergan said. "When you drive for me, you're supposed to watch where the fuck you're going." Lonergan raised the barrel of his .38 revolver and pointed at Lynch's head. "I should give it to you right now, you fucking blind bastard. Like shooting fish in a barrel you say, heh?"

Needles Ferry tried calming the boss down. "Take it easy, Rich," he said. "We'll get another crack at that high and mighty Frankie Yale,"

Eddie Lynch had a tough time living the blunder down. As a matter of fact, in Lonergan's eyes he was a fuckup who didn't deserve a second chance. But Aaron Harms, a good friend of Peg Leg's, intervened on Lynch's behalf and suggested he be given a chance to redeem himself.

Two weeks later, Lonergan dispatched Harms, along with Lynch, to do a hit on another Black Hand gangster, Jimmy "Filezee" DeAmato, who was cutting into the Irish gambling action on the Furman Street piers. The excitable Lonergan addressed them in no uncertain terms. "This ginzo has to get it now!" he said, "and he should be a lot easier to croak than that fucking Yale." Looking into the face of Lynch, Peg Leg added in a sarcastic tone, "Easier, because this chisler is always on the street, Eddie. And you won't have a fucking steering wheel in your hand."

It seemed that Lonergan took each and every opportunity to ridicule Lynch, who promised his boss that this time he would give his very best effort to the assigned job.

It was around ten-fifteen on a Sunday evening in early December when Harms and Lynch spotted DeAmato hoofing it along Hoyt Street in downtown Brooklyn. They decided to park their car and began to shadow the young Italian, who managed to spot the two bloodhounds on his tail. DeAmato livened his pace, eventually making a right onto busy Fulton Street, where people were doing some evening window shopping in front of the swanky department stores located there. Filezee figured he'd lose them by crossing the wide street to the opposite sidewalk, where a large number of people were milling around in front of a Chinese restaurant. Eddie Lynch did, in fact, lose sight of their intended victim for a moment and muttered dejectedly to his partner, "We'd better forget about catching up to him now, Aaron, but maybe, if we keep our distance, the Ginzo will turn down one of the side streets."

"Aw shucks," Harms responded. "If you think I'm gonna pass up this chance, you're crazy!" Harms continued following DeAmato's trail and crossed Fulton Street alone, his eyes once again locked on the brisk-walking target while Lynch hesitated at the corner, expressing his anguish by pleading with his partner as he, too, crossed the thoroughfare.

"I think it's foolish to try to do the work in such a busy place," Lynch said loudly. "Maybe we'll let him go for now. Get him later, you know, on the way back."

DeAmato noticed that for some strange reason the odds against him had been halved and made a decision to stand his ground under a lamppost near the far corner of Fulton Street near Albee Square. He watched the approaching stranger extend an open hand while saying, "Is your name Filezee?"

"Who wants to know?" the Black Hand soldier answered with a sneer.

"I do!" Harms bellowed. With that, he moved his hand inside his coat and came out with a Mauser semi-automatic pistol, which he pointed at the upper body of his intended victim.

Though he was also armed, Yale's hired hand never imagined someone other than a fool would dare pull off a hit with so many bystanders around. When he saw the gun, DeAmato's first impulse was to dive behind a parked automobile to avoid the blast, but instantly changed his tack when he heard the clicking sounds of the enemy gun misfire.

Harms's hands were still trying to get the defective weapon to fire when suddenly and without warning, he found himself knocked off his feet by the Italian, who used his head as a battering ram. DeAmato, with a distinct advantage over the man on the ground, proceeded to stomp and kick Harms, whose screams were never heard by his partner, Lynch, who had already turned the corner. The cautious Lynch concluded that his partner's stubborn and relentless pursuit was a result of the large amount of alcohol he'd consumed that day and made a painful decision to hightail it back to the safety of the car. Lynch didn't feel like being fingered for armed assault, much less for murder.

The sight of the two men battling on the street corner had pedestrians cowering from a distance, aghast at the sight, as some searched

Fulton Street for a policeman. But not one of the spectators intervened in any way, other than vocally.

"That's enough. Let him go now!" somebody shouted as Filezee continued to pummel the Irishman in the face and head with his fists.

He responded by dropping the badly beaten man back to the pavement while kicking the faulty weapon under a parked car. He then directed his shoe at the man's ribs for a final blow, straightened himself up, and checked his trouser pocket to be sure his own pistol was secure, then started to sprint toward Court Street.

Filezee DeAmato was considered by Capone to be a "stand up" kind of a guy. Having been a trusted crony since their boyhood days together, Capone always admired his friend's ability to think clearly and in a businesslike fashion. For that reason, Filezee held an open invitation from Capone to come to Cicero to assist him in running the criminal empire he was forging there. However, DeAmato refused the offer to move from Brooklyn, calling himself a creature of habit who felt most comfortable having his rather large family nearby.

Failing in that regard, Capone did the next best thing. He appointed DeAmato to act as his New York representative in all interstate deals that concerned New York, with the approval and under the protection of Frankie Yale.

. . .

On December 10, 1925, Lonergan called a meeting at his Prince Street headquarters located in a brownstone building near Myrtle Avenue in downtown Brooklyn. In attendance were a still badly bruised Aaron Harms, Needles Ferry, "Ragtime Joe" Howard, Happy Malone, Jimmy Hart, "Sudden Death" Eddie McQuire, Kid Eddie Lynch, Cute Charlie Donnelly, and a number of other White Hand gangsters who witnessed the raving maniac, Peg Leg Lonergan, deliver a verbal onslaught against the Italians.

"My beloved pal, Dinny Meehan, must be turning in his grave at what's happening on the docks," he screamed. "I want to serve notice right here and now that I intend to respond to the looters of the house that he and my brother-in-law, Bill Lovett, built.

"I didn't forget them. Nor did I forget for a second the fucking way they were killed," he said, pounding his fist repeatedly on the table. "Dinny was shot in his pajamas in his own bed and my sister's husband shot and hatcheted to death while he was still asleep too." Lonergan continued his alcohol-inspired diatribe despite shouts of encouragement and renewed oaths of loyalty that sprang from the hearts and mouths of some in the standing-room-only crowd. Most of Richard Lonergan's hirelings were in total agreement with the leader's angry sense of urgency and his promise to "push the Italians off the piers," but some wondered if Lonergan could succeed in his proposal to destroy the Black Hand leadership personified by Frankie Yale, a man who traveled nowhere without extraordinary heavy guard ever since the attempt on his life occurred in his own backyard.

Unlike his brother-in-law, Wild Bill Lovett, who never employed a personal bodyguard, the wooden-legged Lonergan rarely went around by himself. He made sure his flunkies were of the strong-arm type who were not afraid to kill on his command and realized that Aaron Harms had always been loyal to that proposition.

Lonergan's eyes were aflame with anger and his usually neatly combed red hair, which had been parted in the middle, was tossed about during the wild tirade that now seemed to be directed at Kid Eddie, who stood toward the rear of the room listening to his boss while silently praying that he wouldn't be singled out again.

This was the first time Lynch had a chance to tell the others his side of the story concerning the botched hit on DeAmato and confessed that he felt somewhat responsible for the injuries suffered by his partner despite the assurance from Harms that he held no ill will, agreeing that it was a dumb thing for him to go after the Black Hand hood alone on busy Fulton Street.

Regardless of that, Kid Eddie hoped to blend in with the crowd on the ground floor of the Prince Street brownstone while he did his best to avoid Aaron Harms and, most of all, the piercing eyes of Lonergan, who had received Lynch's promise to successfully complete the assignment. But right now, Lynch realized the incident was being promoted to the rest of the mob as an example of the lack of guts shown by "certain members" of his gang.

Lonergan was decked out in a fashionable midnight-blue pinstriped suit as he stood before them, mute for a second, until the gang noticed he was loosening the buttons on his jacket and exhibiting a large caliber weapon. His angry glare reached the sweating face of Kid Eddie, who nearly fainted when he noticed the crowd was silently splitting off to the sides because Peg Leg was pointing the pistol toward the middle of the room where Lynch was standing.

"What would Dinny Meehan or Bill Lovett do with a guy who deserted one of them in the middle of a caper?" Lonergan growled. He seemed to be blaming Kid Eddie alone for their failure to diminish the ranks of the Black Hand organization by two important members.

"Eddie, you're the one who fucked up the hit on that ginzo boss, Yale, then you actually went ahead a few days later and left my good friend Aaron to do an assignment by himself? Why, you fucking yellow rat, I should have killed you a long time ago," Lonergan said, drawing a bead on Lynch, who stood his ground.

"We're gonna crash their little Christmas party at the Adonis Club," the drunken Lonergan announced to his gang. "We're getting rid of Yale and some of his top men that evening and we'll do it without your help, Eddie. Now, get out of my sight before I lose my patience altogether!"

Richard Lonergan had run out of patience on a few other occasions in his young, violent life. As a matter of fact, it is reliably estimated that he was personally responsible for well over twenty murders. One of the more bizarre of Peg Leg's slayings was the shooting death of his own father, John Lonergan, who was killed while attempting to strike Peg Leg's mother with a baseball bat during a family argument.

Lonergan fired three intermittent shots into the ceiling above the head of the trembling Lynch, who dropped to his knees at the first shot, covering his head while white puffs of smoke and bits of plaster rained down on him until the third and final blast rang out. The momentary quiet and the realization that he hadn't been shot after all encouraged Kid Eddie to turn his body toward his boss with a look of pure gratitude on his face. His arms still were partially covering his head as he begged forgiveness.

"I don't deserve to be killed, Richie," Lynch begged. "Please . . . don't do it!"

Lonergan's nervous eyes penetrated Lynch's body like blazing coals while he continued cursing him and repeatedly pounded the table with a bare fist. "Get out of here right now, Eddie," he yelled.

Kid Eddie turned away and strolled to the door, reaching for the doorknob in response to Lonergan's demand to beat it, when another two blasts resounded in his ears. Neither shot was intended to kill him, but were simply insulting reminders of the disrespect he'd earned from the White Hands this day. His refusal to follow Aaron Harms that night had caused Lynch to become an outcast in his element. Shunned by the same guys he considered to be his friends, his bitterness and embarrassment soon forced the Kid to consider getting even with Peg Leg and maybe render himself a service at the same time.

He recognized the foreboding signs of change evidenced by the steamship companies' willingness to do business with the Black Hand and admired their ability to stabilize the dock labor force while they penetrated all phases of the lucrative waterfront rackets.

The future belongs to them, Lynch said to himself, as he made up his mind to use the information he had gathered to good use.

•   •   •

"MAY I SPEAK to Johnny Giustra or Fury Agoglia?" Lynch inquired of the respondent of his telephone call to Cafiero's restaurant. These were names previously mentioned to him as belonging to a couple of hoods who worked for Frankie Yale. Through information acquired from one of his few remaining friends, Lynch learned that both men were frequent customers of this cozy Italian dining room near the corner of President Street in the heart of Batista Balsamo's waterfront section of Brooklyn.

"Who's calling?" answered a voice on the other end of the line.

"This is a friend of theirs. Eddie," Lynch said. "I would appreciate it if you see them, to have either one give me a call."

"Just a moment, sir, I think I see Johnny Giustra coming in the door right now."

Suspicious about the caller who assured him the trip around the corner would be worth the effort, Giustra drove past the meeting place, under the marquee of the Happy Hour film palace on Columbia Street with his two partners, Fury Agoglia and Jack Stabile (alias Stick 'em up Jack), in tow. Stabile waited behind the wheel of his gray coupe, parked alongside the stately clock, which in a few short hours would be the gathering place for crowds of longshoremen, while Giustra and Agoglia strolled across the cobblestone street to hear what this Irishman had to say to their boss.

"Would you object to sitting in the car where we can talk in comfort?" inquired Silk Stockings Giustra, while lifting the collar of his beige overcoat to fend off the cold night air. "I promise you that nobody will offend you in any way, even if what you're offering is bullshit."

Inside the car, seated in the backseat alongside Giustra while Agoglia joined Stabile in the front, Lynch laid out his spiel, including his reluctance to follow the drunken Aaron Harms during his disastrous attempt on the life of Filezee DeAmato, and also revealed that he had been the driver of the Pierce-Arrow that shot up their boss's car on Coney Island Avenue.

"If it wasn't for my losing control of Peg Leg's car, your boss, Frankie Yale, would be dead right now."

"What is it that you want to say to him?" Giustra asked. "Are you looking for a reward or something for screwing up the hit?"

"It's not that at all," answered the disgraced White Hand gangster.

"Why don't you just spit it out and let us decide if it's worth the trouble to bring your story to him?" Giustra remarked, adding, "if it's not bullshit, that is."

Kid Eddie reached into his coat and casually pulled out a small automatic pistol that he displayed by holding it in the open palm of his hand. Johnny Giustra's immediate reaction was to grab hold of the man's wrist, causing the small caliber weapon to drop between his legs while Fury Agoglia pulled out his revolver and pointed it to the passive Irishman's forehead.

"Take the gun, go ahead, any one of you who thinks this is bullshit," Lynch offered. "But when I say another hit is planned on your boss, I know what I'm talking about. This time, it'll be at your annual Christmas party, in a place called the Adonis Club. I've been told that you guys own the place. Am I right?"

Giustra plucked the weapon from the floor of the car while the White Hand hood's eyes stared down the barrel of the pistol now pointed at his face. Lynch offered a challenge to the startled trio. "Go ahead, pull the trigger if you think I'm lying. You can blow my brains out right now if you want to, but it's the truth."

"Relax, Fury," Jack Stabile remarked. "I kind of think he's on the level. What do you think, Johnny?"

"I say it's real strange for him to know about the Christmas party Frank has planned for the club. I think we should bring him to the boss and let him hear what this good man has to say."

· · ·

YALE AGREED WITH the consensus of opinion not long after Kid Eddie Lynch began spilling his guts to him inside his Sunrise Café. He was very convincing and just the type of weasel to betray his boss, Yale told himself, concealing his disdain for Kid Eddie by showering him with smiles of gratitude and plying him with libations gleaned from his private stock.

"If you're so sure of them busting up my Christmas party, I guess I'll have to arrange for a few extra bouncers," said Yale. "Wanna job?"

"No thank you, Mr. Yale," he replied. "If it's all the same with you, I plan on being at home in bed when the shit starts flying inside the Adonis Club. Just keep in mind what I said. You're the main target."

"I'll always remember who warned me about the raid, Eddie, and I appreciate the concern you've shown for a stranger's personal safety," Yale said. "You can be sure that my gratitude will be expressed in a much nicer way when this comes to pass, and we put an end to that Peg Leg fuck."

The next day, Yale placed a call to Capone's headquarters, the Hawthorne Hotel in Cicero, Illinois.

"Alphonso, how would you feel about spending your Christmas here in Brooklyn?" Yale asked.

"I hadn't thought about it, Frank," Capone answered. "Why, what's up?"

"One good turn deserves another they say, and I think I need you to return a piece of work for me, right here in the old neighborhood."

It took little time for Capone to express his willingness to cooperate with the old crew. After all, it was Yale's hand behind the successful hit on Dion O'Banion that allowed him and Torrio to avenge the perceived beer plant swindle perpetrated by the deceased florist.

"Frank, just tell me when I'm needed and I'll be there," Capone replied.

"Well, if you can reach here by the twenty-second, it'll give us some time to go over a few things with the old man before we do the work," Yale said. "I'll have somebody waiting for you at the station, Alphonse. As soon as you find out what time your train arrives in New York, give me a call. Okay?"

"You needn't bother, Frank. I got an idea about driving in. Maybe I'll take Mary and the baby along with me . . . you know, give my mother-in-law a chance to see her grandson."

Seated in the backseat with his wife and child, Capone departed Chicago in his brand-new Packard touring sedan along with two of his hired triggermen, Albert Anselmi and John Scalise, who took turns behind the wheel until they reached the home of Mary's parents at 117 Third Place in the Red Hook section of Brooklyn. Their early arrival allowed them some hours to relax before the briefing session.

· · ·

ON THE EVENING of December 22, the trio from Chicago climbed the steps behind a fish store at 102 Union Street. The business was owned by Batista Balsamo's brother, Dominick, who also maintained a gaming operation in one of the two apartments above the store. They were met at the head of the dimly lit stairs by a youngster who, after identifying himself as a nephew of Balsamo's, directed them to a door in the rear of the building that was partially opened. Soon, a welcoming voice boomed with a Sicilian accent and the door swung open to reveal a room where a crowd of familiar faces were shouting greetings to Capone on the happy occasion of his return to Brooklyn.

Along with Batista Balsamo, the faces belonged to Frankie Yale and his cousins, the Agoglia brothers, Fury and the one called "Sylvie," along with their partner in the Adonis club property, Jack Stabile. Leading his guests to the warmth provided by a black coal stove in a kitchen area, Balsamo tried offering some wine to the trio even before they had a chance to remove their hats and overcoats, which were gathered by the young boy.

Batista Balsamo's voice could only be described as a mellow growl, Sicilian in dialect, with a trace of broken English thrown in.

"This will get your blood warm in a hurry," he chimed, "then, you come inside . . . have a little something to eat."

Batista placed one of his hands on Capone's shoulder while he complimented the young man on his snazzy attire. "Alphonso, it's good to see you looking so well, like a real polished gentleman. I declare, you've matured." Capone smiled and proceeded to tug at the sleeves of the expensive-looking English tweed blazer he wore. Despite the praise heaped on Capone's attire, those who knew Balsamo well would never expect the modest, fifty-seven-year-old man to be caught dead wearing a shirt with a stiff collar such as the one around Capone's thick neck. Batista almost always dressed casually and a cardigan sweater worn over a cotton turtleneck completed Zio's attire that evening. As he continued pouring wine, he talked about "the old days."

"Why, I remember when you were a kid with patches on your trousers, like the day you tried to muscle your way into my Columbia Street territory until a gang from around the corner chased your bunch back to Third Avenue. They wanted to kick the shit out you. Remember?"

Lifting a glass from the tray, Balsamo looked into the gray eyes of the rising star of Chicago's underworld and continued his good-natured kidding. "I'm sure that day was an education for you, Alphonso, wasn't it?"

"It certainly was, Zio Batista," Capone replied. "I learned much about life in general, when I first met up with you." Capone smiled broadly as he raised his glass of wine in celebration of the fraternity they shared. Balsamo returned the toast and took a small sip from his glass before asking, "And what was the most important thing you learned back then, Alphonso?"

"Not to fuck around in Zio Batista's territory, of course," he shot back with a grin on his face. Turning to his henchmen, Capone introduced John Scalise, who was a stranger to the aging mafioso. "Everyone around here calls Batista Balsamo the mayor," Capone declared, "but if you wanna know something, I really think, if this man ever moved his ass to Chicago, he'd be the governor, at least."

His eyes twinkling beneath the cloud of smoke rising from his cigar, Balsamo suggested that he and Capone respond to the clamor coming from the dining room section of the railroad apartment.

"Bring them guys over here, will you, Zio Batista?" he said.

They were sitting around a large, circular table waiting for the last of the invited guests, Capone and his two Chicago heavies, to arrive before digging into the seafood delicacies set in platters before them. Scungilli, shrimps, and pulpo salad as well as clams, oysters on the half shell, lobster tail, and pepper biscuits covered with red gravy were being gulped down and flushed with the excellent wines the Balsamos acquired from neighborhood wine cellars.

After the table was cleared and the kitchen help retired to another part of the house, Balsamo unfolded a piece of wrapping paper on top of the table. It was scrawled with crude images that represented interior portions of the Adonis Club, as well as the surrounding streets.

Capone breathed a sigh of relief when he realized Balsamo had taken great pains in planning the hit by consulting with the present owners of the club, the Agoglia brothers and Jack Stabile. Two of them were his cousins, the other, a trusted friend, who attested to the map's accuracy by ordering a round of applause for Batista, while Capone displayed his approval with a smile and a raised glass.

The Mayor of Columbia Street began with the admonition, "Our success depends on the enemy finding nothing out of the ordinary in the club that evening, For that reason, Alphonso, we can't avoid having outsiders involved. We do this in order to make the intruders feel comfortable."

"I agree with you, Zio Batista," Capone said. "They'll probably enter the club with their guns drawn if they smell a rat."

"You got that right, Alphonso," Balsamo said. "When they enter the place, they'll be looking for familiar faces to pounce on. Frankie Yale's mug won't be around that night, I'll tell you that. And if they find reasons to linger awhile, it'll be their great undoing. You know how we induce them to stay? We offer free sandwiches, pickles, cookies, and such. The Adonis Club spent over two hundred dollars on a spread that'll be right under their noses when they join our happy Christmas party."

"It goes without saying, Zio, you've thought things out to perfection," Capone said. "But how on earth will our bullets find their marks in such a crowded dance hall? I see innocent people getting in the way, maybe catching some slugs too. It'll be a mess with all the witnesses."

"That's part of Stabile's job," Balsamo replied. "He's watching the club's front door and he promises that the crowd will be limited throughout the night to a few employees and only those customers we can trust." Balsamo raised a finger in the air and shook it gently back and forth. Then, pointing in the direction of the two brothers while staring into Capone's eyes, he expounded on his last statement. "Alphonso, your cousins, Sylvie and Fury, they've assured me the customers that'll be in the place can be trusted to keep their mouths shut. They'll be too scared to sing because they know, if they do, their lips will be permanently sealed."

"What about the beat cop?" Capone asked. "There's always the chance a copper will hear the gun play and butt in. No, Zio Batista?"

"My God, you really know how to pick them, Frankie," Balsamo said. "Alphonso is right. That's something to think about."

"Don't worry," the voice belonging to Jack Stabile piped, "I happen to know all the cops who stroll past my club." Rising from his chair, Stabile walked over to the map and placed a finger in a particular spot. "I'll have word sent to the cop on the beat that his good friend, Jack Stabile, wishes to speak with him. When I do, I'll be sure to convince him that he should spend the night patrolling the other side of Fourth Avenue."

Yale jumped into the conversation with an expression of admiration for his former apprentice. "That's why I figured you'd be the right man to manage this job, Alphonso," he said. "Besides, I think Zio Batista did enough to see this thing through. I'm still trying to convince him to leave the actual night's work to you younger guys."

"I agree with you Frank," Capone said. "Zio Batista, I don't mean any disrespect. Everybody in this room realizes you deserve all the credit when the deed is done, but Frankie is right. You sit this one out. Okay?"

Balsamo's face grew pale and sullen, his enthusiasm dwindled by the growing consensus of opinion at the table that for this project he would be delegated to play armchair general. He found little solace when Yale reminded him of his own exclusion from the actual ambush.

"Yeah, but Frank, there's good reason for you not being involved," Balsamo grumbled. "You're the guy they're looking to put on ice!"

Within the hour, as the full layout became clear in his mind, Capone's counsel offered the finishing touches to the scheme Balsamo had brought to the table and he assumed control of the operation.

Directing himself to Sylvia Agoglia, Capone remarked, "It's been a long time since I've laid eyes on the club, cousino. Tonight, after we break up here, how about you showing me around the place a little?"

15

The Peg Leg Murders

THE YALE-AFFILIATED SPEAKEASY incorporated under the title "Adonis Social & Athletic Club" occupied the ground level of a cold-water flat located at 152 Twentieth Street in the Gowanus waterfront section of South Brooklyn. The shabby look of the building's exterior and the fact that it appeared ready to fall down didn't deter the average boozer in the neighborhood from seeking an invitation to enter past its locked doors. Inside, one would be surprised to find that the Adonis Club maintained a rather cozy, friendly atmosphere for members and their guests.

Many of the club's daytime regulars were "longies"—longshoremen whose workshoes hiked the sloping cobblestone streets and blue-slated sidewalks of Twentieth Street for a pitcher of beer or wine.

Although the club had been cited numerous times for being in violation of the Prohibition statute by local law enforcement, a bureaucratic snafu allowed the doors to remain open long enough for the fateful all-day-all-night Christmas party of 1925 to take place. The incident in the Adonis Club would serve to elevate the position of the Mafia pretender to the throne, Frankie Yale, in a Black Hand-inspired effort to lord over the lucrative rackets on the Brooklyn waterfront.

Upon entering the darkened Adonis, Capone followed his cousin, Sylvie Agoglia's, shadowy figure through a long corridor.

"Nothing's really changed about the layout, Al," Agoglia said, "and my partners agree with me, too. It would have been real dumb to put any more dough into this place. As a matter of fact, we get bothered by the police brass so often now that it's almost a relief to lose it. Tomorrow, we'll move what little good stuff we have in here to another location."

"I understand what you're saying, cousin," Capone said. "It don't pay to worry about a joint like this. Not when you can imagine the swell place you'll be exchanging this one for pretty soon."

Agoglia balanced himself on his toes while rubbing his stiff hands together. "How I hate this fucking cold weather," he complained, until his shaking fingers were able to click on a wall lamp that emitted a soft, red glow. The light enabled Capone to distinguish the cloakroom near the entrance and a foyer with a large opening, which led to the main barroom.

The walls throughout the place were covered almost entirely with full-length velvet drapes that shimmered in the drafty club as Agoglia scampered to an adjoining wall. He stuck an arm behind a drape to reach a switch, which turned all the house lights on. "There you are, Al, the same lighting the place will have the night we trim the sails on that Irish shit . . . if he shows up for the party."

Capone raised a finger against his pouting lips as he strolled among the round, wooden dining tables. Agoglia produced a portable oil heater that one of the bartenders used for personal warmth and proceeded to light the wick.

"Say, Sylvie," Capone said, "you claimed the lighting in this joint would be the same tonight as Christmas night."

"That's what I said," Agoglia responded, "because we intend to start the party later in the day this year and because it gets dark so early, the lighting in here will be the same as for any other cold, dark winter night. I promise you one thing, Alphonso. It'll be much warmer in here."

"Well, how about the swagger lamp over the piano?" Capone asked.

"Why, I'll be," Agoglia chuckled. "Leave it to you, Alphonso. You were always the guy with a sixth sense. I was wrong! I forgot a lousy twenty-watt light bulb." Walking toward his cousin with the smoking lantern in one hand and a glass of brandy in the other, Agoglia set the portable heater on the wooden floor and placed the drink on a table where Capone could reach it. "Tell me this, dear cousin," Sylvie said. "What happens if two or three mugs in the joint light their cigars at the same time? Do we cancel the hit because there's too much light?"

Noticing that his cousin wasn't the least bit amused by his joke, Agoglia pushed the brandy closer to Capone, who seemed faraway in thought. The chagrined proprietor decided to get serious and answer his wily cousin's question.

"That lamp is plugged directly into an outlet on the floor behind the piano, Al," he said. "That's why it works independent of all the others."

"Let me ask you another question, cousin Sylvester," Capone said. "Do you think it'd be possible to reserve one particular table for Peg Leg and his boys?"

Agoglia's eyes scanned the dozen or so tables that circled the dance floor while expressing his surprise at the request. "I'm sure that's possible," he answered, "but I thought the idea was to try directing them to the free set-ups near the bar."

Capone climbed a slightly elevated section that included a fifteen-foot-long mahogany bar with a brass footrest. In the far corner of the barroom, a Victrola record player, famous for its quality internal speakers, shared the wall with a large wooden barrel marked ROOT BEER.

Walking back across the dance floor while rubbing his chin, Capone stopped near the piano again and settled his heavy frame on the stool. He remained in that spot for a few seconds until Agoglia heard him say, "I've got a much better idea!"

Agoglia joined his cousin in a dead stare directed at the lampshade that hung over the piano, in close proximity to one particular table.

"If you think it's possible to fill the rest of these tables so as to leave them no choice but to sit at this one, we have a winner here," Capone said, with certainty.

"That won't be much trouble at all," Agoglia said. "As a matter of fact, if you think it's a good idea, I can set up a table to accommodate the free lunch we're providing on one of the nearby tables. But do you really think it's a good idea?"

Capone lifted himself from the stool and reached for the ribbon attached to the small green shade above the piano. He yanked on the cord and switched the light on. It affirmed Sylvester's assertion that the light over the baby grand was on a different circuit.

"This is much too bright," Capone said, squinting his eyes. "I wanna see the dimmest red lamp inside this fixture. Do you hear me?"

After Capone's assurance that the rest of the plan would remain the same as proposed by Batista Balsamo, Agoglia agreed on the new ambush location without fully comprehending what his cousin had in mind. Nevertheless, when he saw his blood relative reach above the piano and carefully proceed to tear the cord from the hanging lamp's switch, Sylvie quipped, "Go ahead, Alphonso, wreck the joint. Because after the Christmas party, the coppers are gonna shut the place down anyhow."

"That's the only damage I'm gonna do to the club, for now," Capone said as he walked with his cocktail in hand. "Do me a favor please, cousin. After you screw the red bulb in, I want you to pose for me by sitting down at Peg Leg's reserved table, that is, the one nearest the piano."

Sylvester Agoglia complied to the request with a grin on his face, holding back his laughter when he finally figured out the scheme. As he sat in a chair, one of six that encircled the "special" table, he noted the minor effect the soft, red glow of the lamp presented to the overall appearance. "Unpretentious," he told himself, "and a rather cheerful touch at that."

He watched Capone striding back and forth in nervous moves that implied to Agoglia that his cousin was trying to visualize the best positions to launch the ambush from. When he saw that Capone was heading for the main light switch, Sylvie drew a pistol from his coat and prepared for the mock battle that was decided seconds after the darkness surrounded him. While his eyes searched the greater portion of the dance hall, Agoglia realized that all he could do was guess where Capone was hiding. He felt like a sitting duck, completely unable to pinpoint Capone's figure in the darkness of his own club. Sightless beyond his immediate location, he heard his cousin's voice coming from somewhere outside the scarlet hue:

"Hey, Sylvie! You'd be dead by now!"

• • •

KID EDDIE CALLED the Adonis Club in the early afternoon of Christmas Day and related to Fury Agoglia that the White Hand leader, with around a half-dozen heavies, were definitely scheduled to show up. "They figure the best time to catch your boss off-guard will be late in the evening, so prepare yourselves around midnight," he said.

"We're ready for them right now," Fury responded, and passed the word to his brother who was conversing with the cigarette girl, Elvira Callahan. Other employees in the place at that time were bartender Tony Desso, piano player George Carozza, and two waiters, Frank Piazza and Ralph Damato, who also served as bouncers. The Agoglias had already advised the beat patrolman, Richard Marano, who was due to work the late-night shift, to keep himself above Fifth Avenue in order to avoid getting involved in the potentially dangerous situation. The officer agreed to keep his mouth shut and did exactly as the brothers advised.

The Christmas party was still going strong shortly after two AM on December 26, 1925, when Mike Sayers, a longshoreman from the nearby Gowanus docks who Stabile recognized as an occasional patron, requested admittance into the club. "I've got some good friends with me, Jackie," he said. "Do you mind?"

"C'mon inside fellows," Stabile responded. "The Adonis Club is always willing to welcome the friends of Lefty Mike." The men streamed past their sponsor, who never did enter the club himself. Instead, it's told that Mike Sayers turned himself around and high-tailed it down the frozen street in order to catch the Third Avenue trolley for his trip back home.

Jack Stabile was the watchdog who prudently stepped outside his post in the bad weather to greet the man and check out the anxious group that appeared to be pushing past the longshoreman, cursing about being cold and needing a drink. Stabile noticed that one of the pack walked with a hobble and recognized the Pierce-Arrow sedan parked on the other side of the trolley tracks.

"Well, you guys are friends with Lefty Sayers?" He inquired in a loud voice, designed to catch the attention of the piano player.

Peg Leg Lonergan, sporting a brown-and-white checkered overcoat, led his flock of hired guns to the cloakroom and through the foyer, while Carozza began clanking out the sounds of "Piano Roll Blues," which served as a prearranged signal. The tune was a reminder to those involved in the ambush to remain alert and to get ready to assume their battery positions.

"What happened to Lefty Mike?" Stabile inquired while leading the group to what he termed "a nice table near the free eats."

"I guess he changed his mind about doing any more drinking tonight," Lonergan said. "Why, is there a problem?" He waited for an answer before sitting down.

"No problem at all, sir," Stabile assured him with a grin. "I'll send a waiter over to take your orders. Oh, by the way fellows, you can help yourselves to the free eats on that table over there."

Along with Lonergan and his best friend, Aaron Harms, Neil "Needles" Ferry, "Rag Time" Joe Howard, Jimmy Hart, and Patrick "Happy" Maloney were all crashing the early morning party. Meanwhile, Harms's bloodshot eyes darted around the club in search of Black Hand gang members, examining each and every dark-haired man in the place until he was certain that neither

Frankie Yale, nor any of his known hirelings, were present in the club.

They warmed up to the atmosphere in the Adonis in short order, availing themselves of the lavish spread and keeping Sylvester Agoglia, an impromptu waiter, busy pouring rounds of whiskey. Stabile reported to Capone, who was tending bar, that the group was "under the influence" when they first arrived and Sylvie could attest to the fact they were quickly becoming a very boisterous group, harder and harder to accommodate. When they noticed a young blond woman, Mae Wilson, strolling arm-in-arm with Stabile toward the dance floor, Peg Leg was already stewed and remarked aloud, "Hey guys, what do you think about a nice, young, Irish lady who'd rather be in the company of dark dagos?"

Knowing the time had come for action, Capone slipped behind the bar to join Fury Agoglia, while Albert Anselmi and John Scalise parted the drapes behind the piano. That action indicated to the tunesmith, Carozza, that it was time for him to bring a smooth conclusion to his piano rendition of "Yes, Sir, That's My Baby." Carozza took his break by walking away from the target area holding an empty glass in his left hand while the other, thrust inside his trouser pocket, gripped the handle of the large-caliber pistol he was carrying. He glanced over a shoulder through the haze of smoke that permeated the air inside the club like a stale fog and smiled at a patron or two in his casual stroll to the phonograph machine, which he set in motion. After soliciting a female singer, Helen Logan, to remain close to the Victrola and to attend to it, George Carozza approached his prescribed position and waited for Sylvie Agoglia's signal.

Sylvester Agoglia had requested, and was granted, the pleasure of striking the first blow of the battle. His action would be directed against the White Hand chieftain personally and that would be the cue for Capone to throw the place into darkness and for the circle of artillery to begin firing.

The moment was ripe when Peg Leg bent down to tug at his wooden leg and lifted himself from his chair. The Irish crime boss shuffled toward the toilet while Capone nodded his approval to his cousin by walking toward the light switch. Sylvie indicated with a smirk and a nod that he was ready to move.

The fear of being intimidated by the six bullies had emptied all the adjacent seats in the house, even forcing some customers to leave the premises altogether. That was a welcome bit of luck for the Capone crew, providing practically all of them with an unobstructed view of their targets in a well-staged crossfire.

Leaving the men's room and walking back through the foyer, Lonergan was dragging his artificial limb when he spotted his waiter, Sylvester Agoglia, and complained angrily in his face.

"Why do these fuckin' places always have the goddamned toilets so far away? Another guy might say, 'Fuck you, ginzo,' and take a leak in one of the corners, but I got too much respect for your boss, Frankie Yale, to do something like that myself. Do you garbeesh?"

"Sure, I understand you, sir, but that name you said, he's not my boss. This place is owned by my brother and a friend."

"You trying to tell me you don't know who I'm talking about? How about another one of your pizzanos, a guy who goes by the name, 'Files,' Ever hear of him?"

"No, sir. Never heard of that guy, either."

Lonergan sneered as he pushed an elbow against Agoglia's chest, forcing the Italian to stagger a bit.

"Outta my way, ginzo," he screeched. Quickly spinning himself around and setting his wooden leg back into motion, Lonergan turned his back on Sylvie and proceeded to walk back to his table. From under his white apron, Sylvie produced a meat cleaver and directed a swift, crashing blow to the skull of the White Hand leader, causing him to scream in agony as Capone plunged the Adonis into darkness.

The tiny, rose-colored niche outlined the mass of confused and terrified bodies that floundered in their seats while barking guns flashed from out of the blackness. Most of the screaming customers retreated to the rear of the club when the shooting started and a few made it out the front door into the cold, early morning street. A barrage totaling more than two dozen slugs were spent, killing two of the five, Aaron Harms and Needles Ferry, who were seated at the table. Needles Ferry was cut down with a bullet to the head and another to his abdomen as he rose from his chair in a desperate attempt to destroy the one remaining light source, the red lamp over the piano.

Aaron Harms received a single, bone-crushing slug through his chest and died on the spot. Jimmy Hart managed to save himself by diving into the darkness and crawling out the front door, sustaining gunshot wounds to the leg and hip in the process, while Happy Malone and Joe Howard escaped without injury, probably because they were on the fringe of the blackout area and the closest ones to the exit.

Within a few ear-splitting seconds, the roar of the firestorm ceased and the sounds of breaking glass were replaced with the more subdued tinkle of Capone crunching debris underfoot as he turned the lights back on. "I don't believe this fuck," he bellowed in the direction of the archway. Capone could not believe his eyes when he saw the Irish crime boss heading toward him, like a ghost, rising from the grim shadows while bleeding heavily from the savage blow delivered to his cranium. Peg Leg's body stiffened and he appeared ready to stumble to his knees again as he staggered forward in an unmanageable attempt to get to the street. Capone observed the pitiful condition of the Irish boss, concluding that the tremendous amount of blood gushing from his head and the glazed look in his eyes meant that Sylvie had delivered on his promise to finish him off. Nevertheless, Capone fired two more shots at close range. One hit Lonergan in the forehead while the other plowed into his upper back as the momentum carried him outside the open door and onto the curb.

Scalise grabbed a damp bar towel, wiped his weapon clean, and tossed the pistol into a corner, reminding the others to do the same, lest they be picked up with a smoking gun in their possession.

Sometime around four AM, after being notified that the expected problem with the White Hand gang was over, Patrolman Marano ventured down Twentieth Street. About halfway down the block, the cop spotted the figure of a man sprawled face-down in front of the Adonis Club. The street was dark and quiet as the policeman clawed his flashlight from under his jacket and directed the beam down to the pavement. It revealed a well-dressed male with red hair, in a pool of blood.

"God only knows what I'll find inside," Officer Marano told himself as he entered the dark club. He avoided inspecting the dance floor and instead walked a bloody trail through the foyer to a pay phone on the wall, where he excitedly called the desk to report the scene of carnage. Within the hour, the Homicide Squad was sifting through the rubble.

Tablecloths placed over the three bodies probably caused the conflicting reports in the tabloids regarding the identification of individual murder victims. The New York *Daily News*, on December 26, wrote that the man found in the gutter was Needles Ferry, while a reporter for the *Brooklyn Eagle* claimed the man lying in the street with the massive wound to the skull was Aaron Harms. Considering the results of the autopsies performed at Kings County Hospital and studying them, we are drawn to a different conclusion. After reading the autopsy reports on all three victims, Dr. Reza Khatib, chief of neurosurgery at Brooklyn Hospital, agreed with the authors, who received their information concerning the gruesome event from somebody who was in the club at the time.

"Laceration" to the victim's brain would lead Dr. Sam Lawrence Basso, a fine Brooklyn physician for over thirty years, to concur, "The report issued by the medical examiner indicates that only one victim sustained a laceration to the skull as well as a bullet wound to the head and body."

That victim found in the gutter was Richard Lonergan, who died as violently as he had lived, with a slug in his head, another in his back, and his head split open.

Reporters asked Lonergan's sister, Anna, who she thought was responsible for the multiple slayings. She attributed the slaughter to immigrants, saying, "I don't know, but you can bet it was no Irish

Americans like ourselves who would stage a mean murder like this on a Christmas night."

Of the three White Hand gangsters who fled the ambush, Happy Malone and Joe Howard managed to make it safely back to Myrtle Avenue. However, the troubles of their companion, Jimmy Hart, were far from over. Mysteriously cropping up miles away, on Flushing and Throop Avenues, police noticed Hart, struggling along the street with gunshot wounds in his leg. They promptly called an ambulance that took him to Cumberland Hospital, where he was treated and placed in a curtained section for recovery while his family was notified.

Early that afternoon, when he was informed that the prognosis for Jimmy Hart was good, Kid Eddie Lynch, the Irish turncoat, showed his grief by placing another call to Cafiero's Restaurant. Johnny Giustra listened to him describe Hart's reported anger.

"Tell Frankie that Jimmy Hart is a prime candidate to spill the beans to the coppers," Lynch whispered.

Soon afterward, a black sedan sped through the downtown streets delivering a neatly dressed couple with a bouquet of roses in hand to Brooklyn's Cumberland Hospital. Al Capone was familiar with the patient, Jimmy Hart, simply because he was one of those responsible for his being in the hospital in the first place. Following Yale's advice, he brought a gun moll, Concetta "Connie" Morganti, along with him for good reasons. Morganti had been an employee of the hospital in the past and she assured her male companion of "easy access through the hospital with her at his side." That could prove very useful in the event of a police presence, because they had no way of knowing whether Hart had already fingered their mug shots.

Hart remained unguarded by the authorities who hadn't tied this particular shooting to the early morning mass murder at the Adonis Club. Hart had told a story of some Christmas revelers in an automobile who drove by throwing lead at him on the same corner they picked him up at. He lay in bed drifting in and out of consciousness unaware that his own likeness was being shown and identified as one of the men involved in the melee by the club's cigarette girl, Elvira

Callahan. Hart lay peacefully asleep when they arrived. Only a female relative sat by his side, waiting for him to awaken from his drug-induced slumber. Capone peeked behind the half-drawn screen and whispered to the sentinel, "Excuse me, lady, is that my friend Jimmy Hart in this bed?"

"Yes, sir, it is," she replied, "but I don't think he's gonna open his eyes for a while. He's asleep. His condition is very hopeful, thank God! If you leave your name, I'll make sure he knows that you were here."

"That's all right, I guess, but do you mind if I put these flowers on the cabinet near his bed?" After receiving her permission to do so, Capone took a small step backward and looked her in the eye. "Shucks," he said, "these here flowers could stand a little water."

Getting up from her chair, she extended her arms to receive the bunch of roses and disappeared from sight for a moment. That was enough time for Capone to awaken the disoriented Jimmy Hart, who thought he was having a nightmare.

"Hey, Jimmy, pal, how are you?" Capone asked in a sweet voice. "What have you said to the cops, eh?" The chunky, scarfaced man whose facial expression didn't match his speech, beamed over Hart's helpless body, causing the White Hand mobster to choke on his own saliva.

Capone so terrified Hart that he simply responded by shaking his head back and forth, indicating he hadn't squawked. Sweat poured down Hart's face and his eyes were full of tears as he swore an oath of silence.

Connie met the woman coming back with the flowers and distracted her from the bedside by claiming she'd lost a valuable ring somewhere near the hallway. Long after they left, Hart's companion still searched under the bed and in the corners of the room for the nonexistent ring.

Hart lived by the underworld code of silence and it was unlikely that he would have reported his involvement in the calamitous sortie into Black Hand territory regardless, but this brazen act on the part of the rival mob cemented his resolve to remain quiet.

After questioning Elvira Callahan and others known to be employed by the club, the brass urged that Jimmy Hart be placed under arrest and a police guard assigned to his beside. His ordeal would continue throughout his hospital stay as he continued to vehemently deny knowledge of one of the most horrific gangland homicides to occur in New York City history.

When Detective Charles Hickey asked him how he traveled such a distance when he was so badly wounded, from the Adonis Club to Flushing Avenue, Hart replied, "I flew there, don't you see them wings on me back? I'm a seagull. Don't you know? Now, please officer, let me be to rest awhile. You could be better spending your time trying to pinch those who shot me up around Flushing Avenue."

Meanwhile, the police came up with the names of Anthony Desso, a bartender, and more importantly, Sylvester Agoglia, who was recorded on the club's registration certificate as an official of the Adonis Social & Athletic Club. The Agoglia brothers, of course, denied being anywhere near the place on the night in question. The list of names grew to include an individual described by the *Brooklyn Eagle* as a bouncer at the Adonis Club that night, thought to be a Chicago torpedo, Alphonse Capone.

By December 31, the tally of suspects climbed to nine men (including the three White Hand survivors) who were due for arraignment in Brooklyn Supreme Court when a hectic scene erupted in chambers and spilled out the door. It was revealed that a female voice had called the police station on Empire Boulevard, leaving an ominous message.

"Get word to the courthouse on Adam Street that if Peg Leg's pal, John Patrick Malone, has any idea of talking to the judge, or anyone else regarding the murders at the Adonis Club, and he goes free, tell him he'll be shot dead, no further than the courthouse steps," the woman said.

After Malone's attorney relayed the threat to his nervous client, Malone broke the silence only to concede to the fact that he was present in the club. However, when the lights went out, he heard gunfire and just ran. When asked if he was able to recall any of those present in the club before it was plunged into darkness, he claimed he was drunk and couldn't be sure.

Police suspected Capone and his cousin, Sylvester, of being the main assassins, but this could not be backed up with either testimony or material evidence. After spending a few days in jail on suspicion of murder, they both posted bail and were released. When they appeared in court, their counsel, Samuel Liebowitz, produced a sworn affidavit signed by Happy Malone and Joe Howard exonerating all the employees of the club for any wrongdoing. Their stories had a completely different spin to those offered by other witnesses. The two White Hand gangsters claimed they paid little attention to some strangers who entered the club just before the place went dark and also swore that these phantoms were responsible for the killings.

Judge Francis McCloskey had no choice but to dismiss charges against everyone involved including Jimmy Hart, who left the hospital shortly thereafter to find his personal fortunes had actually increased with the untimely passing of his White Hand boss, Lonergan.

"We got people ready to move into the new rackets that'll be springing up like mushrooms now that we control every pier in Brooklyn," Yale said at a banquet held in the Sunrise Café. The banquet was attended by Yale, Liebowitz, the Mangano brothers, Philip and Vincent, Albert Anastasia, "Little Augie" Pisano, "Silk Stockings" Giustra, and Batista Balsamo.

The honored guest was Al Capone and the occasion was to celebrate gaining near-unconditional control of all the docks and warehouse rackets in Brooklyn.

"We have agreed to allow Charlie Donnelly, "Rag Time" Joe Howard, Jimmy Hart, and a few more of Peg Leg's crew to operate the public loading operations on the old Pearl Street dock and that's it!" Yale said. He steadied the drink in his hand while he continued to address the nefarious assembly. "If they're not satisfied, we'll take that away from them too."

The anticipated increase in gang warfare that the police assumed would certainly follow the Peg Leg murders never materialized. Instead, only sporadic, relatively minor skirmishes occurred in Brooklyn and these were promptly squashed by Yale with the help of Cosa Nostra "experts" such as Don Vincenzo Mangano, "Silk Stockings" Johnny Giustra, and the powerhouse, Albert Anastasia, an enforcer who later in life would be dubbed by the press "Lord High Executioner" of Murder Incorporated.

Capone's business interests in Chicago warranted his immediate attention, but that didn't spoil his triumphant return as the undisputed boss of the most powerful criminal organization in Chicago, with tentacles that reached far beyond the restrictive territorial limits laid down in 1922 by his ex-boss, Johnny Torrio.

Eventually, most of Al Capone's business rivals would be either forced into a tributary alliance with his organization, or else join the dwindling list of those who complained about his methods.

Acknowledgments

We wish to acknowledge the following people who greatly assisted us by providing facts relevant to the life of young Al Capone: Frank Galluccio; Gido Bianco, who was a prime source of beneficial information during the 1970's and early 1980's; Ciro Favaro, Mickey Donnelly, Mary Savarese, and NYPD Detective Nicholas Scarcella.

For their encouragement and support, we thank our brothers Eugene, Dominick, and Joseph, as well as William's children: Joseph, Helen and Connie Ann, William's wife Catherine, John's grandson's Gregory Deliso, John Martinez and John Mistretta, and Judy Galestro. Special thanks to our good friend and writer Robert Schoenberg, author of Mr. Capone.

Special thanks also go out to our agent, Steven Harris, a real gentleman and without a doubt the best in his profession. If not for his guidance and superior ability to act as teacher, coach and referee, this book would have never been realized.

We offer a final salute to our editor, Mark Weinstein. Thanks for all the help you provided with your patience and understanding of the difficulties inherent in the writings of two former longshoremen.

About the Authors

Hilton Flores

WILLIAM BALSAMO, considered by many to be one of the world's premier Capone historians, has invested more than twenty-five years in researching and writing this unique book. He is the author of *Under the Clock*, now in its fifth printing, and served as a consultant to both Brian DePalma's blockbuster 1987 film, *The Untouchables*, as well as to the companion book for the 1994 Fox TV special, *Loyalty and Betrayal: The Story of the American Mob*, produced by Nicholas Pillegi (*Wiseguy, Casino*). Mr. Balsamo's many television appearances include the *Sally Jesse Raphael Show*, *The Joe Franklin Show*, *The Geraldo Rivera Show*, and various documentary features on the History Channel, A&E, The Learning Channel, Discovery Channel, Travel Channel, and, most recently, the Bio Channel.

YOUNG AL CAPONE

JOHN BALSAMO is the chief executive of SUPERDON INC., a company that markets board games. Previous to that, John worked on the Brooklyn waterfront for more than thirty years while compiling extensive material regarding the life of young Capone.

Index